THE LIVES OF OBJECTS

CLASS | NEW
2 | STUDIES
0 | IN
0 | RELIGION

EDITED BY Kathryn Lofton AND John Lardas Modern

THE LIVES OF OBJECTS

Material Culture, Experience,
and the Real in the History
of Early Christianity

MAIA KOTROSITS

The University of Chicago Press
Chicago and London

The University of Chicago Press, Chicago 60637

The University of Chicago Press, Ltd., London

Published 2020

Printed in the United States of America

29 28 27 26 25 24 23 22 21 20   1 2 3 4 5

ISBN-13: 978-0-226-70744-0 (cloth)

ISBN-13: 978-0-226-70758-7 (paper)

ISBN-13: 978-0-226-70761-7 (e-book)

DOI: https://doi.org/10.7208/chicago/9780226707617.001.0001

Library of Congress Cataloging-in-Publication Data

Names: Kotrosits, Maia, author.

Title: The lives of objects : material culture, experience, and the real in the history of early Christianity / Maia Kotrosits.

Other titles: Class 200, new studies in religion.

Description: Chicago : University of Chicago Press, 2020. | Series: Class 200: new studies in religion | Includes bibliographical references and index.

Identifiers: LCCN 2019042826 | ISBN 9780226707440 (cloth) | ISBN 9780226707587 (paperback) | ISBN 9780226707617 (ebook)

Subjects: LCSH: Material culture—Religious aspects—Christianity. | Civilization, Greco-Roman. | Church history—Primitive and early church, ca. 30-600. | Judaism—History.

Classification: LCC BR163 .K68 2020 | DDC 270.1—dc23

LC record available at https://lccn.loc.gov/2019042826

CONTENTS

**Might it not be that the main point
of the performance is a denial of deadness . . . ?**

D. W. WINNICOTT, "THE MANIC DEFENCE"

INTRODUCTION

The Lives of Objects

You move from your home, are perhaps forced to move, and are packing up. You are feeling numb. You pack objects, now both alien and familiar, heavy and strange in your hands: objects that made more sense in the landscape of a life, however provisional. Now their thingness, their density feels more distinct, their value questionable or intensified. You pack them, you give or throw them away. They go on to live a different life, take on different uses, accrue more or less value, or become trash.

Despite their unreliable value and mobility of meaning, given the swiftness of time and the unpredictability of change, objects can take on a curious solidity, a steadiness. As remnants, they contain pasts by externalizing memories, for one, but their obvious form of presence might also offer a more subliminal reassurance that *some* things, some *things*, remain (whether we'd like them to or not). In and among all the confused narratives of what happened, the postmortems for a moment not ever fully concluded, the subtexts and whys, the repeated reconfigurations of proximity to and distance from people and places, there is the blunt and unequivocal object.

How might we interrupt this apparent solidity of things?

This is a book about the lives of objects considered through a history of the ancient Mediterranean. It is about the nonobvious histories of obvious physical artifacts, and about the ways in which, across time and geography, colonial relations and collectives crystallize in the tangible, material world. It is about the ways in which aliveness and deadness, agency and objectification—fully political categories—were points of ongoing reflection in ancient worlds, no less than contemporary ones. I render the ancient Mediterranean in terms of its subterranean social content, and read themes

of life and death, vitality and breakdown, in both ancient and contemporary literature as they touch questions of political self-determination (sovereignty) and cultural solvency. In this way, the ancient world, and particularly what we call early Christian literature, is not the exclusive focus of this
book as much as it is the needle's eye for considering a more expansive set of
historical, sociopolitical, and theoretical questions. The ancient world and
its remains offer condensed illustrations for the ways people grapple with
the materiality of life.

But this is also, and perhaps more, a book about objects of *attachment* —
those relationships, figures, and elements that live on in the psyche — and
the dynamic place of those objects, as considered through the history of
what has been designated as early Christianity. It is about the subtle intonations and furtive psychic content of those things that consistently draw
ancient attention and/or scholarly energies: ruins, statues of the gods and
emperors, the "bad" student. And it is about the elaborate worlds we devise,
especially the ways the worlds we devise make some things (people, experiences) matter more than others — make them more material. My interests
are both historical and historiographical, focused not only on making sense
of ancient lives and experiences, but also on how we imaginatively reconstruct those lives or experiences.

In other words, this book approaches materiality (and what is implied
by it) both critically and expansively. It destabilizes material objects as such,
their "realness," mostly by noticing that their stability is a product of *psychological work*. It points to other, seemingly less solid things as no less actual or
significant. Inflected by theories of the psyche, it is a series of meditations on
the tensions between fantasy and reality, readability and the illegible, physical elements and their subtexts. It mixes and moves between ancient history
and contemporary cultural studies to ask: What appears real to us? What
appears to us *at all*, and why?

MATERIALISMS AND OBJECTS OF INTEREST

This project began with a curiosity about the renewed attraction (an attraction I share) to material culture in the ancient world — those more distinctly
physical elements of the ancient cultural landscape. Numerous fields across
the humanities have witnessed a swell of revived interest in the tangible
artifacts and processes that form the often underacknowledged basis for

scholarly work. To name a few in studies of the ancient Mediterranean: manuscript variations, book production, and the dating of long-dried ink on papyrus; inscriptions in situ; architectural remains and the reliefs that decorate them; burial practices; the spatial organization of houses and marketplaces; the sizes of dining rooms where various groups met for banquets; the assortment of objects—crowns, clay pots, and weapons, described in scrupulous specificity—held by ancient hands.[1]

In a mostly parallel development, over the past fifteen years or so, concentrated in cultural studies, literary studies, queer studies, and philosophy, the collective attention has settled on the sensible world and our mechanisms for sensing it. Social theories of emotion and affect—a basic capacity to feel, be moved, or respond—emerged out of a kind of frustration or weariness with the linguistic turn, of which these same fields were prime propagators.[2] The linguistic turn, the shift toward analyzing the ways in which language or discourse both constructs what is perceived as real and funds power relations in the social world, was characterized, at least in part, by a fist shaken at the Cartesian formulation "I think therefore I am" (*cogito ergo sum*) and the sovereign, knowing subject it emblematized. These new materialist theories that turned to the sensible world and its affective impressions on us heightened the gesture. In social theories of emotion, bodies course with social forces, and dominant narrative histories are countered with attention to the more seemingly ephemeral effects of these forces.[3] Feeling—that which seems most personal, internal to us—is an experience of social incursion, one that forms us and those collectives to which we belong. In new materialism, the already shaky subject-object opposition and human-animal divide began to disintegrate, producing a world ever more vivid and dynamic, one crackling with liveliness, uncertain fluidity, and strange affinities.[4]

In studies of ancient societies, the world of words, at once ethereal and noisy, has given way to the somewhat stark and quiet, but comfortingly palpable, world of things. But these quiet things, these objects of our affection, cull no small amount of words around them. Likewise, even the list of curiosities attending the materialist turn in studies of the ancient Mediterranean, especially, so many of which are about writing in some form, suggests we haven't turned (or can't or won't turn) away from utterances. Indeed there seems to be a kind of tension issuing from the collective turn away from linguistic analyses and toward various kinds of materialist ones. The tension, I want to suggest, is an epistemological one: a tension about "thereness," or what those of us who do history might traditionally call data or evidence.[5] Objects and spaces, codices and temples, can be seen or touched, if not by us, than by someone. They offer a distinct sense of not just ground-edness, but legitimacy in an enterprise like ancient history that can seem, not without reason, marginal and capricious if not downright whimsical. Likewise the linguistic turn and its associated relativities around what con-stitutes the real might feel a little too friendly, to put it gently, to a political climate now operating (at least in the United States) more explicitly in the realm of "alternative facts."

I've been riveted by the materialist turn in studies of the ancient world(s). This is less because of the verifiability or legitimacy it promises than because the linguistic turn in the field abetted an already problematic overattention to the statistically minor practice of literary production for understanding the ancient Mediterranean. With the linguistic turn came not just questions about the construction of reality through discourse, but a fantasy that writing could tell us everything. Material objects represent and often preserve a certain element of intractability in the writing of history. Less pliable than language, material objects can't or don't always do what you want them to.[6]

The materialist attachments in contemporary theory circles have like-wise circulated around, and wobbled on, the question of thereness and the real. Feelings are ephemeral, after all, and the attraction to ghosts and haunt-ing as thought-figures in some of this work, especially in queer theory, illus-trated the way affective historiography endeavored to unseat those tradi-tional forms of history and renditions of reality that maligned subjective experiences (especially minoritized ones) and their expression as insubstan-tial, negligible, or indulgent.[7] And yet some of this work was founded on a desire to engage with work in the so-called hard sciences, to be grounded in some biological particulars of human experience, even at the risk of the essentialism so disavowed by poststructuralist theory.[8] When affect indi-cates not feelings but rather an elemental, if unevenly distributed, capacity of all existent things, the force of the work is in its *reanimation* of a world rendered dull and still by a disillusioned modernism.[9] But the central place of the sciences in so much new materialist theory suggests not simply some further, if still tentative, erosion of familiar disciplinary divides. Humani-ties scholars' blending of work in the sciences (associated with the concrete) with work in the humanities (associated with the interpretive) more dis-tinctly suggests a desire on the part of the humanities to touch something more *solid*, to make contact with certain externalities that have been fore-closed in the self-referential focus of poststructuralist theory.[10]

This book is not just born of these tensions across fields, but seeks to intensify and stage them. I am dissatisfied with the ontological bombast and universalizing around language so characteristic of the body of literature housed under the linguistic turn (Derrida, Foucault, Lacan). But I can't turn away, and so I play out renegotiations of some of those figures and their claims on other terms. Besides, the linguistic turn as indebted to psychoanalytic theory brought with it something I do not wish to leave behind: it sheltered in it a certain relativization of the visible and the obvious. As suggested by the now clichéd iceberg analogy for the unconscious, in which most of the substance of the psyche exists below the observable surface, psychoanalytic epistemologies taught that what we see is only a fraction of what we get, and that even then we don't always know what we're getting. That is, the unconscious presents us with striking intimacy the limits of our knowing. The observable is but a tantalizing hint of the total picture. Thus "symptomatic" readings emerged with the linguistic turn. In symptomatic readings, the words on the page were manifestations of the much larger, infinitely more complicated and consequential world of the unsaid. The coherence and unity of meaning, like the coherence and unity of the person, are undone by the implicit associations of the said, which offer a glimpse into the forces and conflicts at work behind the scenes.[11]

Not incidentally, the ancient world was an important analogue for the psyche for Freud. Actually, it was the ruins of the ancient world that he evoked: "Now let us, but a flight of imagination, suppose that Rome is not a human habitation but a psychical entity with a similarly long and copious past — an entity, that is to say, in which nothing that has once come into existence will have passed away and all the earlier phases of development continue to exist alongside the latest one."[12] Commenting on this passage, Shane Butler notices the counterintuitive use of Rome as a place where *nothing* is lost, "[W]here [Freud] gives us a scenario of potentially total recall (the return of the forgotten or repressed), the Romantic imagination had instead surveyed, with melancholic desire, a scene of irremediable destruction."[13] For Freud, the remains of Rome/the psyche call forth and necessitate attending to a much broader, deeper scene. Thus this book offers some provocations in chapter 2, "Citizens of Fallen Cities," on the place of ruins in postcolonial (and psychosocial) landscapes of the ancient and modern worlds. Of course ruins, as objects that gesture toward absence and erasure, occupy an uncertain place in relationship to materiality from the get-go.

But psychoanalysis is nothing if not a history. What's more, it is a history in which, as Adam Phillips puts it, what we might normally think of as facts are neither obvious nor necessarily the most relevant dimensions of that history.[14] Psychoanalysis is also a history of objects. It is most definitively so in the object-relations school of psychoanalysis tracing back to Melanie Klein. In object-relations, relationships are rendered into discrete, even concretized forms that we consume or internalize. The relationship between mother and child becomes concretized in the breast, for example. Psychoanalysis likewise demonstrates how thoroughly the past, as that which we think is dead or over, is animating the present as we relive our traumas, repeat our primary relationships, and build our worlds and ourselves out of bits and pieces of bygone people and events. In the Freudian scheme, the human psyche contains impersonal, inhuman parts (the id or the "it" being the prime example), and the psyche is the place in which subjects and objects are made. It is the place where subjects and objects are distinguished and no longer easily distinguishable. That is to say, part of the materialism of psychoanalysis is that it treats objects and matter or what matters as elastic.[15]

Can our renewed interest in what physically remains of the past hold this more ample notion of thereness? Can it hold this destabilization of relevant facts, and especially this subtle inquiry into the mind-work around objectification and the animate that psychoanalysis (for one) provokes? Can it afford not to? How will we be responsible to the ephemeral dimensions of life that typically seem immaterial in considerations of history but are the very substance of our own experience?

Before I address these questions more directly, I want to claim some of the subtexts and historical assumptions that underpin the readings here. I want to also map some of the theories that inflect my narratives or get elaborated in a more methodical way.

STAGING THE REAL: ON FANTASY
AS A HISTORICAL CATEGORY

In a piece on the history of dream interpretation ("The Future of Dreams: From Freud to Artemidorus") thirty years ago, S. R. F. Price observed the heavy hand of psychoanalytic (specifically Freudian) approaches to human experience and the structure of the self on understandings of ancient dreams. In so doing, he argued vehemently against modern psychoanalytic readings of ancient literature and figures. His reasons are both historical and ethical or ideological: Freud's internalized, introspective model of the human psyche constitutes a "radical break" from ancient notions of the self.[16] The "asocial, apolitical nature" of Freudian theory, with its focus on individuals, is "unlikely to be informative historically," Price writes. "It might be illuminating for the biographies of individuals, but it cannot make sense of the cultural configurations specific to that society."[17] Critiquing not just the universalism but the "ethnocentric and Whiggish tendencies" of psychological readings of historical figures,[18] Price (rightly, I think) suggests we put both Freud's introspective approach to dreams and Artemidorus's predictive approach to dreams into cultural perspective.

For all of Price's steep rhetoric, he illustrates a circulating sentiment regarding the application of psychoanalytic theory to ancient history and literature.[19] Obviously Price's conviction that the individual or personal/subjective offers us little if any read on culture is unfounded. That presumption has been undone by feminist epistemologies and recent theories of affect after and indebted to them. Individuals and their experiences are knit into social fabrics at the most intimate of levels, and so there is genuine historical traction and heat generated in thinking through those more apparently individual experiences, in the same way that, post-Foucault, texts have been understood as being less about individual authors and more about cultural discourses. Likewise I would quarrel with a hardened distinction between modern and ancient people, with its ironically essentialist tendencies. Such a perspective insists that ancient people are *absolutely* different from modern ones, and that therefore their experiences, no matter how apparently compatible, should not be submitted to modern rubrics.

While certain specified assumptions from psychoanalytic thinkers might sustain hits in these pages (most notably perhaps in chapter 6, "Penetration and Its Discontents"), those hits are not taken in the name of history. Do we really think that ancient people had no ulterior motives? Do we believe they were transparent to themselves, or that because they didn't think in predominantly individualist terms, there was no depth at an individual level? One can note the ways terms and concepts in both the contemporary and the ancient world might point (sometimes awkwardly or partially) to compatible experiences, and do so without imputing a specific historical understanding of the structure of the person.[20]

Indeed fantasy (*phantasia* in ancient Greek) is one such concept that points toward compatible, transhistorical experiences of creativity, invention, and imagination. Ancient minds were active as, for instance, Jaś Elsner has demonstrated in *Roman Eyes: Visuality and Subjectivity in Art and Text*.

Ancient visual culture stirred and provoked the imaginations of its onlookers. In fact Elsner's very thesis that ancient people *formed their subjectivity* through viewing and being viewed would seem to require not just narrative creativity on the part of ancient people, but some level of internalized
self-reflection. And ancient people had dreams, as Patricia Cox Miller has
richly catalogued. Dreams were not only sleep experiences, and while they
were often thought to arise from an external source (a place, in Homer and
Ovid at least, near the land of the dead), Miller notes the clearly psychological implications and corollaries of the place from which dreams emerge.[21]
In Ovid in particular this place is "chthonic": dark, shadowy, and where
personified emotions live, what we might think of as the externalized kin
of the unconscious.[22]

Miller describes what she calls the "oneiric imagination" in the ancient
world, which "confounds the conventional distinction between (real) thing
and (false) copy."[23] Even with a certain suspicion circling around images in
antiquity—a suspicion that itself testifies to the fluidity of real thing and
false copy—encountering a figure in a dream often meant encountering the
figure itself.[24] Likewise, statuary had an eerie doubleness about it. As de-
picting gods in statue form became more dominant as a cultural practice,
these representations shaped senses of who the gods were. By the second
and third centuries, dreamers encounter the gods in dreams *as their statues*,
Miller notes, and indeed statues regularly moved, interacted with, and appeared alive to observers.[25] The visual representation of the gods, and the
effect of that liveliness on notions—or fantasies—of Roman power in the
provinces, provide an important pretext for rereading Tertullian's relationship to Roman power in chapter 4 ("Tertullian of Carthage and the Materiality of Power"). But on a basic level, it is clear that the liveliness of statues and
the discourses negotiating the truthfulness of images suggest not just active
inner lives, but *a fluidity and constant negotiation of what is real.*

These ancient negotiations invite comparisons with later and more
contemporary experiences of reckonings with the hazy boundaries of subjects and objects, animate and inanimate—including in our historical and
anthropological descriptions (as I discuss in chapter 1, "Objects Made Real").
The place of fantasy, not as a counterpoint to reality, but as *constituting it*, is a
thread I pull throughout the book in various ways. In psychoanalytic theory,
fantasy is the psyche representing the world and the self to itself, a continual
and endlessly adaptive attempt to make sense of relationships, feelings, and
contradictions in an incoherent self and world. Much psychoanalytic work
on fantasy proceeds from the work of Melanie Klein, who theorized phan-

tasy (with a *PH*) as distinct from the normal kinds of daydreaming and daily flights of fancy of fantasy with an *F*. Phantasy is especially characteristic of the earliest phases of child development and happens mostly in relationship to the mother or the breast. But it persists over time as a psychic process. As Klein writes in *Envy and Gratitude*, "Phantasies—becoming more elaborate and referring to a wider range of objects and situations—continue through-out development and accompany all activities; they never stop playing a great part in all mental life."[26]

Consequently, fantasy and imagination signify more than fiction or myth. They rather evoke a set of psychosocial processes that assemble dis-parate elements of a noncoherent world into a working if also frequently contradictory set of devised scenarios. In *The Fantasy of Feminist History*, for instance, feminist historian Joan Wallach Scott leverages fantasy to de-scribe the ways in which feminist historians place themselves into a histori-cal and monolithic continuum of women, thereby stabilizing the category of "woman." What makes such affiliations across time, geography, and other material differences possible, if not "woman" as a fixed identifier? Scott uses the work of Slavoj Žižek and Jacques Lacan, describing fantasy as a "setting for desire" and as a "tightly condensed" narrative that gets staged to arrange and work out wishes and fears.[27] Fantasy is both a social and an individual process. However, its psychoanalytic underpinning means that no one con-trols the process. Fantasy has a life of its own.

One of Scott's most striking observations is the persistence of the figure of female orator in feminist histories, which "projects women into mas-culine public space, where they experience the pleasures and dangers of transgressing social and sexual boundaries"—a fantasy that feminist histo-rians themselves do or hope to embody.[28] The figure of the female orator, emblematized by the woman at the podium speaking publicly that Scott tracks through feminist histories, inspires my own interest in another fanta-sy figure, one that gnaws at and inspires so much of contemporary academic life: that of the Public Intellectual. In my last chapter, "Darkening the Disci-pline," Scott's use of fantasy is amplified by Robyn Wiegman's spellbinding account in her book *Object Lessons* of the affective force and fantasies of political agency undergirding certain identity-based disciplines.

Scott's critique of feminist history however is not that it engages in fantasy. Nor is Wiegman imagining we should divest ourselves of certain political aspirations. Rather Scott critiques what gets *naturalized* in the pro-cess of writing these histories. Fantasy is an inevitable dimension of psychic life, and so likewise of historical work. Obviously I don't dispute the inevitability of fantasy as a strong dimension of any sense-making we might do of the world (past or present). But I still want to approach the real, which is foreclosed as an available, assimilable possibility, particularly in theories indebted to Jacques Lacan, which place the real (or rather, the Real) in near-absolute opposition to any form of representation. So on the one hand, I want us to reckon with the way fantasy constructs what we construe as reality and the ways reality is not available to us as we hope. On the other, I resonate with the desire for the real that has been articulated both self-consciously and unselfconsciously in contemporary and ancient studies. I persist in the belief that we must reckon with what is *outside* our devised worlds, as well. I want to have my cake and eat it too, I suppose, even while I know I'll still leave the table a little bit hungry.

My (our) ongoing and unresolved push-and-pull between fantasy, reality-as-fantasy, and the real in any attempts to describe a world is managed in this book through recourse to something like reality-testing in psychoanalysis. Reality testing doesn't mean "facing" reality; it means the relational process by which fantasies are suddenly seen as nontotalizing, *as fantastical*, and the process through which one must revise one's narrative. The question I pose in the first chapter, "Objects Made Real," is: what happens if we construe history (and pedagogy, in chapter 7) as an ongoing process of reality-testing and fantasy-revision? What if we understand it as a process that might provide fleeting or even chance run-ins with the real, on terms other than our own—largely by grappling with the pieces that our fantasies do not, cannot hold? We cannot fully manage the real, but perhaps we can set the stage for it. There may even be ways to think about (gasp) representing it—a tabooed notion since the linguistic turn. These questions and propositions appear most prominently in that chapter, but as an extended meditation on the theoretical questions that gave rise to the rest of the project's pieces, they underwrite so much of this book.

Fundamental to fantasy/phantasy in psychoanalytic theory is the life of objects in the psyche. In object-relations theory, the lineage of which Klein is a significant member, the self is formed (in infancy and childhood, particularly) through the internalization of others as images or "objects," or even part-objects. Fantasy/phantasy is the imaginative work of relating to these images or objects. In Klein, objects are projected or introjected, and thus are the arbiters of the boundary between inside and outside:

> From the beginning the ego introjects objects 'good' and 'bad', for both of
> which the mother's breast is the prototype—for good objects when the

child obtains it, for bad ones when it fails him. But it is because the baby projects its own aggression on to these objects that it feels them to be 'bad' and not only in that they frustrate its desires: the child conceives of them as actually dangerous—persecutors who it fears will devour it, scoop out the inside of its body, cut it to pieces, poison it—in short, compassing its destruction by all the means which sadism can devise. These imagos, which are a phantasmically distorted picture of the real objects upon which they are based, become installed not only in the outside world but, by the process of incorporation, also within the ego.[29]

In Klein, objects "disintegrate" as they are hastily parceled off into "good" and "bad" pieces. This can become a state of anxious desperation, in which the ego seeks ever more urgently to deny the incorporation of the whole, mixed, complicated object. There is loss, since the object has been rent into bits and pieces, its wholeness destroyed. The guilt of destruction fuels an attempt to reassemble the object into a whole, restore it, bring it back to life, which Klein only belatedly and almost scandalously describes as "love."[30] "Love" then appears as an attempt not just to restore the object, but to let it be real, which in this case is a complicated mix of good and bad.

The term "object" derives from Freud—the object is the telos of drives. It is the flat recipient of desire; that which gets invested with desire. The implicit gendering of the object is clear even in Klein's account above, in which the infant is a default "he" whose central object is the breast—that biological reduction and synecdoche of womanhood. In the past few decades, psychoanalytic theory-in-practice has struggled with the notion of the object, as it imagines the child as a single subject in a field of psychic instruments. Jessica Benjamin, most prominent among proponents of what is called the relational perspective, describes her discontentment with the one-person model as a function of her needing to reconcile psychoanalysis with its feminist critiques. Of course the primacy of the breast as the object after which all objects are modeled points to the prickly difficulties of maintaining the term "object" at all. The relationalist perspective theorizes not one subject and its objects, but the dynamism between two (or multiple) centers of subjectivity. In her work, Benjamin theorizes "intersubjectivity," which posits that individual subjectivity is born, somewhat paradoxically, out of dependence on one's others for recognition.[31] Importantly, as I discuss in chapter 1, she does not negate the intrapsychic process of fantasy and the objects that come with it: she rather suggests that intersubjective and intrapsychic processes be held in tension with one another.

Like the artist Pygmalion, a character in Ovid's *Metamorphoses*, whose woman-statue animates before his very eyes (and whom I discuss in chapter 1), one might say theory has sought in various ways and places to bring its own woman-object to life, to make her real. But one might note that psychoanalytic theories of fantasy/phantasy, particularly those in Klein and Benjamin, have also offered us a way of thinking about how it is that a human being could become an object in the first place. They describe the conflicted and imaginative processes that both open and foreclose realms of possibility. That is to say that psychoanalysis not only depicts a subject that struggles with ideal images and reality. More generally, it witnesses to psychic states that, in their navigation of the ongoing life of objects, resonate with the ancient oneiric imagination too.

BODY OBJECTS AND THE SOCIAL BODY

The fluidity between subject and object has appeared with particularly poignant critical traction in postcolonial and critical race theories. Who is seen as a locus of experience, as being substantial in and of themselves rather than instrumental or subsidiary to the worlds of others? Who manages to reach the echelons of the human? These questions are politically differentiated and racially arbitrated. Scholars from Frantz Fanon and Hortense Spillers to Anne Cheng and Antonio Viego have also played out in psychoanalytic terms the logics, injunctions, and curses of racialized identities. Anne Cheng, for example, describes racial identification of any kind as a melancholic process, one that "affects both dominant white culture and racial others; indeed racial melancholia describes the dynamics that constitute their mutual definition through exclusion."[32] In racial melancholia, the loss of being what one cannot be is both admitted and denied, as one incorporates the object/other that one cannot be. But this process, according to Cheng, creates a kind of "Moebius strip," a slide between objects and subjects.[33]

Of course, some psychic objects become cultural objects much more easily and readily than others. "The melancholic eats the lost object—feeds on it, as it were," Cheng writes, suggesting connections to the work of Kyla Wazana Tompkins, for instance. Tompkins draws attention to the ways cultural eating practices and discourses produced racialized national citizens in the nineteenth-century United States, a "consolidation of racist ideologies in the intimate workings of the body politic."[34] The edible Black body that Tompkins tracks, epitomized in chocolate fetishization, might be understood as one way these racial psychosocial processes materialize. Similarly, to be a racialized subject is not just to be an object in a particular way. It is also to occupy a space between life and death, to be a dead subject, or a ghostly citizen, haunting the citizen body since, as Michel Foucault and biopolitical theories after him have demonstrated, life, sustenance, dis-ease or debility, and death themselves are political distributions.[35] I discuss ecologies of social life, and the ways eating and digestion process belonging and its contingencies, in chapters 3 and 5 ("Histories Unwritten in Stone," "The Perils of Translation").

This collection of race-critical work suggests moving toward what, according to Lana Lin, psychoanalysis has often been hesitant to do, and that is think about material objects and psychic objects together. Her book *Freud's Jaw* performs an "expanded notion of object relations," which "contends with objects that are not 'properly' psychoanalytic, namely the psychic life of things as opposed to persons."[36] Reading Freud, Eve Sedgwick, and Audre Lorde's negotiation of their long-term illness with cancer, Lin recounts their relationships with physical objects, particularly body-objects—including the cancerous breast in the case of Sedgwick and Lorde. "In showing how morbidity is negotiated through nonhuman objects," Lin writes, "I intend to give psychoanalytically informed criticism a more nuanced discussion around material culture."[37]

In the present book, I move between and merge psychic and more literal objects (or: instantiations of materiality). Here too ancient material elements express negotiations of morbidity, as well as many other things, including—most especially—ethnic or national dissolution and diaspora re-formation.[38] There was an almost ubiquitous cultural preoccupation with bodily integrity and bodily breakdown subtending the Greco-Roman world. This preoccupation showed up in a variety of forms. Novels of the first and second centuries repeat motifs of dismemberment, near death, or false death; medical literature intensifies and proliferates; healing gods and more general interests in healing practices mushroom. The arena's battle dramas, enactments of torture, and other forms of disciplinary violence, whether real or imagined, provided prolonged, lurid encounters with the crumbling, or even implosion, of ambitions of bodily integrity. Queries about what dimensions of the person might be immortal, divine, or otherwise indestructible were especially hotly debated when they focused in on that most heavy of cosmic substances, the flesh. Body *parts*, specifically, loomed in the ancient imagination—a constancy of limbs and organs—ones either disjoined physically or through discourse that, like that of the Greek orator Aelius Aristides, isolates and catalogues somatic particulars.

What does it mean for the body to become an object (an object for use, an object of thought) or a collection of them? We know on some level what makes it possible: the animate—what counts as a life—is a socially derived distinction, as many have observed. And the objectification of human beings is a corollary to the ways certain lives are seen to matter more than others, or not at all.[39] In other words, that people can become objects has everything to do with what in the larger social body counts as a life in the first place.[40] So the question is not only, How does objectification happen? It is also, What is happening when animate and inanimate are no longer salient distinctions—when, for instance, the French Martinique poet Aimé Césaire merges with the ruins of his landscape? What is happening when one carves up or cordons off dimensions of that forest of elements composing selfhood into distinguishable parts—a mouth from its voice, the voice from its speaker, the flesh from that which keeps it warm? How does experience get parsed in such moments of suspended animation? It is often literally parsed: truncated, boxed, parceled into manageable pieces. Conversely, what happens when objects take on a life of their own? What are the experiential subtexts for those moments when the social body expands to accommodate a host of things?

Not insignificantly, the object in psychoanalytic theory also regularly interrupts the subject's imagined reality. In Lacan's mirror stage, the stage in which the child begins to associate themselves with the image they see reflected back to them in the mirror, the ego is constructed out of a sense of the body as a comprehensible whole. It is a mistaking of the mirror image for reality, and a retrojection of that image. The self was, in that well-known formulation, "always already" cogent. But the conceit of that mirror image, the fantasy of it, follows the subject. So the fragmented body—*le corps morcelé*, the "body in bits and pieces," and what Lacan associates with "the real"— haunts the subject by arising in the spectral form of dreams and nightmares.[41] *Le corps morcelé* is an uncanny twin to the terracotta votives— myriad and fragmentary—that lived in the literal underground of Corinth and (as I argue in chapter 2) seemed to haunt the imagination of the apostle Paul as he stretches his rhetoric like a skin over the miscellany of his interlocutors. This is one instance in which we see the real and the material collide—which is to say that they are not always and already the same. In other words, "the material" and material objects are not real by virtue of their materiality. They can, however, create encounters with the real in the moments in which they interject in or fail to conform to dominant (fantastical) realities. These body-objects make their return by disturbing the slumber of the social body that has assumed that its own intact image was real.

LOST OBJECTS: LOSING THE "NATION" IN THE HISTORIES OF CHRISTIANITY AND JUDAISM

Studies centered on nations, nationalism, and sovereignty have swept through the humanities. This is mostly due to the growing resurgence of nationalism across the globe, as well as the increasing prominence of Indigenous studies, especially in Canada. The study of the ancient Mediterranean — and particularly of Christianity and Judaism — has, with few exceptions, sidestepped this movement.[42] A significant part of the reason for the inattention to nations and nationalism is that there is simply nothing like the contemporary idea of the nation (the nation-state as a geopolitical entity) in the ancient world. What is translated as "nation," the ancient Greek term *ethnos*, rather meant something like ethnic peoplehood, though still one with (as I'll elaborate more) emphatically geographical referents. It is the loss of that form of belonging — the loss of it in colonial antiquity, and the loss of it in histories of Judaism and Christianity — that I would like to examine and, in the case of the latter, for which I'd like to adjust.

Another reason for the absence of the nation with reference to Christianity and Judaism might be that evoking the term thrusts one into a modern political minefield. As I write this, white nationalist Christians march in Charlottesville, and Zionist aspirations and Israeli military operations continue to shrink and impair Palestine. Both of these movements take place in the name of a national, religious, and racial sovereignty ostensibly or almost lost and in need of reclamation. The response to these nationalisms, too, has often been in the key of a nation now lost. It is modern nationalism, with its naturalized racial and geographical reverberations, that tends to make some uneasy with bringing sovereignty and ethnicity to ancient literature.[43] To talk of sovereignty in Christian and Jewish literature, even with a healthy dose of historical differentiation, is to potentially find oneself aligned with these causes, if subtly.

Thus for some it might seem counterintuitive if not completely disorienting to use ethnicity and sovereignty as primary frames for understanding the texts I collect here. (This is less true for diaspora, which appears prominently in this book, and only as tied to ancient forms of ethnic peoplehood.) Ethnic peoplehood has only rarely seemed like a significant historical preoccupation or even a preoccupation at all for Roman period Jewish or Christian literature.[44] This is most obviously because of the notion of Judaism and Christianity as religions: separate, if entangled, ones. "Religion" and all that it draws up with it have taken some hits in recent years.[45] Although many modern historians of the ancient world who want to retain the category do so with some pretty steep qualifications, the baggage that surrounds that term—an abstract, transcultural, and nongeographical entity, revolving around a particular set of beliefs—is still heavy. But what we might call religion—a set of practices and assumptions in relationship to the gods—was tied to basically every facet of ancient life, making it hard to particularize and extricate. Even if it works tentatively to describe a set of practices, religion fails as a way to think about social collectives and belonging in antiquity, especially given the general nonexclusivity of devotion to gods in the ancient world.

Ethnic peoplehood, on the other hand, was arguably one of the most salient categories, if not *the* most salient category, for self-understanding in antiquity. Shy as we might be about the racial and geographical implications of the term nation, peoplehood in the ancient Mediterranean was imagined in unequivocally physical and geographical terms, if less distinctly naturalized ones. I would even go so far as to argue that peoplehood was simply not legible without some sort of geographic reference, even while that geography was not clear, continuous, or uncontested. What constituted Judea even just in the Roman period—previously Judaea, and before that Judah and Israel—for instance, was a moving target over time. Of course the Romans remapped many portions of the Mediterranean after conquering them. Nonetheless, "religion" and even "culture," terms that become more portable (if not quite extractable) over the course of time, are largely dependent on histories of territorialization. There was the culture *of X place*, and the reason this is important is precisely that place was so thorny and so completely imbricated in Roman imperial and other past frames of conquest. (This is why I will from here on use "Judean" rather than "Jewish" as a qualifier for this period.)

In fact, the reason ethnic peoplehood and sovereignty are not obvious to us as thematics in ancient literature, especially in the first through third centuries, is because of the colonial/imperial erasure of those forms of belonging. Claiming to belong to a people in the ancient Mediterranean was to make immediate reference to such specific and constructed geographies. However, there was one variation: when one claimed "Romanness." In contrast to classical Greek notions of citizenship, which were grounded in the city (*polis*) and civic responsibility, Roman citizenship was expressed translocally as both familial and a particular kind of submission to Roman law, a submission that was imagined to enable freedom.[46] *Romanitas* was to accept Roman values as superior, but it additionally implied a surrender of previous local attachments.[47] The Roman ethnographic enterprise of describing and stereotyping the peoples Rome conquered was not in contradiction with the goal to incorporate "other" peoples.[48] In this way, the Antonine Edict of 212 CE, which granted citizenship "universally" across the empire,[49] was not a signal moment of transformation as much as the formal articulation of a long-held set of goals and values—so much so that this edict was in later history attributed to various other emperors, including Hadrian, who ruled almost a century earlier.[50]

Universalism and particularity are not opposites; they rather operate in a dependent tension with one another.[51] The imperial tendency to press disparate peoples and their traditions or cultures into similar molds— producing them as different kinds of philosophy, for instance[52]—is both particularizing *and* universalizing. Imperial authorities sought to locate and target populations by various means, and to do so for physical eradication and/or cultural assimilation.[53] Judea's tentative and limited autonomy into the middle of the first century CE, and then its stagger and collapse, are simply part of the more extensive and simultaneous movements of boundary expansion and refigured relation to imperial authorities.[54]

We might say then that the early empire's intensive focus on ethnic particularity through ethnography and affiliated mapping practices worked to parlay these particularities into a heightened investment in universal Roman belonging (cosmic rule over the inhabited world or *oikoumene*). In some instances, this perhaps gave more localized forms of belonging, however imperially structured, additional traction for Rome's conquered peoples.[55] Therefore it also gave the loss of that object, that imperially constructed particularity, more poignancy. But the slow erasure of localized attachments and movement toward more status-conscious subjection to Roman law and *paterfamilias* (legal male head of the family)[56] are contemporaneous with and strikingly similar to the delocalization of rhetoric in so much "Jewish" and "early Christian" (read: Judean) literature. In this literature we see an increasing emphasis on family (and status within it, as in the household codes) instead of nation as the primary structure of self-understanding, and then later a growing attachment to the universalizing terms "Judaism" and "Christianity."[57] Orthodoxy and heresy debates of the second through fourth centuries and their rhetoric of authenticity mimic ethnographic discourse *because they grow out of ethnographic discourse.*[58] More specifically, they grow out of the diaspora rhetoric of authenticity, and take flight within this delocalized landscape.

But we must read ancient literature through and against this deletion. My own attempt at doing so materializes in chapters 2, 3, 4, and 5, as I seek to recover a history of the almost negligible (at its moment) production of "Christians," as well as that lost object of the nation (*ethnos*) and the ways in which that loss was felt and/or refused by those who suffered it.

Regarding the production of Christians, one historical proposal and presumption here deserves some elaboration: that Christianity, as an analytical object, and attachments to it need to be more thoroughly scrutinized and denaturalized. In my previous book, *Rethinking Early Christian Identity*, I logged restlessness with the reliance of the field on the notion of "Christian literature," which leads to somewhat circular readings: what do these Christian texts tell us about being Christian? But I took seriously, and still do, the lateness of the appearance of the term Christian (after most of the New Testament was ostensibly written), in combination with the fact that even long after the term was coined, there was nothing at all socially unique about the people called Christians. This means that understanding nearly any first-through third-century text housed under that term with recourse to some discrete, if diverse, phenomena is wildly anachronistic and profoundly problematic for trying to get a sense of what kinds of social lives and collectivities these texts archived.

My point of departure in both this book and my previous one is thus not anything like Christians or Christianity in the ancient world. It is ethnic peoplehood and diasporic culture, including (but not exclusively) Judean culture in the ancient Mediterranean. It is the standard MO to understand ancient Mediterranean culture in general, and Judean traditions and belonging specifically, as offering "context" within which to articulate the dimensions of ancient Christian discourses/beliefs/practices—ones that are, somehow, unique or creative adaptations. This still feels a little like the background model that contextual historical studies were meant to replace. Reversing the ordinary flow of analysis, I suggest instead that what we think of as early Christian literature, as it is embroiled in ethnic questions of collective self-understanding, offers a fresh angle for getting at ancient culture in the first and second centuries. What's more, I argue that it can contribute generally to understandings of peoplehood, diaspora, and colonization across time. In other words, when we're not attempting to locate, define, or differentiate Christians in antiquity—the marker of belonging to a *contemporary field*, rather than indicating a social movement in antiquity—the literature in which scholars of early Christianity have been trained might actually help us focalize underexplored facets of history more generally.

Interestingly, most of the casual pushback I received for *Rethinking Early Christian Identity* was for nearly dispensing with Christians and Christianity for first- and second-century literature that has borne those names. The more sympathetic objections showed up as questions such as "But what do we call this literature then?" or "But what are we studying then?" My proposals that those themes seen to be most fundamentally and uniquely Christian were simply mundane responses to diasporic and colonial conditions also were sometimes greeted with a kind of apologetic shrug: "I just don't see it." My stubbornness drives me to double-down on my original propositions and inquire about how disciplines overdetermine and legitimize certain objects of study over others. Questioning "Christians" produces disciplinary crises. This pushback also drives me to inquire about the ways certain beloved objects (such as martyrdom, as I discuss in chapters 4 and 5) dominate our historical frames to the degree that they take on the status of reality, even if the form our love takes is some moderate deconstruction.

FINAL WORDS: ON DISCIPLINARITY
AND BELONGING

Psychoanalysis began as a form of interpretation that tried to lay claim to itself as a science. Its inability to pass as a science, however, is not incidental to its increasing marginalization outside of theory circles. But that means that part of what then drives (pun intended) psychoanalysis at its inception is a longing for modernist legitimacy, to be seen as real, even as it has created a legacy of unsettling any modernist sense of the real. The founding tension (preserving a place and desire for the real, while reconstructing the psychic processes that produce it) is a creative one, I think, and one I try to replicate across this book.

At the same time, legibility and disciplinary mechanisms are a substantial preoccupation here, and became more so with each chapter I wrote. I am interested in scenes of law and justice in antiquity, as well as those disciplinary scenes of contemporary academe, and the fantasy lives they respectively engender. What are the laws, both written and unwritten, that determine what materializes, what appears as real in those scenes? How might we surface experiences that don't register on dominant grids of legibility (whether past or present) or that fall by the wayside of disciplinary operations? The first chapter theorizes on the ways historical description might interrupt or work around dominant grids of legibility for what counts as real. But these questions appear again in chapter 4 with the third-century North African writer Tertullian of Carthage and his own captivation with legibility and recognition in Roman scenes of law and justice (and the invention of a Christian population in those scenes). Chapter 5 considers legibility and translation in other, roughly contemporaneous, juridical scenes, as well as the violence associated with translation in colonial lives. In chapter 6 I relativize the penetration grid, as it is often called, as the overriding framework for understanding erotic relations in antiquity, suggesting that the very function of such grids is to render certain experiences illegible. Penetration has also been an overdetermining model for relationality in contemporary theory, though, so I borrow from the Acts of Paul and Thecla to articulate an erotic relationality off the grid and work around the surface/depth binaries and traumatic injury that penetration implies. And the final chapter asks about some particular disciplinary fantasies about teacherly agency and scholarly political intervention, observing the ways those fantasies actually might constrain and limit the political potentialities of our scholarship and classrooms. In all of these cases, I pose questions about how we imagine various systems of power to operate and why we imagine them as such, recognizing all along that one of the ways these systems of power operate is by shaping vivid imaginations.

Indeed the academic disciplines to which I speak in this book are also at issue. While I am a historian of early Christianity, I have been writing to and in conversation with the adjacent and overlapping fields of classics, Jewish studies, literary studies, diaspora studies, anthropology, gender and sexuality studies, and others. Still, the impulse for this intervention feels as if it falls to the side of any of these frames of reference. Cultural studies—which theorizes diaspora, gender, sexuality, and more—has not taken a particular interest in the ancient world, and certainly not anything associated with ancient Christianity. Classical studies, by virtue of its canon, centers on Greek and Latin people and literature, which almost necessarily relegates other people or literatures to secondary or derivative status. Jewish studies has only rarely integrated New Testament literature as part of its overall capture of ancient Judean literature and culture. And given that so much of my work keeps pressing against specifically Christian belonging in antiquity as the overriding object of study or object of attachment, early Christian studies feels like a poor fit, too. And yet, here we are.

As may be clear by now, while I do want to propose some fairly comprehensive orientation changes for the way "Christianity" is configured within the literature and social world of the ancient Mediterranean, this is not a standard or conventional historical project. First of all, the title of the book is somewhat ironic, since I am not directly describing individual archaeological objects—the dimensions of a wall, the specific cartonage in a codex—but rather expanding, almost to the point of breakage, our ideas of what we might take material culture to mean in the first place. Again, taking inspiration from psychoanalytic theory, I want to know not only how more overtly material things live on in the imagination, but how materiality as such is an imaginative negotiation.

Second, the overriding goal of this book is not comprehensiveness. This book is rather a series of historically specific illustrations and provocations for ways to approach not just the social world of antiquity, but the materiality of history, differently. As such, the collection of materials that I address cuts across time, geography, and affiliation—though not unconditionally. There are certain texts (the Gospel of Mark and the letters of Ignatius, for example) that are more dense with the themes I want to accentuate, so I confer disproportionate degrees of attention on them. I often do so recursively, returning again and again to particular materials that won't quite let me go. On the axis of ancient literature, I touch on writers from the classical Greek writer Herodotus to Tertullian of (Roman) Carthage—roughly the fifth century BCE to the third century CE. I address the Israelite/Judean books of Daniel and 4 Maccabees, as well as the texts of the New Testament and so-called Christian texts associated with the New Testament but outside of the biblical canon (such as the Gospel of Peter and the Acts of Paul and Thecla), and in a more familiar move place them alongside Greek writers like Pausanias and Aelius Aristides.

Trained in ancient literature, but always with my head someplace else, I can't (won't) read ancient literature as if it's a time capsule or as if there's some absolute difference that must be respected between then and now, especially since "then" and "now" are also heterogeneous fields. So along with ancient material, I gather thematically resonant, more contemporary literary works on the social, political, and personal reverberations of matters of life and death (torture, decay, illness, healing, revival), ones that speak to or from other fields. Sometimes these contemporary reflections help fore-ground certain elements of ancient materials, sometimes ancient materials bring submerged facets of contemporary experience to the surface. In some chapters, ancient history and texts predominate; in others contemporary material and directly theoretical concerns take over. While I'm not on the hunt for universal human experiences, I do get satisfaction out of unex-pected points of contact along all kinds of lines. I feel that these points of contact, when not seen as threatening the compartmentalization that mod-ern academia so encourages, can fill out our sense of history in both the long and the short view. Perhaps more than that, I hope they can deepen our understanding of the forces that make and break our material lives, the forces that shape the ways we live and die.

OBJECTS MADE REAL

The Art of Description

There are certain experiences, which the Greeks call phantasiai and the Romans visiones, whereby things absent are presented to our imagination with such extreme vividness that they seem actually to be before our very eyes.

QUINTILIAN, INSTITUTIO ORATORIA 6.2.29

From birth, therefore, the human being is concerned with the problem of the relationship between what is objectively perceived and what is subjectively conceived of.

D. W. WINNICOTT, PLAYING AND REALITY

Traditional forms of historical description, especially as they interact with and rely on material culture, have yielded a lot. Requiring meticulous attention to grainy details and quirky specificity, traditional forms of description demand that we reckon with the particular. They provoke us to double-check, look again, return to the *thing itself*—to ask if we've truly captured what it is we hope to capture. Like a string on a balloon, material specificity can keep us from floating off into the ether. And yet: the *thing itself*, the object we seek to describe, is possible only through a set of imaginative processes and assumed postures. As a form of apprehension, objectivity objectifies. The *thing itself* is a product of knowledge that "bears no trace of the knower"—at least presumably.[1]

The simple fact that living beings get objectified should change our relationship to material objects. The question is, how? It could mean that we further fetishize objects, our fear of their liveliness recapitulated into a sense of awe or preciousness—a near obsessional return to their surfaces and limns.[2] Or it could mean we entertain them, and our co-implication with them, with more humility.

In the *Metamorphoses*, Ovid tells the story of Pygmalion, an artist who falls in love with a sculpture of his own making. The sculpture is, perhaps predictably, a sculpture of a woman, and Pygmalion's motivation is his hatred of women.[3] Wanting a woman for sex but not marriage, and fearing boredom, Pygmalion makes a sculpture so perfect, and yet so compelling, that he becomes deeply infatuated with her and she comes to life. The way her awakening into liveliness proceeds, however, is that at first Pygmalion marvels at her vivid realness and her extraordinary beauty: she *seems* to be real to him. Then, as he touches and kisses her, her hard flesh awakens under the weight of his hand. Her blood flows under her skin, and she begins to kiss back.

There are a number of fantasies at play in this story. There is, for example, the fantasy of the artist whose own creations are both more ideal, and perhaps even more real, than life itself. There is the fantasy of the ideal woman. There is the fantasy of sex without personal entanglement; the fantasy of autonomous desire. Then there is also the misogynistic fantasy attending the woman-as-object: that after rendering her an object, his desire could awaken her into a type of humanity whose only attendant agency is to legitimate his use of her by making her return his affection.

In this chapter I reflect on fantasy, reality, and the art of description. I pause on some instances of the "extreme vividness" of things in antiquity, as the first-century Roman rhetorician Quintilian puts it, instances vibrating with uncertainty between liveliness and deadness, as they appear in various ancient narratives—and I consider scholarship's response to some of them. I usher these instances toward questions of the real and objectification that weigh on description as an anthropological, literary, and historical pursuit. Description in these fields has provoked grappling with the agency and autonomy of the objects they wish to chronicle, as they wonder and worry over the extent to which one can be in contact with and then represent reality. The story of Pygmalion is a cautionary tale inasmuch as one imagines that description "brings things to life," only to turn them into a source and instrument of narcissistic gratification. So I keep Pygmalion in mind as I ask how fantasy and object-relations in psychoanalytic theory might help us think through our tangled relationship with the real and find earnest ways to represent realities. The subtext here, however, is that this chapter narrates in more overtly theoretical form what I hope this book's other chapters accomplish.

WHEN OBJECTS SPEAK

Jaś Elsner takes up the story of Pygmalion and some of its attendant fantasies in his book *Roman Eyes*. He uses these fantasies to think about the ways in which subjectivity and the real were configured in tandem with, and through, visual representation and the act of seeing, or "the gaze," at large. As a part of a whole terrain of ancient struggles with the "deceptiveness of realism," Elsner notes that Ovid's telling of the story departs from some earlier versions, in that it is a sculpture not of Aphrodite, but simply of a mortal woman: "Ovid concentrates the story around the problem of realism, which, while it is transgressive in making the marble or ivory flesh, is precisely *not* a problem of the human transgressing the divine."[4] Ovid focuses on Pygmalion's self-deception, such that Pygmalion becomes "a symbol of the deception which lies at the heart of realism."[5] Even as the statue becomes more real to Pygmalion, the text presents Pygmalion as increasingly delusional. Thus, "[t]he erotic myth of Pygmalion's statue turned to flesh is as much an assertion of absence as it is of fulfillment."[6]

While Elsner concentrates on epistemologies of sight, it might likewise be noted that Ovid gives at least as much attention to touch: Pygmalion feels the hardness of her breast yield to his hand. Her lips become warm. Every touch makes her softer, like wax, until he feels her vein pulse under his fingers. In this way, Pygmalion's desire for realness depends on tactile verisimilitude. She's got to *feel* real, not just look real. But as Elsner notes, "'Realism' in art necessarily evokes a myth of 'reality.'"[7] That is to say, realism is already a fantastical imagination of what the world is "really like."

Perhaps more interesting than desires for the real and their impossible fulfillment, though, is the fact that Pygmalion's fantasy coincides with masculine desire and the objectification of women. The description of Pygmalion caressing the frozen woman-object resonates all too painfully with women's mundane and almost constant experiences of unwanted touch, and their numbed or disassociated responses to them. And again, she appears as lively only with, and as responsive to, his want. His creation of a woman-object is a function of his wish to instrumentalize a woman for sex, and thus his sculpture literalizes his misogyny. In fact the story reads almost as a sudden, if circumscribed, recognition of women's subjectivity—a fear, or wish, or simply a way of registering the possibility that those rendered objects by the masculine gaze might "animate," might suddenly become something *more* than object. Tucked into this chilling and apparently comical tale, we find the acknowledgment, somewhere, of the ways those things that have been rendered dead matter, those objects of one's manipulation, have the potential to (a)rouse, to suddenly appear real in ways they did not before.

The woman-object is a reminder of the ways realness appears and disappears with different forms of apprehension and recognition. Indeed deadened experiences of the world, like the one I imagine the woman-object in the *Metamorphoses* has, so often derive from the erasure of one's subjectivity, the imagination that one was not a life at all. One becomes both more and less material: a dense mass, a knot of limbs, a piece of castaway debris, at the same time one is disjoined from the network of human sympathies and identifications that make one's experience matter. In objectification, experience is effaced to produce a body as thing. So what if the fantasy of Pygmalion was not that his beloved *objet d'art* becomes real? What if the fantasy was that she was ever an object in the first place?

Ovid's Pygmalion is certainly not the only uncanny instance of objects-made-real in antiquity. As Elsner and Patricia Cox Miller illustrate, visual representations of many kinds—particularly statues and statues of the gods—were ambiguous in their substance and nature.[8] Images were described regularly as moving in strange, disarming ways and were understood as "deceptive" for this same disarming vividness. Miller's book *Corporeal Imagination: Signifying the Holy in Late Ancient Christianity*, like Elsner's *Roman Eyes*, argues for the role of the imagination, especially in the visual register, in the building of the real in the ancient world. She argues that the literary practice of image description (*ekphrasis*), especially in late antiquity, could conjure holy figures into a form of presence before those devoted to them, and icons managed to conflate image and real presence, producing a kind of "tangible vision."[9] Icons had more than power. They had agency.

Miller argues, in fact, for another kind of "materialist turn," one taking place in late antiquity, which mitigated (not without contestation) the "ontological separation between matter and spirit."[10] She suggests that late ancient Christianity appropriates matter as a "locus of religious meaning" that also meant a positive re-valencing of the material world.[11] It's not clear to me that the instances Miller collects are symptoms of any kind of pronounced turn in orientation characteristic of what's become periodized as "late antiquity." It seems that these instances of relics and saints' images were rather moments of intensification in a longer-running, and not at all especially Christian, set of practices and recognitions. Elsner's work demonstrates this, since it addresses *ekphrasis* in similar terms.

What is more conspicuous, however, is the way in which the fluidity between god, human, and object often reflects on or interrupts proclaimed or accepted realities, ones that periodically and differentially render humans as objects. Pygmalion's story is one instance. But in the Gospel of Peter, an extracanonical account of Jesus's torture, death, and resurrection, we find another, when the cross on which Jesus dies makes a lively appearance:

> But that stone which was pushed against the door, having rolled itself away, moved to the side, and the tomb opened, and both the young men went in. And so those soldiers, having seen this, woke the centurion and the elders (for they were also there guarding). And while they were explaining what they had seen, again they see three men who had come out from the tomb, with the two supporting the other one, and a cross following them, and the head of the two reaching to the heavens, but the head of the one being led out by them going beyond the heavens. And they were hearing a voice from the heavens saying, 'Have you preached to those that sleep?' And an answer was heard from the cross: 'Yes.' (Gospel of Peter 10, my translation)

The Gospel of Peter has received its fair share of attention, mostly owing to the details in the scene above. Jesus appears larger than life, gigantic, and the cross on which he died meanders behind him, even speaking back to a voice from above. It would seem to be patently unrealistic.

New Testament scholars have struggled with this apparently anomalous scene. Mark Goodacre for instance argues that the text does not depict a walking, talking cross at all, that the talking cross is an eighth-century scribal transmission error. He suggests that the text should be read as "the crucified [one]" who is speaking back to the voice in the heavens: "The idea of a walking, talking cross is almost unbelievably absurd," he argues, "all the more so given the lack of precedent for it in the text, in which the cross was earlier completely inanimate, and did not enter the tomb with Jesus at burial."[12]

Contesting Goodacre's reading, Paul Foster situates the enormous figures and the animate cross among other, related "miraculous phenomena" in the Gospel of Peter. He writes, "Underlying the desire to emend the text of Gos. Pet. 10.39–42 is the assumption that the original author would not have envisaged the bizarre scene in which an inanimate object, such as the cross, becomes both mobile and articulate. From a modern perspective, one would be correct to share such concerns, especially in relation to judging the historical likelihood of the events described."[13] Foster goes on to note, however, that other moments of animacy appear in the Gospel of Peter: it is not that the stone has been rolled away from the tomb, suggesting an outside agent as in the canonical versions of this story; it is rather that the stone has "rolled itself" away.[14] Likewise, the text describes the ground shaking as Jesus's dead body is laid upon it (6:21).[15] Thus, according to Foster, the Gospel of Peter "affirms the sanctity (if not the divinity) of the body placed on the ground by having the earth shake. Therefore, in the mindset of the Gospel of Peter, even the inanimate world trembles in recognition of the significance of what has taken place."[16]

While Foster offers a rebuttal to Goodacre's plea for emendation, and recognizes a wider context for the animacy of things in antiquity, he still situates the walking, talking cross relative to "apocryphal" traditions, suggesting that the canonical gospels offer less fantastical accounts.[17] It's curious though, that both Foster and Goodacre register a level of surprise at the largeness of Jesus's body and the speaking cross but don't pose the same questions about realism for the walking, talking postcrucifixion Jesus himself. Why is the animacy of a dead body more "realistic" or less fantastical than the animacy of the wood on which it dies?

These responses to the Gospel of Peter echo certain elements of the tussles about authenticity that surround the Secret Gospel of Mark, another extracanonical fragment that has provoked scholarly intrigue for its apparent depiction of a homoerotic encounter between Jesus and another man. Alexis Waller has explored these debates over the Secret Gospel of Mark, a text either discovered or fabricated by Morton Smith in the 1950s. This text has engendered both a homophobic distancing of the text from the ancient Christian past and hopes for alternative histories of sexuality within Christian tradition.[18] Waller observes how much the fragment has become "an object of longing and repulsion, a marker and maker of alternative narratives—be they ancient and 'authentically historical,' or modern fictions—of early Christian traditions, as well as an incitement to emotionally charged debates about methods and ethics in reconstructing the past."[19] Whether in the scholarly "defense" of Christian tradition from Smith's potential and sur-

reptitious queer contamination of ancient history, or in the utopian imagination of a gay Jesus, the fragment and its reception provide an illustration
of the "felt investments that saturate the rhetoric of forgery and authenticity,
mark the boundaries of what counts as evidence."[20] In attempting to pry
apart the real and the imagined, the discourse of forgery and authenticity
denies, according to Waller, the powerful fantastical and affective work that
funds historical reconstruction in the first place.

   This scholarship on the Gospel of Peter is undoubtedly another instance in which distinguishing between fantasy and the real means protecting certain (presumably) theological commitments, including the special
authenticity of canonical literature. It presents a hiccup in the modernist
project of history with its focus on facts, as it renders the real and the fantastical themselves as contingent on imaginative projections of what is and
is not possible. But the (fantastical) project of determining what counts as
authentic or real is not *only* modernist, even if modernist tendencies toward
rooting out the real are especially exaggerated.[21]

   If ancient statuary and other visual representations collected a range of
ancient reflections on questions of truth and reality, testifying to the slender
margin between the animate and the inanimate, the Gospel of Peter exploits
this slender margin, with its revived corpse and living cross, its incredulous
soldiers in the early morning haze, rubbing their eyes in disbelief and trying to describe and come up with a coherent or perhaps convincing report
for Pilate about what they have seen. But notably the objects made real in
this instance, the ones that disturb the soldiers' sense of the real, are an instrument of torture and the (objectified) body that was strapped to it. The
walking, talking cross, while appearing substantively different to scholars
accustomed to the animate body of a crucified Jesus, expresses something
quite similar to that crucified body. They are each representative of the ways
torture, and more generally criminalization and forms of discipline and justice, render human beings as the raw materials of power.[22]

   I obviously resonate with Waller's sensitive critique of scholarship's
straight-faced, and simultaneously highly fanciful, adjudication of the question of "the real Jesus," relevant to both the Secret Gospel of Mark and the
Gospel of Peter. And while I don't share a longing for the real Jesus per se,
I am sympathetic to the question of adjudicating the real. The problem is
that the real, whether in the ancient world or contemporary one, is precisely
what is up for grabs.

   It is not incidental that "adjudicating the real" in biblical studies and
studies of the ancient world often has recourse to material cultural ele-

ments, as when Goodacre presses scribal practices into service for his argument, for example. These details—manuscripts, ink, missing or reappearing fragments—make a difference. But they also become alibis and, more than that, *replacements* for a set of negotiations with our access to the real that scholarship rarely confronts.

So how might we configure the material and the real in relationship to one another?

I would like to broaden this question such that it is not only about "what happened" in the ancient world, but more about description *as practice*. Is there a way to take the political and imaginative dimensions of reality seriously—as well as the problems of representation—and still ask earnestly how we might meet and receive real moments and things, and render them with words?

LITERATURE, TOUCH, AND
THE "REALLY REAL"

I sought something beyond this: I wanted to find in the past real bodies and living voices, and if I knew that I could not find these—the bodies having long moldered away and the voices fallen silent—I could at least seize upon those traces that could be close to actual experience.

STEPHEN GREENBLATT, "A TOUCH OF THE REAL"

Paralleling Ovid and those others of the ancient world who sought to navigate questions of reality and imagination, subjectivity and what stands outside of it, the fields of anthropology, literary studies, and historical studies have had many and varied arbitrations between what might be parsed as the real and the literary, or interiority and exteriority. Hayden White, Clifford Geertz, and Michel Foucault have been primary figures through which these arbitrations often take place. Each of these figures engendered their own certain dogmas about how to manage the problem of cultural representation in relationship to "the world as it is," or—in less ontological terms—language's outside: White through his account of the inevitable force of narrative in history, an account that nonetheless preserves a place for "real events" (if inaccessible ones), Geertz through his double commitments (and divided reception) along both empiricist and cultural constructivist lines, and Foucault (along with Jacques Derrida) through potent proclamations about a world powered and strictly delimited by profligate discourses.[23]

Literary critic and Renaissance scholar Stephen Greenblatt's articulations of New Historicism, a mode of reading literature as symptomatic of the culture that produces it, have mediated between Geertz and Foucault.[24] While indebted to Foucault's theorizing of power as formative of culture,[25] Greenblatt has also proclaimed a most un-Foucauldian commitment: a devotion to experience as referent. In a volume circulating around the work of Geertz, in fact, Greenblatt claims this devotion baldly, also marking his affinity for Geertz's literary background.[26] Geertz, after all, describes culture as an "acted document," and he remarks that ethnography is "like trying to read (in the sense of 'construct a reading of') a manuscript—foreign, faded, full of ellipses, incoherencies, suspicious emendations, and tendentious commentaries." This is nonetheless a manuscript "written not in conventionalized graphs of sound but in transient examples of shaped behavior."[27] Geertz made a case for "thick description," a form of anthropological description motivated by the rich, context-specific import of a given cultural instance. Thick description is interested in cultural significance. For Greenblatt, not only did Geertz help conjure a real world through the imaginary of literature, that is "the ways in which everyday institutions and bodies get recorded."[28] He also drew from Geertz to show "the ways in which poetry, drama, and prose fiction play themselves out in the everyday world, since men and women repeatedly find themselves in effect speaking the language of the literary not only in their public performances but also in their most intimate or passionate moments."[29]

More recently, however, queer theory and cultural studies scholar Heather Love has pushed back against the literary studies interest in Geertz, as it is claimed by Greenblatt. In "Close Reading and Thin Description" (2013), Love notices that Geertz's "thick description," which attends to "intention, emotion, cognition, depth," rests on a distinction made by Gilbert Ryle. Ryle contrasts it (naturally) with "thin description," which for him means unadorned, plain accounts of human behavior. She also notices that Geertz himself actually *relies* on thin description as prerequisite to thick description.[30] What does it mean, she wonders, that humanities scholars, and particularly literary critics, have been solely invested in *thick* description, and even suspicious of the empiricism implied by a stricter interest in observable behaviors?[31] She suggests that "[i]n literary and cultural studies, where fieldwork is not essential to the work scholars do, 'Thick Description' is taken up as a wholesale critique of empiricism, whereas Geertz's aim was to build a better empiricism."[32] She specifically critiques Greenblatt for his recourse to a real that is "defined in relationship to the textual," noting that "[t]hin description has no role in such a world."[33]

While Love herself has spent her intellectual energy on questions of emotion, depth, and feeling (see her 2009 book *Feeling Backward: Loss and the Politics of Queer Theory*), in "Close Reading" she angles for a different form of literary practice. Greenblatt's single use of real being not quite enough, Love is inspired by Bruno Latour's interest in "what the real world is really like."[34] She fears that in its indebtedness to the linguistic turn, literary criticism will lose track of the "hard surfaces of life," including attention to behaviors as such, something Geertz also hoped to preserve.[35] Contrasting surface versus depth, and hard observational realness versus (soft) literary realness (though not devaluing the latter), Love wants to pause on microsociological description and invite a "reluctance to speculate about the interior life of one's research subjects."[36]

Claiming reading as a social science, Love questions "the dismissal in the humanities of empirical methods as naïve and objectifying."[37] Indeed it seems that the ethics of her reading, her emphatic aspiration toward the doubly real, itself comes from a fear of objectification—or at least a wariness about the dominance of the describer in the frame. She wants to move our attention more concertedly to the specificities of that which is being described. Her illustration, however, in one place, is the book as material object: "Treating the book as a material object, a commodity, or a social fact, these methods put books back in contact with hard surfaces of life including trade, industry, craft traditions, marketplaces, publics, geography, and discourse networks."[38] She elaborates: "Surface reading makes reading central, but it focuses on aspects of texts often seen as too obvious to be of interest. In this sense, it is descriptive: it defers virtuosic interpretation in order to attempt to formulate an accurate account of what the text is *like*."[39]

The literary real is not real enough, not nearly as real as the book as material object (which, significantly, includes its implication in "discourse networks"). Love and Greenblatt thus play out the very tension that has long funded biblical studies and early Christian studies. And of course it should be noted that biblical studies and early Christian studies have already long been onto the materiality of texts. Geertz is an implicit hero in so much of the social science and sociohistorical wing of these fields, and for much more than simply his notion of what constitutes description.[40] But one might notice that what we typically call "thick description" in these fields actually tends to look more like thin description. Judging by its casual evocations at conferences and in scholarly conversations by scholars of ancient Christianity, at least, it tends to mean *detailed description*, often of behaviors, conditions, or interactions. If literary critics have leaned into the thickness of thick description, those of us studying the ancient world have collectively leaned away, hardly preoccupying ourselves with the murkier, more elusive kinds of questions to which Geertz wishes to attend.[41]

Love is not the only one to notice the dual dimensions of description in Geertz's work, that is, interest in the empirical on the one hand, and the meaning-driven and depth-oriented on the other. Geertz's reception at large has followed these two lines. He too was critiqued for being too strongly objectivist, or at least belatedly reclining back into objectivist investments,[42] even as he was accused, to quote Sherry Ortner, of "carrying anthropology into some abyss of uncontrolled subjectivism, nominalism, and constructionism."[43] (See Geertz's proclamation that "[w]hat we call our data are really our own constructions of other people's constructions of what they and their compatriots are up to.")[44] In a recent book on experimental ethnographic writing, entitled *Crumpled Paper Boat*, for instance, Geertz is evoked two times. In the introduction, the writers borrow his name as a call back to the ethnographic responsibility to report "faithfully and rationally on the circumstances of [ethnographers'] encounters."[45] In a later essay, Anand Pandian evokes Geertz to remind readers that "ethnography depends upon the powers of fiction, *fictio*, from the Latin *fingere*, to make, mold, form, and shape."[46]

While this volume prizes the reflexive turn in anthropology, it nonetheless frames itself through a need to account for the real. The authors build on the suggestion by Michael Taussig that ethnographic writing is a "seeing that doubts itself," as well as his notion that in ethnography "[s]omewhere, somehow, real reality breaks through the scrim," despite the ethnographer. In the introduction, the authors hesitate around the real, and carefully define it: "[R]eality is always suffused with something more, some other face, some other dimension, something intangible, evanescent, resistant to analytical decomposition."[47] What would it mean, they ask, "to reveal aspects of the real at the very limits of the perceptible?"[48] The real here, too, is described through materiality and touch: "Take the reality of this book too as something tangible, tactile, materially present, something like the sea, perhaps even a marine jelly, stirred by tremors and undulations, always in motion, perpetually liable to mutual transformation with its readers."[49]

Crumpled Paper Boat emerged out of a seminar entitled "Literary Anthropology" and seeks to take up "experimental modes of writing as ways of lingering with the vicissitudes and implications of empirical encounters."[50] The contributors assert that an investment in the literary dimensions of ethnography is not a matter of reclaiming fiction against documentary: "Instead, we need to approach an ethnographic mode that somehow presses — in Michel Serres's terms — close to the turbulence preceding the emergences of an intelligible, discursively knowable world. Literary writing, Serres argues, in its capacity to body forth this aspect of the world at its limits, may be no less truthful than science."[51]

The rhetorical opposition between the literary and science, a field itself teeming with narratives of varying sorts, is an interesting move. They also share a worry that ethnographic description "freezes" life, deadens it, and they long to catch life as it moves and changes.[52] But perhaps more interesting is the link between the literary and the section that follows: *Responsibility*. Ethnography is an ethical and political enterprise, the authors note, in that like poetry, it "makes the dead matter."[53] But, they note, "There is both responsibility and delicacy in this task of taking up the speech and silence of others, and then giving those elements the reach of another world."[54] The colonialist legacies surrounding anthropology linger around this project implicitly. That last sentence, in particular, seems to house postcolonial feminist theorist Gayatri Spivak's now legendary provocation, "Can the subaltern speak?" somewhere underground.

All of these descriptive projects are, with differing levels of explicitness, bothered by colonial encounters and orientalist legacies. Description is knowledge production, and these descriptive projects are worried about the violences, potential and actual, of encountering and describing "others." They theorize "doing justice" (shall we say) to objects of study.[55] This work is not simply hoping for less presumption, but issuing a plea, something like, "Pygmalion, *let her live.*"

We should note though that neither Pygmalion's self-concept as an artist (a sculptor, who "makes, molds, forms and shapes"), nor his hyperattentive touch of the woman, as he assesses her detail with aching deliberation, saves him from his objectifying fantasies. We certainly can't divest ourselves of the literary ("generic") dimensions of historical description or forget that description is knowledge production rather than knowledge acquisition. But neither should we lose sight of the outside: the obstinately present, the world as it is beyond us and our knowing.

Rey Chow, in a critique of the self-referentiality so characteristic of poststructuralism (for which Jacques Lacan is an important genealogical figure), notes that self-referentiality was imagined as an ethical check on the temptations and dangers of colonialist modes of encounter. Yet, she argues, the foreclosure of referentiality, in which there is no outside to representations of others, "really does not offer a way of thinking other than by turning (what is thought) inward."[56] She observes that this "compulsive interiorization," which offers an important critique of knowledge production about cultural others, nonetheless centers the dominant cultural subject. It is a "tendency to reject externally observable difference," not only leaving those outside the system of signification as only ghostly traces of that system, but lacking any kind of political traction.[57]

For Love and the writers in *Crumpled Paper Boat*, who are pushing back on the linguistic turn in their own ways, as well, materiality appears associated with or even *as* that outside. That kind of force accorded material things parallels some premium values of much research in biblical and early Christian studies. The parallel is unexpected, however, since the linguistic turn is not exhausted in biblical and early Christian studies (nor has it been fully engaged). Likewise the fact that material objects are thoroughly fetishized and eroticized in studies of the ancient world suggests that "the material" is not and cannot be interchangeable with the real, especially since material objects in particular can ignite fantasies *by trading on the real*.

"The material" is and is not what we want: it only holds the promise and the threat of the real with its unassimilable physical presence.

WHEN OBJECTS LIVE ON

In *Playing and Reality*, psychoanalyst D. W. Winnicott theorizes at length on one of his most fundamental contributions: a theory of transitional objects. Transitional objects are physical objects (a toy, a blanket) that accompany the infant through the internal transition from a sense of omnipotence (the mother and her breast are always available, and thus I am in charge of the mother) to the recognition of her separateness, and thus the infant's realization that the mother is not under the infant's control.[58] The "transition" indicates a period of suspense, an "intermediate state between a baby's inability and his growing ability to recognize and accept reality."[59] The transitional object, which might for instance mitigate separation anxiety, has a number of important qualities. Among them: the infant must largely control the object and any changes it undergoes, the object must withstand and survive both loving and hating, and the object must be a tangible thing. It must seem to "give warmth, or to move, or to have texture, or to do something that seems to show it has vitality or reality of its own."[60]

Contrasting the transitional object with the internal objects of Melanie Klein, Winnicott argues that his object must be a possession.[61] It must be something unequivocally outside the infant—something that belongs to the larger world, a shared reality. "The transitional object is never under magical control like the internal object, nor is it outside control as the real mother is."[62] The object ties the infant/subject to the world—the world, as it were, outside their head, even while (at least in the case of the transitional object) the object itself is still functioning with respect to internal life. Over time, at least typically, "disillusionment" takes place. The "good enough" parents adapt less and less to the infant's every need, and the child eventually disinvests from the transitional object. Importantly, however, some transitional objects become fetish objects and "persist as a characteristic of the adult sexual life."[63] And Winnicott remarks, "It is assumed here that the task of reality-acceptance is never completed, that no human being is free from the strain of relating inner and outer reality, and that relief from this strain is provided by an intermediate area of experience . . . which is not challenged."[64]

Transitional objects for Winnicott help the child find where the boundaries of the child end and the world and those others outside begin, so that the world is no longer an extension or projection of the child's will. Their tangibility, their textural specificity, is what makes such objects usable for this negotiation with the outside. But it is not the exteriority of the object *itself* that needs to be negotiated; the object occupies the middle space, the suspense from the tension of illusion/disillusionment. Again, physical things, those things we can touch and hold, do not carry the force of the real. Instead, they provide something obdurate and still manipulable to intervene in the sense of omnipotence, and give solace when the illusion of omnipotence shatters. For Winnicott, the "real" is a world of others who do not bend to our will, who cannot and do not conform to our illusions.

Winnicott stresses persistence and survival. A major function of the object is its survival of the child's (or subject's) aggression and hatred, their desired or imagined destruction of the object. This is true for both transitional objects and internal objects (like the mother, the breast, etc.), which he discusses later in the same book. Winnicott describes a developmental movement from object-relating and object-use—a movement from fantasy-driven relationship with the internal object (object-relating) and a relationship in which the object is no longer under the child's total control (object-use).[65] This movement occurs through the aggressive, imagined destruction of the object, a form of vengeance because the object does not do what the child wants or needs it to do. However, the survival of the object, the fact that the object is *not actually destroyed*, means the child can "live a life in the world of objects." Winnicott writes of object-use that "[t]his is a position that can be arrived at by the individual in early stages of emotional growth only through the actual survival of cathected objects that are at the time in process of becoming destroyed because real, becoming real because destroyed."[66]

Klein's account of this destruction is thorough and brooding, at times graphic, as the child tears the woman-object-mother into bits and pieces, devours her, in part out of terror.[67] Then, out of guilt, and seeing the mother as an external reality that did not perish, the child finds use (object-use) for the bit pieces, or at least some of them, sometimes even taping them together with restless hands: a form of art. It is this state of recompense, the reparative position, that Eve Sedgwick recounts in her book *Touching Feeling*, though in a much happier key.[68]

Jessica Benjamin's own reading of Winnicott and the movement between object-relating and object-use in *Like Subjects, Love Objects* picks up on the psychosocial and, more to the point, gendered subtexts of this scene: What is the psychic process that produces the infant's recognition of the mother, the primary object, as a separate domain of subjectivity? And how might we use psychoanalysis to theorize domination, especially under the regime of binary gender differentiation? Her theorizing of intersubjectivity ("the capacity to recognize the other as an independent subject") involves a tension between connection to others and differentiation from them, "between the assertion of self and recognition of the other."[69] It is a paradox, in which one can discover oneself as subject only by bumping up against the failure of the world to meet our demands of it: "To the extent that the mother herself is placed outside, she can be loved; then separation is truly the other side of connection to the other."[70] It is the recognition of the mother as a similar center of inner experience, with her own will and her own feelings.

The exteriority of the mother is not an *absolute* exteriority, however. Benjamin theorizes a give and take, in which recognition of the other as capable of inner experience involves the possibility for contact with the mother-object-other, not just through encountering the failure of will, but through shared reality—eating at the same table, as it were. "Separate minds can attune."[71] If such shared reality sounds a little too rosy, too satisfying,

Benjamin emphasizes that such a reality, while attainable, is ephemeral: "Again, this movement refers not to a one-time sequence or final accomplishment but to an ongoing tension between complementarity and mutuality."[72]

Throughout Benjamin's book, it is clear that we need not eradicate fantasy or aggression (as if we could). These are inevitable and constitutive dimensions of psychic life. It is rather the breakdown of the tension between intrapsychic and intersubjective processes that is the danger. "Fantasy must endeavor to eat reality in order for the subject to taste the difference between them. And reality must survive the devouring of the unconscious in order to be more than mere repression, and thus to truly include the discovery of an other," Benjamin writes.[73] Fantasy and reality are measured against each other, and it is only when the world and its constituency fall outside our imaginary command, upon our reckoning with the way the world goes on despite our wanting it destroyed, that we have the chance, a brief one, to touch something real.

Although it still functions in Benjamin and Winnicott as that which is outside subjective fantasy, reality for them is importantly not a pure concept but a concretely relational one. This is quite contrary to Jacques Lacan's bald, severe, and abstract Real: an existential cliff. One dimension of the tripartite division of psychic experience (along with the symbolic and the imaginary), the real for Lacan has no fundamental content, since it is coextensive with "lack," or the gulf at the center of subjectivity.[74] While still tied to hunger and loss, reality in Benjamin and Winnicott appears as simpler, more terrestrial: when someone or something doesn't deliver on exactly what you want or demand, and when there is the consequent opportunity to be with someone or something in and across the gap of differentiation.[75]

Borrowing from Winnicott and Benjamin: if those of us engaged in historical and anthropological or literary description have worried about the destructiveness and aggression in our enterprise, it seems that there is no avoiding it, at least on an intrapsychic level. The aggression arises from a world that cannot conform to our visions of it, even if those visions are under constant *re*-vision. How to not literalize our destructiveness, how to preempt the enacting and actualizing of it, is another question. I would imagine that question has many possible answers, especially since the ways that aggression—our feeling the humiliation of our loss of power—takes many forms and has many kinds of recipients. But on a basic level, rather than being an act of waking the world and its objects up, bringing them to life, in another scene of imagined omnipotence, description might be most real at moments when the practice *wakes up the describer*. It is most real when prompted by the unyielding presence of something or someone else, something or someone the describer can't consume, even as it is a venue for the describer to revise and elaborate their fantasies.[76]

If we take the real to be as Benjamin and Winnicott describe it, "reality" is always a relational encounter after disjoint, perhaps even an embarrassing one. It is not a singular, abstract abyss, but rather an ongoing set of encounters (many realities) with a world of objects that relativize us and what we want out of them. So the real is before us—though not in the artifact per se any more than the stuffed animal. It might be equally in the chair we stumble over in the middle of the night or the dream it woke us from. It is before us in statues when they will not surrender to our touch; strangers or intimates when they give us something different from what we want. It is in the populated world of objects inasmuch as they interrupt our sleepwalking with assertions or indifference.

APPROACHING REALITY WITH WORDS

Returning to Pygmalion: the artist's narcissism and presumed omnipotence are not mitigated by either his attentiveness to material details or his sense of himself as an artist. In fact both of these things aid and abet Pygmalion's elaboration and enjoyment of his power. We are ever in danger of marveling at our own virtuoso performances of fantasized omnipotence and/or trying to explain away talking crosses. I am not attempting to adjust for these dangers, or to imagine a description free from the risks of objectification and power. But I do think description can be conceived of along other lines, and therein lies some space for thinking through how we might reclaim an earnest, if never quite secure, relationship between words and realities.

Because of its debt to Lacan, who understood the real as what the symbolic (language) excludes, poststructuralism implicitly portrays the task of approaching reality with words as naïve at best: reality and language are in existential tension with one another. Language engenders realities, but the real is signification's excess—what language cannot capture.[77] This singularity of the symbolic may not be imperative for reading Lacan.[78] But left unqualified, this understanding of language casts a wide net: words, all communicative modes of exchange seem equally suspicious. Any act of description then would be, in this paradigm, to craft a reality (and/or engage a discursively structured one), creating its own unassimilable remainders. I don't wish to deny the power of words; it's rather that the poststructuralist paradigm of language doesn't leave much room for the interaction of multiple systems of representation.

There have been interventions into the extremity and existential power of language that poststructuralism has passed down, in which multitudes of words, linguistic structures, and symbolizations get condensed and abstracted into a unified concept known simply as *Language*—the tower of Babel before God's jealousy. For instance, the monolinguism that Jacques Derrida theorizes, and that poststructuralist theory generally prefers as its analytical object, postulates a speaking subject always and necessarily captured and violently translated into the dominant idiom.[79] But as Rey Chow has observed in her book *Not Like a Native Speaker*, it is consequential that Derrida was writing from and theorizing out of a particularized experience as a French colonial subject. Derrida's move from language to Language, Chow argues, leaves little room for thinking about the inequalities between languages (or, I would add, about nondominant forms of symbolization) since it universalizes dominant ones.[80]

Chow has addressed the colonial problem of the multiplicity and inequality of languages in various places in her work. After her critique of poststructuralism's foreclosure of referentiality in *The Age of the World Target*, Chow speaks to comparison in literary studies, and the problem of "world literature": "The universalist concept of all the literatures of the world being held together as a totality, one that transcends restrictive national and linguistic boundaries, remains an enormously appealing one to many people."[81] Not only does the project of comparative literary studies rest on a foundational universalism, it also imagines a kind of parity, a "peer-like equality and mutuality among those being compared."[82] Comparative literary studies thus relies simultaneously on a kind of cosmopolitan multilinguism and on translation as its prerequisites, while imagining (out of ethical hopefulness) that languages can be placed in nonhierarchical positions alongside one another.[83] The lack of attention to differential histories of language and the very production of such particularized national identities through colonial frameworks create an implicit paradigm of "Europe and Its Others," according to Chow, which "stabilizes Europe as the grid of intelligibility to which may be added more and more others."[84]

While poststructuralism typically takes "language" as an undifferentiated whole, of which there are only (equally problematic) iterations, Chow invites not just pluralizing our notion of language, but disentangling language from grids of intelligibility.[85] It remains true that words shape and often overdetermine. Words capture, and fail to capture. And all communication is an act of translation, moving from one domain of experience to another. But Chow's emphasis on the "uneven distribution of cultural capital among languages" is a reminder that some acts of translation cost more or differently than others; some languages speak more loudly than others.[86]

This is not to romanticize any system of representation as self-contained or neutral, or (for heaven's sake) any language as more authentic than others. It is to say that not just different languages, but also different idioms or representations within what we might cast as a "single" language, have distinct weights and currency. (Chow notes that the singularity of any national language is a construct essential to globalism and global studies.) It is also to say that *because* commanding idioms have the power to crystallize and gel certain experiences — make them more possible, more recognizable — we might want to pay special attention to nondominant languages and the particularities of what they express. They might meaningfully provide access to or even create forms of encounter with what dominant grids can't actualize.

Grids of legibility mean that some people, things, or experiences appear more real, more material than others, a phenomenon to which we are all accountable. Yet trying to describe any given experience with words is not necessarily or exactly the same, not just as fraught, as pressing experiences through dominant grids — the macro-level ordering tendencies of a discourse. Not all descriptions are equal.

We might understand the art of historical description then as a highwire walk, as we teeter on the line between our indebtedness to grids with their deadening effects and our insistence on chronicling ever more precisely the ways objects live; between a sincere confidence in the potential of words to express the lives of others and the lapses in our capacities to hear objects when they speak. We can, I think, maintain a trust in words to enable contact, to express *something* without capturing it — but perhaps only if we're talking about, around, and outside the governing idioms. In that case while it may not be an absolute Real that we touch, we might still touch a lot of other significant, if less high-flown, realities in our descriptions. But what else could matter?

CITIZENS OF FALLEN CITIES

Ruins, Diaspora, and the
Material Unconscious

Psychoanalytic theories since Freud paint the psyche not only as strewn with objects, but as a site of ruin: an accumulation of remains. But these objects and remains are not passive or dead; they are revived again and again as they become the rich, conflicted materials out of which one builds one's own self and vision of the world—a reality. While Freud more concertedly associated the psyche with ruins, this is the subtext for so many other descriptions of psychic processes: Klein's infant must reckon with the destroyed pieces of her mother, the relics of her own rage, and piece them together anew; Lacan's subject is imagined over and against the disassembled body, a body that is always only a glance away, on the other side of the looking glass, as it were. Attachment emerges alongside aggression. Loss recapitulates itself as reconstruction.

What happens, however, when ruins are treated as more than useful metaphors for ordinary individual and internal psychic processes? What happens when these psychic processes are placed alongside literal, physical ruins? What new things might we see? In what follows, I describe Rome's ruins not only as the results of sociopolitical processes but as signs and symptoms—externalizations—of less immediately visible processes of destruction. Rome built, of course, and built copiously: cities, roads, aqueducts, temples, libraries, baths.[1] But what sleeps in the underground of that construction?

ROMAN RUINATION

There are few storylines more persistent than those of rise and fall: the promise of splendor, perhaps even a stretch of vitality, good fortune, success—and then, of course, things fall apart. Leaders plummet from grace, celebrities descend into addiction, economies crash, nations perish.

But stories of rise and fall are heavy-handed narratives, ones whose work is less to describe any kind of historical reality than to moralize and bemoan.[2] Too much fortune, too much success (or, perhaps, too much *enjoyment* of success), is a vice of the doomed: a parable of excess. The fall of Rome is a favorite trope, one that appears with regularity in contemporary literature or popular news outlets, always with some theory about precisely *why* it fell. The primary error tends to look exactly like whatever the United States is also losing its grip on. Such theories implicitly suggest that if the Romans had just done things right, they would have achieved almost eternal rule, and so we might too. Americans seek but also fear the demise of American power.

People in the ancient world(s) of the Near East and the Mediterranean also understood history as a series of cycles of swells and downfalls. That's surely how we've inherited it. They saw humans subject to the capriciousness of the gods or the storminess of Fate, figures undone by their own corruption or bad judgment.[3] Stories about the rise and fall of cities were not only a frequent literary convention of ancient life but, as Ann Suter observes, a convention that helped shape collectives through shared memory. This was mainly a dramatized and invented shared history, though, since archaeological evidence often doesn't corroborate those laments or narratives of sudden, total, or irreversible collapse.[4] Stories of rise and fall were also pedagogical, warning against improper rule or disloyalty to a god. Of course they were also reflections on impermanence, attempting to give meaning and sense to the fragility of life.

There is a dimension of these tales of ruin, both ancient and contemporary, that is simply dramatized and universal existential grief. "Vanity, vanity, all is vanity"—like a puff of air we, along with our achievements, disappear into the ether. And yet the standardization and the often universalized melancholy of the narrative camouflage and express something else: a real sense, an actual intuition, that something is falling, or has fallen, apart. The people telling these tales are experiencing breakdown.

Ruination does attend the city, the temple, the kingdom, the nation, it turns out, but not as its inevitable future as much as its constitutive feature, and from the very start. Sociopolitical entities indeed *build* themselves through ruination, through processes of decay and degeneration,[5] processes that are then naturalized or hidden from view. This is the kind of ruination that preoccupies me: not a dramatic decline or falling away from glory (except as tale), but a distinct and constant experience of sociopolitical life. Ruination is a means through which political ascendency and power are built. Sovereignty is fashioned in and from ruins.

While narratives of rise and fall are common in ancient literature broadly, they take on special appeal in the Roman period. Stories of bygone peoples and places, of imperial resurrections of cities, of collectives emerging from the rubble signal something of a preoccupation with ruin, one modern people seem to share. As I'll suggest here, they demonstrate the ways ruins are a kind of material social agent, the ways in which they are vital and active participants in social life.

The Roman empire was quite explicit about connecting its own dominance with the destruction of other entities. But the fall of cities in narrative representations of Rome's founding, especially in the early Roman period, betrayed some finer reflections, and some more delicate titrations. Just as Rome was beginning to prevail in the Mediterranean, and particularly as it was conquering Greece, reflections on the fall of Troy were also finding their way into Roman literature. The fabled Troy, the fall of which enabled Greek dominance, gets retold in Ovid's *Metamorphoses*, Virgil's *Aeneid*, and Seneca's *Troades*, for example. In such retellings, there is an implicit gloating over the Greeks, implying that the Greeks, too, will someday be subject to the same fate to which they subjected the Trojans.[6] But there is at the same time a sympathetic identification with Troy. It is not simply a claim of lineage between Rome and Troy, but a "displacement" and projection of Rome's worries of its own fall onto its prototypes.[7] Troy is Rome's predecessor and model, as well as that which needs to be destroyed in order for Rome to become itself.[8]

Troy is a kind of eternal city: it does not fully fall because its progeny will found a city greater than those before or after.[9] Its fall is even part of its immortality, part of what makes it so deeply memorable.[10] But it is also a signal instance for contemplating the costs and complexities of war. The *Aeneid* ends with ambivalence regarding victory. Not only does the Trojan prince Aeneas hesitate to kill Turnus, doing so in a fit of rage rather than calculated or heroic justice, but Aeneas is the only member of his royal family to live, suggesting that the costs of war are both moral and distinctly personal.[11]

Seneca's *Troades*, too, involves some painful queries about the price of military triumph. Seneca describes the way two Trojan children are killed in front of a Greek audience that is simultaneously moved by the beauty and sadness of the deaths and still committed to the killing. It is presumably meant to resonate with Roman audiences who also expressed a mix of longing admiration of and hardly mitigated aggression toward their captured rivals.[12] The impact of the scene is, in Jo-Ann Shelton's words, "to prompt the Roman audience to consider the detriment to Roman morality of the perverse demands that prisoners of war face torment and death with a courageous defiance"—even as that was what occasioned the Romans to fight them in the first place.[13]

To fall, to die beautifully, to be incorporated into Rome all involved grief and wounding, but also promised different forms of immortality. To survive, to overthrow, to dominate, though, likewise meant grief—an unvoiced acknowledgment that one's own demise was only a matter of time, and thus a sympathetic attachment (one both too little and too late) to the ones who perish in order for Rome to live.

We can echo and assume the ancient literature's naturalization of the "life cycle" of empires as simply the obvious course of history, or we can ask more difficult and historically specific questions. Individuals are, after all, threaded into an ecology in which the life and sustenance of some are inextricably tied to the deprivation and deaths of others. Precarity and vulnerability, while universal dimensions of life, are deeply political. It is an ecology in which forms of violence and protection, sustenance and neglect, are strategic uses of power. Your safety might be my intensified vulnerability, my livelihood might mean your peril, and that relationship is neither incidental nor unmediated.

Attempts to characterize the Roman Mediterranean, in both the field of classics and in early Christian studies, have circled around whether the Roman empire's relative longevity and success were a mark of its stability and robust structural machinery, or whether it was always on some level precarious - not just unwieldy, but seething with fear, frustration, and anxiety. Were things impressively sound or were they falling apart? Thinking about ruination and the inherent destructiveness of sociopolitical life, however, leads to the answer that they are in some sense both. Whatever structural stability, whatever durability any sociopolitical entity achieves is not possible without divestments large and small. Strong structure implies profound breakdown. Perhaps more importantly, the social body *feels that*. But the social body also feels that in complicated, oblique, and hardly predictable ways.

To put it more bluntly, if there is simply no kind of sociopolitical belonging that doesn't involve, even demand, destruction, how does this ecology and the destruction out of which political entities are built wear on their inhabitants themselves? How does the knowledge that protectedness goes hand in hand with violence express itself symptomatically or experientially? What are people doing with that knowledge? How can we better account for the social productivity of destruction? Where and in which ways is the ruin wrought by nation- or empire- building unnervingly prolific?

BABYLON'S FALL

Sovereignty and civic or social belonging—particularly diasporic belonging —materialized in and through ruins in antiquity. The Revelation to John offers a condensed and dramatic illustration of the ways in which aspirations of sovereignty, felt senses of disintegration, and the paradoxes of belonging often coalesce. In a pinnacle scene in Revelation, the Whore of Babylon, the archvillain in the book and a representation for Rome, is dramatically vanquished. Strangely, it is also the first time the Whore of Babylon appears, at least named as such. In fact, Babylon's introduction in chapter 16 begins not with her clownish majesty, but first with her judgment: "God remembered great Babylon and gave her the wine-cup of the fury of his wrath" (16:19), and a few verses later, "Come, I will show you the judgment of the Great Whore who is seated on many waters" (17:1). Babylon is always already fallen.

To invoke Babylon is to invoke ruin and destruction. Babylon is of course the entity that destroyed Solomon's temple, which is one of the more obvious reasons Revelation, written in the decades after Rome destroys the second Jerusalem temple, evokes it here to speak about Rome. Babylon, by the first century, is also an empire that has seen its day. So calling up "Babylon" as a figure both immortalizes it as the epitome of empire and represents the current imperial menace and its allure as on their way out.

Revelation is a narrative of rise and fall: it sees the destruction of Rome (and the world) as the pretext for the descent from heaven of a new, perfected Jerusalem that will be ruled by God and house God's faithful. While it is typically and nearly exclusively understood as a Christian text with Christian ideological or social interests, several scholars have highlighted the ethnic and diasporic investments of Revelation.[14] The text doesn't ever refer to Christians, and the term Christian isn't in circulation in the late first century, the moment when Revelation is likely written. So there's no reason not to take the predominance of Israel or Judea as *ethnos* or people as a sign of the text's main point of reference. Indeed this is a story of a blood-ritual cleansing of the impurities brought on by foreign rulers and cooperation with them. A story in which a population figured as a multiplication of the twelve tribes of Israel is liberated and given a new kingdom to replace the recently crushed one, a kingdom ruled exclusively by Israel's god, could hardly be seen another way.

Revelation seems to be a pretty straightforward tale of comeuppance. It imagines Judean dominance in place of Roman dominance, Yahweh's destructiveness in place of Rome's: a subjected population's longing for self-determination and revenge. Scholarship has for decades read this book as a response to the extremity of Roman violence, specifically the bloody and spectacular events enacted in amphitheaters across the empire, and the Roman-Judean war of the 60s CE that culminated in the destruction of Jerusalem and its temple.[15] It is, however, far from clear what Revelation's author would have actually seen, writing from Asia Minor (present-day Turkey) decades after the war and in a region in which amphitheaters, at least at that time, were few and far between.[16] As I'll discuss in more detail in chapter 4, concrete knowledge of or interaction with Roman officials in the provinces cannot be taken for granted. Locals in these areas sometimes gathered their knowledge of the powers-that-be from the impressive construction projects for which Rome was so famous, and a kind of fantastical elaboration of visual propaganda, of which there was much in Asia Minor.[17] The visual propaganda expressed Roman power in sometimes graphic and exorbitant terms—emperors stood as gods over the subdued bodies of those they conquered.[18] And yet few provincials would ever in their lifetimes catch so much as a glimpse of an actual Roman authority figure; perhaps at best they might encounter a local elite proxy for Roman power. So it is not a coincidence then that Revelation matches so precisely these representations.

Neither is it a coincidence that Revelation's triumphal final vision is an extravagant (re)construction project, a new Jerusalem. The illustrious architecture combined with rumors of the war, stories of historical Roman seizures of territory, and vivid depictions of raw power through the images of emperors were perhaps all the author knew of Roman rule. Thus Revelation's fantasy of dominance, whether Rome's or its own, is drawn up in the very fantastical terms the Roman empire provided. As a function of Rome's own stark self-representations, Revelation is not reflective of the way Roman administration and power operated on the ground across the empire generally. But in the face of Rome's reconfigurations of belonging—its incorporation of locals into Roman procedures and structures, at the same times as local cultures shifted, combined, and lost pieces of their histories—Revelation's fantasies of power, of destruction and reconstruction, offer a magnification of what was perhaps a more long-term, and less immediately visible, but no less damaging colonial insidiousness. In other words, this hyperbolic fantasy of Roman power gives shape to psycho-social corrosion and injury that seek a ready language for their articulation. As it perhaps does for readers now.

Revelation not only demonstrates that sovereignty had a deep hold on the ancient imagination. It also reflects the ultimate inextricability of colonial powers and the populations they rule, as ruins make the constituencies of one entity hard or even impossible to separate from the other. Rome presented its power as extreme and alluring, and Revelation makes implicit reference to its own sense of empire's allure.[19] Babylon is, after all, a whore—nothing if not a gendered and sexualized figuration of those twin colonial experiences of magnetism and revulsion. The whore of Babylon and her own destruction in the text impart violent, consumptive desire, and shame for having ever wanted her.

Babylon as Rome implies ruin on several levels. "She" causes ruin and is ruined—in a sexually humiliated fashion. But Babylon as a figuration seems to have fragmentation and decay plaguing it on other, less straightforward levels. For instance, the tower of Babel story in Genesis 11, a comment on the Babylonian empire's power and technological prowess, embeds social dissolution in Babel/Babylon's very project. The city and impressive tower are built in order to prevent scattering, to solidify unity amongst the people, but God punishes humanity, confusing their language and scattering them across the world. The building project is thwarted by Yahweh even before it can be completed—"they stopped building the city"—pointing to foiled potential, a fall before Babel got to enjoy its rise. The scattering that Yahweh performs, though, is ambiguous. This may be a story of Yahweh's judgment on Babylon, a critique of Babylon as "mere babble."[20] But the story seems to be a diasporic origin story at the same time, since Babylon represents Israel's own diffusion and scattering.

This concurrent identification and disidentification with Babylon and moralizing on Babylon's achievements and glory are, as Erin Runions has so strikingly demonstrated, part of the biblical discourse of Babylon:

> Even within the revenge fantasy against Babylon in the book of Jeremiah, there is an implicit identification between Babylon and Judah, representing an ambiguity between them. In the middle of the oracles against Babylon, we find a short poem that seems to speak positively of Babylon as God's weapon (51:20–23). . . . Conversely, a negative identification between Judah and Babylon occurs, as Hill notices, when the oracles against Babylon mimic the language of the earlier oracles against Judah.[21]

Likewise, in second Isaiah, Babylon explicitly and blasphemously takes up the language of God, suggesting not only (as the story of Babel does) that Babylon's power pales in comparison to God's, but that Babylon is a cheap imitation of God.[22] Second Isaiah's figuration of Babylon as a queenly but humiliated woman is likely where Revelation draws its inspiration for Babylon as whore, though Revelation admittedly extends the analogy considerably.[23]

Even more uncomfortable than identification and disidentification between Israel or Judea and Babylon or Rome are a tension and collusion between Yahweh and Babylon/Rome. In Jeremiah, Babylon is both a metaphor for exile and landlessness and a representation of "the possibility of a future for Judah."[24] Babylon's violence, while interrupting Judah's sovereignty, ironically strengthens and enables it as a collective. The explanation for Babylon's conquest is that God "uses" Babylon to punish his people, largely for cultural accommodation—a theme steadily repeated throughout Israel's history. That instrumentalization not only manages to negotiate questions of God's power in a time of helplessness, but suggests that God *uses Babylon* as a disciplinary mechanism to *show how thoroughly Israel belongs to God*. In other words, "God's people" are most definitively God's people when given over to another power.

God's judgment of "his" people, while uncomfortable for its victim blaming, thus imagines a disciplinary power outside of the current, overarching political one (a theme to which I'll return in later chapters, as well). It is a redescription of a destructive (imperial) act that coalesces a people, and the collusion between God and Babylon is at once an acknowledgment of and rhetorical and imaginative response to the hair-raising ambiguity of colonial life. Of course God's judgment and anger are not only the imagined source-behind-the-source of the temple's destruction but also the engine

behind visions of Babylon's ruin. God "restores" his people through defeat
of Babylon, and these visions portray Babylon as "the antagonist against
which to claim transcendent sovereignty and authority."[25] In Revelation this
dependence of Israel's sovereignty on empire's defeat is especially conspicuous, since the swallowing up of Babylon/Rome is tied so closely to the new
Jerusalem's descent from the heavens, a vision that ends with the lamb and
its followers taking up the divine throne.

The new Jerusalem is a city immune from ruin,[26] and is thus imagined
in contrast to both the real Jerusalem and Babylon. The new Jerusalem is
not just *imagined in contrast* to the real Jerusalem and Babylon, though; it is
figured out of the ruins of both Jerusalem and Babylon—ruins that, it turns
out, are pretty difficult to differentiate. Chapter 11, for instance, begins with
reference to the destruction of Jerusalem:

> Then I was given a measuring rod like a staff, and I was told, 'Come and
> measure the temple of God and the altar and those who worship there,
> but do not measure the court outside the temple; leave that out, for it is
> given over to the nations, and they will trample over the holy city for
> forty-two months. (Revelation 11:1–2)

Revelation goes on to describe the "two witnesses" who will prophesy in
sackcloth, promising fiery destruction to anyone who dares harm them (vv.
4–5). After their prophecy, however, the beast will come up and "make war
on them and conquer them and kill them, and their dead bodies will lie in
the street of the great city that is prophetically called Sodom and Egypt,
where also their Lord was crucified" (vv. 7–8). After the two prophets are
raised, one tenth of the city is destroyed in an earthquake (v. 13).

Is this latter part of the passage talking about Jerusalem, Rome, or
both?[27] In the first part of chapter 11, Jerusalem is called "the holy city," and
this city in verse 8 is called "the great city," terms that are not mutually exclusive but also seem to be distinguishing. If it would then seem that the
"great city" that is "called Sodom and Egypt" references Rome, that reference is interrupted by the reference to the place "where also their Lord was
crucified." That would be closer to Jerusalem (at least according to gospel
tradition).

"Sodom and Egypt" is itself an incoherent referent. While Sodom and
Egypt, like Babylon, are both used to figure cultural otherness and sexual/
cultural impurity, both also represent diasporically complicated elements
of Israel's history. Egypt is the oppressive imperial presence through and

against which an "original" Israel articulates itself, even as it is clear that "Egyptianness" is also constitutive of Israelite belonging from the get-go (most notably in the Egyptian lineage and name of Moses). Sodom also figures as a too-close-for-comfort contaminating force in Israel's history. Not only is it the home of choice for Lot, morally dubious kin of Abraham (cf. Genesis 13:12) and the immoral city from which he is narrowly saved (cf. Genesis 19:1–29). But as if testifying to the ambiguity and contagion of Sodom and its destructiveness and destruction, Lot's wife is turned into a pillar of salt for simply, and perhaps sympathetically, looking back as it burns (Genesis 25:26).[28] Sodom is also thus like Babylon in its virtual synonymity with destruction, and its position as the foreign place that one might make one's home, and that one must come out of to be saved from iniquity and God's judgment of it.

This confusion of cities certainly matches the open-ended referentiality of Revelation at large,[29] but it is particularly significant, even moving, from a postcolonial or diaspora perspective. The question of which city, or whose city, is being ruined is evoked by Jerusalem itself, since from economic, political, and even cultural standpoints, it was somewhat typical for the ancient Mediterranean: Jerusalem becomes Rome in chapter 11 because Jerusalem was in effect a Roman city.[30] The associative drift from Jerusalem to Rome expresses not just ambivalence about Jerusalem as a (complicated) place but, implicitly, a question of which is one's "home" city. I don't mean "home" city in any literal sense of trying to place Revelation or its writer in a particular location. Rather, consonant with diaspora theories, I mean that Rome and Jerusalem are "home" cities in that they are emblematic cities that are figures for constituencies and kinds of belonging. "Babylon" in fact specifically evokes the question of the ambiguities of home, since there is such a wide set of attitudes and affective associations with it in Hebrew literature, and there was at least the sense that plenty of those exiled to Babylon didn't want to leave when they finally had the chance.[31]

The visions of Babylon's fall suggest that the ruin of Jerusalem and the ruin of "Babylon" are implicated in each other. In fact, if Babel tells us anything, as both diaspora origin story and story of Babylon's untimely fall, a signal of God's power and God's defensive vulnerability, it tells us that ruin and ruination themselves represent strange materials and moments through which constituencies are at once born and confused, and in which the presumed lines between life and death, power and vulnerability, are corroded.

The Judean and Roman historian Josephus, writing and responding to roughly the same long moment in Judea's history as Revelation, has his own reading of the Tower of Babel story, one that also mixes referents. Josephus, a Judean general who helped lead the revolts that catalyzed the Roman-Judean war, instrumentalizes the story as an allegory to disparage the very revolts in which he took part, suggesting that hubris was what led to the downfall and scattering at both Babel and Jerusalem.[32] Josephus thus reads the Babel story in line with so many other tales of rise and fall: as a moral tale about excess. But what is surprising is the very fact that Babel is *Jerusalem* in this reading, not Rome. Rome is of course the more obvious equation to make with Babel—and Josephus surely knows that that equation circulates in Judean conversation and literature. But his mix-up is telling, and resonant with his larger position: captured by the Romans toward the end of the war, only to write both an account of the war and a history of Israel in Flavian Rome, Josephus is nothing if not illustrative of the doubleness of colonial and diasporic belongings. His allegiances are notoriously foggy and hard to parse: If he's writing from Rome, can his account of the war be trusted? And how compromised is he as an ambassador of tradition?[33]

These questions are loaded ones, and ones that register anxieties about cultural authenticity and ideological purity. Of course his account can be trusted, but less as an account of events or the "truth" of tradition (whatever that is) than as a source among others for how Judean collective self-understanding worked itself out in relationship to Rome in this period. Rome had a long and complicated relationship with Israel, long before the conquest by Pompey in 63 BCE, and one that involved various forms of collusion and cooperation, as well as conquest. 1 Maccabees, for instance, describes the Roman Senate briefly helping secure Judean political independence from the Seleucids in the second century BCE.[34] Whatever the political actualities were, there is at least the notion that Rome once had a less antagonistic place in Judea's aspirations for sovereignty than it did later on. Indeed, in this story, Rome *enables* Judean political sovereignty—not long before it then claims Judea as a province.

It seems, however, that these are not contradictions, and that Judean aspirations for sovereignty in this period are constantly being figured *through* Rome, rather than despite it. In *Antiquities*, for instance, Josephus suggests that the Greek term *Ioudaioi* (referencing the inhabitants of Judah) is coined after the return from the Babylonian exile, despite the fact that the term doesn't seem to exist until the first century BCE and does not have much traction until at least a century later.[35] For Josephus, though, it is importantly after exile and return, after the destruction that Babylon inflicts, not before, that *Ioudaioi* (best rendered "Judeans") become a people or nation (*ethnos*). Josephus's descriptions of the war are associatively close to the language and drama of Revelation, with virtual rivers of blood, mountains of fire, and heaping piles of bodies.[36] Likewise one can find resonance between Josephus's emphasis on the destructive articulation of the Judean god's sovereignty and that of Revelation. But the long-running (and implicit) comparison between Babylon and Rome here in Josephus confirms, as does Revelation, that imperial ruination is not antithetical to Judean expressions of belonging; it engenders them.

FEELING WRECKED

Ruins and ruined places are not just leftover scraps. They are manifestations of social and ecological processes, ones that often become naturalized in the material of ruins themselves. Evidence of imperial or colonial (and in the present, capitalist) muscle, ruins often seem to be obvious in their meaning, and this obviousness gets taken up by diasporic (or other) populations that claim them. Ruins become evidence of a shared past that precedes that destruction, even while that shared past is always being reinvented. Whether physical or metaphorical, ruins are nothing if not socially useful: fetishized, romanticized, renarrated, or reclaimed, they provide endless fodder for collective self-reflection.[37] But ruins can't be bent at will—not completely, anyway. In their stubborn persistence and framing of landscapes, ruins are active material participants, too.[38] Physical ruins often refuse to move or be moved, making resettlement impossible, demanding that they be incorporated into new buildings, or that construction projects work around them, for instance. They often get renarrated exactly because they can't be buried or cleared away. In that way, they physicalize the unyielding heaviness or obstinacy of the past, and in doing so, dynamically shape the ongoing present.

While the Roman Mediterranean was not measurably more chaotic than previous periods, and while the vibrancy and independence of the vaunted Greek city (*polis*) was both overstated and hardly dissolved,[39] some Greek writers in particular seemed preoccupied with a sense that things had deteriorated—they were fascinated by ruins. Ruins indeed become an important site for the articulation of Greek self-understanding after Roman conquest. Take, for instance, Pausanias and pseudo-Longinus, two Greek writers of the Roman imperial period who, respectively, tour the architecture and literature of Greece's past. James Porter has described the way ruins function in Pausanias and Longinus as fragments through which longings for wholeness can be expressed and satisfied, or at least satisfied imaginatively. Pausanias and Longinus, like their contemporaries, prefer to skip over artifacts from the more complicated Hellenistic period, focusing on those from the vaunted classical Greece. The effect, Porter suggests is

> the imaginary wholeness of a Greece that is made to contrast sharply with the ruined condition of the monuments presented. Pausanias dwells upon monuments that are in fragments. Longinus serves up an antique past that is itself in fragments, and deliberately so, in the form of quotations torn from their original seats and contexts. The invitation to readers is that they restore the ruins in their minds.[40]

This "restoration" is one in which Pausanias participates and which creates an idealized notion of Greece and Greek belonging. Pausanias has recourse to both the brief period of Greece's political sovereignty and a much more expansive idea of "Greekness" and the Greek people.[41] According to Porter, Pausanias, fully part of the set of trends and sensibilities traditionally housed under the term "second sophistic," is among other writers who "embrace and exploit the uncertainties of their [Greek] identity." They do so by fashioning their own identity in the midst of the generalized anxiety about belonging in the social flux of the Roman Mediterranean.[42] Ruins in the ancient Mediterranean are plentiful, and not only do they foreground the destructiveness of imperial life, but that ubiquitous rubble becomes the very material through which one's distinctness is claimed and elaborated.

Porter draws attention to a particular passage in Pausanias on Megalopolis that offers a glimpse into what fallen cities evoked for those who considered them. In that passage, Pausanias laments how Megalopolis, "viewed with the highest hopes by the Greeks, now lies mostly in ruins, shorn of all its beauty and ancient prosperity" (8.33.1).[43] Pausanias compares it to other great cities that likewise have fallen from their glory—Nineveh, Mycenae, and, notably, Babylon—describing them as now small, desolate, and modest. He waxes on the inevitability of change, God's will, the workings of Fortune, and how "transient and frail are the affairs of man" (8.33.4).[44]

Pausanias's marveling at contingency, and his articulation of a relationship between the ruined and the magnificent, point to the way ruins impart a sense of the sublime, that which is "wondrous and miraculous, the outsized and the venerable, and above all what lies beyond reach in the present."[45] Ruins are tangible objects that produce a sense of a numinous absence, something outside of ordinary comprehension, but something *felt*; seeing and not being able to see are complementary partners in producing a sense of the sublime. So the fragmentary, metonymic nature of ruins is part of what makes them sublime—they are the trace of something incomprehensible.[46] For Pausanias, his travel and participation in the rituals of ancient Greece through the broken pieces that continue on into his present are what produce the elevated fantasy of a numinous entity, an entity to which he emphatically claims belonging.

The generality embedded in Megalopolis's very name (Greek for "great city"), and the philosophizing on the similar, inevitable fates of other cities—often metonyms for empires—casts a distanced "this too shall pass" glance on the places themselves. There is tension then between these cities' exceptional grandeur and their ordinary ephemerality. Notably, Pausanias is less impressed with the grandeur of the cities than with the wonders of Fortune and her capriciousness.[47] Nonetheless, ruins point both to the magnificence of the city and to its precariousness—indeed, the more magnificent the city, the more precarious its position for Pausanias, as if he is performing his own moralizing reading of the tower of Babel story. Pausanias finds himself enamored most with Greece in its relatively short moment of political sovereignty.[48] Yet his use of ruins to elaborate that vision suggests that the project of sovereignty is always plagued by the inescapable life cycles of political entities. Ruins are the erosion of the exceptionalism on which political sovereignty is so often predicated, the divine sanction of political dominance troubled by the volatility of divine will.

The tension between exceptionalism and unexceptional ephemerality resides in Revelation's own implicit recourse to ruins. The new Jerusalem is a literal restoration of the old Jerusalem in much the same way Pausanias's Greece is dreamt through its remains—it is a perfection of the old city, gathering in all those followers of the lamb and those who are faithful to God. When we read Revelation as a work of fantasizing and mourning Judea's destruction (both actual and figurative) and negotiating diasporic belonging in its wake (rather than, say, as a text about any specifically Christian persecution, social conflicts, or negotiation of empire), it seems Revelation's new Jerusalem is like Pausanias's Greece. Each is a strategically inaccessible place, a sublime place, that not only gets figured in and through ruins but carries important diasporic social traction. Contra Pausanias, though, who wonders at the strange workings of fate and divine will and restores Greece through memory (thus doing his diasporic work in the register of the past),[49] Revelation imagines the physical restoration of Jerusalem as the restoration of God's will, doing its diasporic work in the register of the future.

Greek and Roman self-understandings were mutually constituting, even while they were antagonistic. The Roman-funded revival of Greek philosophy and literature and its coincidence with the most robust moment in the life of the Roman empire is only one example, if a prominent one. The power of Rome to restore cultural identity out of ruins in particular, however, appears in the speeches of the second-century Greek orator Aelius Aristides. His orations on Smyrna, which include extravagant praise for the city's beauty and prosperity, a lament to Zeus for its fall after an earthquake, and a plea to the emperor Marcus Aurelius to restore the city, illustrate the arc in which a civic or political entity is immortalized in and through its destruction. In his letter to Marcus Aurelius, Aristides appeals to the healing and restorative capacities of the emperor, who restored cities in Italy "which long ago were sick" (Smyrnaean Oration [SO]19.10), going on to say that "the restoration of the whole city belongs to you, to whom the gods have given such great resources" (SO 19.13).

In Aristides' palinode, which recounts the promised revival of Smyrna, the revitalizing capacity of Rome is more pronounced:

> But now all that pertains to a mournful tune and to unpleasing dress and whose praise originates from grief has gone away. The continent wears white; Greece assembles to see a happy plot; the city, as if in a play, has changed its age and once more is rejuvenated, being both old and new, as is the tale of the phoenix which is resurrected from itself. (SO 20.19)

Rome's restoration of Smyrna will enable a return to the past, it seems, as Aristides writes, "O blessed are the older men who will reach that day in which they will see Smyrna with her old beauty. Blessed the boys who will suffer no loss, but will behold their country such as it was when their parents dwelled in it" (SO 20.22).

Smyrna's restoration, too, echoes the descent of the heavenly Jerusalem in Revelation, and not just in the ways in which its residents might come "home" again. Smyrna was, after all, "by its nature . . . the very model of a city" according to Aristides: "I think, if an image of some city had to appear in heaven . . . this city's image would have prevailed to appear" (SO 17.8).

Aristides describes Smyrna as both idealized and anthropomorphized, regularly taking on the figuration of a highly adorned and beautiful woman. "Its name is completely appropriate to this city and to no other. For it is a 'bosom' in its gentleness, utility, beauty and form" (SO 17.2). Like the figuration of Babylon as whore, or the new Jerusalem as bride, Smyrna's female form is part of a larger discourse in which cities were depicted as somatic and, obviously, gendered. Likewise, in his lament for Smyrna's fall, Aristides figures the city as the body of the people who belong to it: "Such is the head which you have taken from our people; such is the eye which you have plucked out!" (SO 17.8). Thus ruined cities aren't just emblematic or constructive of constituencies; they also seem to reflect or express the somatic experiences of those constituencies.[50] In other words, the ruined city is not just the ruination of architecture, not just the sign of the decimation of an entity or the crushing of its aspirations of self-determination. As a figure, the city in ruins expressed in a dramatic way the subjective experience of degradation and breakdown in its people.

In fact, ruins are where the monumental meets the personal, and where what we might call "social architecture" is literal, concrete, and distinctly material. Aimé Césaire, the twentieth-century politician and poet from French colonial Martinique, captures this convergence of monumental and personal, this literal materialization of social forces, in his poem "Solid":[51]

> Goddamn it they have secured the universe and everything weighs –
> everything—the gravity's plumb line having settled on the facile
> foundation of solidity—the uranium veins the gardens' statues perverse
> amours the street that only feigns being fluid not to mention the river
> with its pace more sluggish than my feet no exception for the sun which
> stopped its clouds now forever fixed. "Ten-shun!" it is by the way the
> order that resounds constantly from one end to the other of this strange
> army of despair. The world became fixed. The stone is fixed. The
> universal false move is fixed and tell me about your crazy girl manners
> encircled by the world that encircles a river in which each human couple
> is ordered to dip twice and whence moreover the bona fide bovine of
> debacle with its ranch of crosiers and roots will never emerge.
> I am a stone covered with ruins. I am an island hooded with guano. I am
> a pyramid erected by an immemorially disappeared dynasty an elephant
> herd a mosquito sting a small town aggrandized by crime unless it be by
> the Pacific War or the Atlantic Charter. There are people claiming that
> they could rebuild a man from his mere smile. That is why I make sure
> not to leave my teeth impressions on the putty of the air.
> Face of man you will not budge
> you are caught in the ferocious graphs of my wrinkles.

Césaire describes the colonized landscape and its inhabitants (which imply one another) as "fixed," strewn with shit and wreckage, and colonialism as hardening or deadening even that which seems dynamic or alive—the sun, the river, the road.[52] The solidity of the colonized world is juxtaposed with the ghostly, with the ephemeral and disappeared. Not only does the first-person speaker in the poem become "a stone covered with ruins . . . an island hooded with guano . . . a pyramid erected by an immemorially disappeared dynasty," but the speaker refuses to be "rebuilt": to rebuild or be rebuilt perhaps would not only undo the testimony of colonial damage, but also further the colonial edifice of unshakability. While Pausanius occupies a different position relative to colonial power, Césaire's recognition that one *feels like crumbled stone* makes more understandable Pausanias's writing and investment in ruins, especially his deadened tone (interpreted as neutral description), which is only occasionally cut by a philosophical wistfulness.[53]

This affiliation between ruined entities and the somatic experiences of their constituencies appears periodically and sometimes quite pointedly in Judean literature of the Hellenistic and Roman periods. In the book of Daniel, for instance (another book evoking Babylon, in fact), Israelite figures' repeated survival of physical danger and destruction (the fiery furnace, the den of lions) parallels the indestructible, incorruptible kingdom that their god promises. More specifically one finds in this book repeated themes of decline, destruction, indestructibility, sovereignty, and restoration or rising. In one storyline in chapter 2, Daniel, an Israelite in exile in Babylon, saves himself from death by knowing and interpreting King Nebuchadnezzar of Babylon's dream– a dream about the decline and fall of various kingdoms. In Daniel's reading of the dream, the kingdoms that replace one another are symbolized by a statue composed of metals declining in value (gold, silver, bronze, and iron mixed with clay) — and Nebuchadnezzar himself is the gold head of the statue. The dream culminates, however, with a kingdom (i.e., Israel) that will not fall. Indeed, it is a kingdom that "will not be corrupted" and will "crush and abolish those kingdoms and it will stand forever" (Daniel 2:44). In the next chapter, when Nebuchadnezzar insists that everyone bow down to and worship the gold statue he has built (one not unlike that in his dream) or be thrown into the furnace, three Judean men refuse. Nebuchadnezzar, seeing Shadrach, Meshach, and Abednego emerge unscathed from the furnace, comments, "Lo, I see four men unbound and walking in the fire, and no ruin [*phthora*] has come to them" (3:92).

In the following chapter, we find Daniel interpreting another dream Nebuchadnezzar has of his own downfall—this time symbolized by a tree cut down. As Nebuchadnezzar hears his fate delivered by Daniel, the text jumps to a year later, in which Nebuchadnezzar is pictured strolling on the walls and through the towers, saying proudly to himself, "This is the great Babylon, which I have built by the might of my power, and it will be called my royal house" (4:27). But then a voice from heaven tells him he will lose his power by sunrise. Immediately, he is exiled from civilization and is treated like an animal, being fed like oxen and growing his hair and nails long like a bird (4:33). Posing questions about power and what lasts, and noticing that sovereignty has its ironies, the text both implicitly and directly associates ruin and restoration along geopolitical, material, and personal or subjective lines. Ruins seem to reveal not just the slipperiness of sovereignty but a related uncertainty about what it is to be human.

Interestingly, the book of Daniel's narrative trajectory is one in which faith in God is continually rewarded with avoidance of destruction of varying sorts, and wisdom and savvy with positions of power under foreign kings.[54] It is an improbable and idealized picture of diasporic negotiation, in which the diasporic subject manages to ascend to the heart of colonial administrations while they themselves stay steadfast and culturally intact, even as kings lose their minds.[55] No threat is more harrowing than God, it turns out, who produces *real* ruination, often of cosmic proportions, compared with the inconsequential dangers imposed by foreign authorities. Indeed, Daniel's faith is never in question in the book of Daniel. The text prefers to focus on the faithfulness or unfaithfulness of foreign rulers, most compellingly through Nebuchadnezzar's haunting dreams, his idol worship, and his frightened concession about the sovereignty of the "most high" god. Anxiety about destruction circulates around Babylon and its rulers, perhaps out of sympathetic attachment to and identification with them. The result is a displacement of worries about colonial ruination onto the colonial figures themselves.[56] As a text, Daniel thus charts a narrow path in which colonial ruin and the felt dangers of the ruinous God are imagined, against the odds, as avoidable.

For Revelation on the other hand, even while it alludes heavily to Daniel, the possibility of ruination is never fully displaced from its aspirations, and is so more thoroughly unsettling. The untouchable new Jerusalem, that utopian ideal of sovereignty that is seemingly immune from destruction, still carries the hints of ruin within it: by the end, the lamb standing as if slaughtered, that graphic reference to violence and dehumanizing victimhood, resides in the center of the divine throne. Revelation's own dramatic bid for (imagined) political viability in the new Jerusalem thus contains an implicit acknowledgment of the vulnerability at the heart of its project.[57]

The lamb, standing as if slaughtered, is not just a symbol for violence and victimhood in a general way. The lamb also carries specific associations with the destroyed temple—less because of any associations with sacrifice than because Revelation states that in the new Jerusalem, there is no temple, "for its temple is Lord God the Almighty and the Lamb" (Rev. 21:22).[58] Revelation is not the only text of this period to associate Jesus and the temple, however. The Letter to the Hebrews makes of Jesus both high priest and the sacrifice to end all sacrifices, even suggesting that his flesh is the temple curtain (Heb. 10:20), making Jesus's vulnerability and fleshiness a constitutive, material part of the indestructible heavenly temple. Just as distinctly, the Gospel of John has Jesus claim that he will resurrect the destroyed temple in three days, but as if all hope for the physical temple seemed useless or silly, the text clarifies that he was "speaking of the temple of his body" (John 2:21).[59]

In the Gospel of Mark, the earliest of the gospels and seemingly written in the immediate aftermath of the Roman-Judean war, the associations between Jesus's body and the temple appear differently. At the scene of Jesus's crucifixion, Jesus's humiliating torture and death are dramatized as or alongside the destruction of the temple in the war. He calls out that God has abandoned him, is mocked for his helplessness, and just as he breathes his last breath and cries out, the temple curtain is torn in two. Earlier in the story, the gospel makes the association of Jesus's body with or as the temple, or at least needs to account for that association, but retracts it by calling it "false testimony."

> Some stood up and gave false testimony against him, saying, "We heard him say, 'I will destroy this temple that is made with hands, and in three days I will build another, not made with hands.'" But even on this point their testimony did not agree. (Mark 14:57–59)

As we will see in chapter 5, the question of testimony and truth is a significant theme in Mark. But later in the story, Jesus is taunted with these same words, which he ostensibly did not speak, while on the cross: "Those who passed by derided him, shaking their heads and saying, 'Aha! You who would destroy the temple and build it in three days, save yourself, and come down from the cross!'" (15:29–30).

While the text of Mark shies away from calling Jesus's body "another temple," or a rebuilt temple, it does not see an association between Jesus's body and the temple itself as problematic. It would seem then that the Gospel of Mark's initial retraction around the association of Jesus with the temple is simply about the association of Jesus's *resurrection* with the temple. The text rather presses the point that the association of Jesus's body with the temple is that *both are in ruins*.[60]

For the Gospel of Mark, not incidentally, both Jesus and the temple were always already fallen, given that both are predicted (at least in the narrative) regularly and in advance of their occurrence. The "little apocalypse" in Mark 13, which I discuss more in the next chapter, in fact offers something of a phenomenology of ruin, since its *ex eventu* character means to describe *what things feel like now*, in Mark's present. Even apart from the "little apocalypse" of chapter 13, the Gospel of Mark depicts an entire landscape of ruin in its attention to the destitute, hungry, injured, near-dead, stigmatized, and condemned.[61] The story of the Gerasene demoniac, a possessed man consigned to live in the tombs, has been most explored for its colonial resonances,[62] and is as evocative as the crucifixion scene in its associations between colonial experiences of deadness and physical structures. However, the stories of the Gerasene demoniac and of Jesus's crucifixion are only where the larger understanding of colonization as ruination, as at once destructuring and objectifying, makes itself most overt.[63]

While different in their specific aims and historical conditions, the Gospel of John, Revelation, and the Letter to the Hebrews are all embarking on diasporic restoration projects, apparent recuperations of sovereignty through ruins. For the Gospel of Mark, on the other hand, the project of sovereignty—understood both as an imagination of personal self-determination and as collective political autonomy—is itself still in ruins, though, importantly, contingent affiliations and moments of vitality are still possible.[64] As we shall see over the course of this book, the Gospel of Mark is a dark forest of diasporic themes. But each of these texts testifies to the stony, deadening effects and breakdowns of colonial captivity.[65] Christ as seemingly mortally wounded animal and heavenly temple, as destroyed structure that is also surprisingly vital, chronicles ruination as a process that renders material remnants lively, even sublime, and figures people as "remains," decaying part-objects.

DISJOINTS IN THE SOCIAL BODY
AND THE MATERIAL UNCONSCIOUS

The ruined Jesus might also be seen as having diasporic resonances especially given how closely his crucified and resurrected body is tied to collectivity, and not just in Revelation's lamb that leads the faithful to occupy the
throne of the new Jerusalem.[66] In Paul's letters to the Corinthians, in which
the wholeness and coherence of the social body, which meets "in Christ,"
are a primary concern, ruination is both what funds and what threatens a
sense of belonging in the Corinthian gatherings.

Especially in the Corinthian correspondence we see Paul longing for
not just social wholeness, but a very particular kind of social wholeness. He
repeatedly attempts to smooth over the frictions and rough edges of community life. He evokes the language of concord in an apparently anxious
address to disagreements in the community.[67] He conjures the image of the
perfectly functioning, intact body as metaphor for idealized collectivity.[68]
His language around women and gender in the Corinthian correspondence
largely maintains gendered hierarchies, and he consistently polices, or at
least attempts to police, propriety.[69] He's worried about sex, illness, and
eating—the most carnal of experiences, of course, but also and not incidentally ones that erode senses of boundedness or physical intactness.[70] He's
worried about how the community is seen from the outside, and whether
they will be legible to others: "If the whole gathering comes together, and
all speak in tongues, and an unbeliever or outsider comes in, will they not
say you are out of your minds?" (1 Cor. 14:23). Paul notes in 1 Cor. 14 that
he himself can and does speak in tongues, but that those who are speaking
in tongues should speak one at a time and have an interpreter.[71] Shameful
exhibition worries Paul in 1 Cor. 4:9 : "For I think that God has exhibited
us apostles as last of all, as though sentenced to death, because we have become a spectacle to the world, to angels and to mortals" (1 Cor. 4:9). And
of course in 1 Cor. 11, "Any man who prays or prophesies with something
on his head disgraces his head, but any woman who prays or prophesies
with her head unveiled disgraces her head—it is one and the same thing as
having her head shaved, for if a woman is not covered, let her cut off her
hair." The Corinthians, for their part, seem to be a little less worried, even
seem to be occasionally experimenting and playing with the boundaries of
inside/outside, experimenting with vulnerability and power, even and espe-

cially along gendered lines.[72] While much of Paul's language can be chalked up to standard ancient rhetoric and more specifically rhetoric surrounding ancient association gatherings in general, it nonetheless naturalizes hierarchical social relations, not to mention tightly delineated boundaries.

But the landscape in which Paul and the Corinthians are preoccupied with the boundaries of the social body causes them to reverberate not with an assured security, but rather with tenuous and idealized fantasies of collective completeness — ones that nonetheless have social traction. Indeed, the recent (or at least presidential) renewed obsession with wall-building in the United States, while part of a whole set of assertively anti-immigration, white nationalist, and masculinist policies and rhetorics, perhaps offers us a bit of an angle on Corinthians. Physical walls become important to collectives precisely at the moments in which national sovereignty is under distinct pressure, if not rapidly disintegrating.[73] Likewise, the carefully monitored boundaries of the social body — meaning both the social collective and the social construction of the individual body — have to do with wanting to "reclaim" a kind of sovereignty, one largely fantasized and unavailable, as a diasporic collective.[74]

The portrait that has been painted of the correspondence and the landscape of Corinth is one in which questions of collectivity and belonging are at the fore.[75] First-century Corinth was indeed a large and complex urban center for Panhellenic culture, and with a highly mobile population, including migrant populations, military personnel, and members of the merchant class.[76] Corinth was certainly then characterized by various kinds of uproot and social fragmentation in its immediate and more long-term context, a center of cultural interaction and exchange. It was a city whose grandeur and appeal, as well as its perhaps inherent variety and disarray, are indebted to Roman ruination and colonization since it was destroyed by the Romans in the second century BCE and rebuilt in the first century BCE as a Roman colony. Although Corinth was emblematic of Greek identity at large in the Roman era, its Greekness was reclaimed, colonially reconstituted, rather than continuous.

The Asklepios sanctuary on the outskirts of Corinth was renovated at the founding of Roman Corinth in 44 BCE, though very little survives from the Roman period of the cult — there is an inscription, and there are some second- and third-century coins attesting to the life of the cult.[77] Bronwen Wickkiser, in her work on this sanctuary, asks why specifically this cult of a healing god would have been appealing to a Roman colony of freedmen: the cult of Asklepios had a lot of "cultural baggage," in that it was both important to Greek cultural imagination and history, and imported by the Romans.[78] The story of Asklepios arriving in Rome by boat in the form a snake to heal the third-century plague was a staple of first-century BCE Roman literature. So Wickkiser asks, "Which Asklepios did the colonists establish?"[79] Was it an attempt to reinstate Asklepios of Greek Corinth, or import the (more) Roman god Aesculapius? This is not an either/or question, of course, since again, the revivification of classical Greek elements was itself a Roman colonial project. More interesting though, Asklepios was the son of Apollo, one of the divine patrons of Julius Caesar and Augustus, and Ovid's *Metamorphoses* parallels the Apollo/Asklepios relationship to that of Julius Caesar and Augustus.[80] As Wickkiser notes, "In the wake of Actium, the medical skills of Asklepios would have served as the perfect metaphor for Augustus' skills at healing a state torn apart by civil war."[81] This is another instance of the ways in which the life-giving and restoring capacities of the god echo or are otherwise tied to the restoration and resuscitation of the social body, and in particular, perhaps, the restoration of Corinth.

I'm struck by the image of the votive dedications that are often found in archaeological excavations near Asklepios sanctuaries: the terracotta casts of hands, feet, arms, breasts, heads, fingers that were hung or placed in the sanctuary, out of either hope or gratitude for healing. These terracotta dedications were indeed found in Corinth, though they are dated earlier than the Roman period. However, the image of these body parts, these eyes and limbs and bellies and heads, injured, sick, and collected, buried under the ground at the edges of Corinth as people were walking around, perhaps has a kind of social and psychological poetry about it. It resonates with the collection of people, the mixed and fragmented population, of Corinth at large. It is the subtext buried underneath the Corinthian correspondence's body talk, especially (but not only) chapter 12 ("For the body is one and has many members.")

In his book *The Practice of Diaspora*, Brent Hayes Edwards offers a generous description of the social and literary processes that gave birth to Black internationalism in the early twentieth century. He points to the politics of translation in creating links between Black intellectuals, especially in New York and Paris, and the ways differences are negotiated and bridged in the production of Black transnationalist (later termed "diaspora") movements. One really significant dimension of this is the bridging of inflections of Blackness as it appears in different languages and different class constituencies—Negro in English, Negre and then Noir in French, and then *hommes de couleur*. Edwards is interested how collectivity was articulated (and he uses the word "articulated" strategically) without essentialist and nationalist formations. How were the divides between these terms, which signified sometimes very different things, bridged? He borrows from Stuart Hall's use of the word "articulation," which refers not only to giving expression to something, but to a "joint," a place in the body where things connect, and thus to how things might connect while maintaining "difference within unity."[82] The joint is, he notes, a point of both connection and separation. He thus also draws from the meanings of the French word *décalage*, which might be translated as "gap, discrepancy, time-lag, or interval."[83] His project takes inspiration from Black internationalism of the 1920s and '30s to "rethink the workings of race" through *décalage*, that is, through *disjoint*, the points of "misunderstanding, bad faith, and unhappy translation" that constitute a "necessary haunting" of the social body.[84] That is, the points of *décalage* or disjoint, where things don't properly meet up, prevent the social body from naturalizing itself readily.

As interpreters of Corinthians have long noted, there are indeed "disjoints" in the letters, ones that Paul both responds to and seems to illustrate. "Now I appeal to you," he begins the letter, "by the name of our Lord Jesus Christ, that all of you be in agreement and there be no divisions among you" (1:10). Paul's responses themselves titrate between his own divisive rhetoric and his attempts to hold things together. Indeed Paul responds not only to questions of marriage and sexuality (1 Cor. 7), of what to eat (1 Cor. 8–10), of to whom they "belong" (1 Cor. 11–17), and of how to act in the gatherings, but to differences in opinion on resurrection (1 Cor. 15), as well. The Corinthians seem to have understood resurrection as a felt vitality in the present as opposed to Paul's deferred promise of a new kind of body after death and the defeat of worldly powers.[85]

Paul's collapse into anxiety, into hierarchy, into hard lines, and into a future resurrection rather than a present one presents problems for certain ethical and politicized interpretations of the letters. It is also par for the diasporic course, as the ground beneath his feet is not just shifting and unsteady, but full of the vestiges of the fragmentation of other peoples, the fractured figures and forms of bygone eras. Paul worries there is not enough to hold the Corinthians together; he craves wholeness, a resurrected body untouched by death and disease. That is, he craves a kind of sovereignty, and he tacitly acknowledges that can't possibly happen in the world as he knows it. In Second Corinthians, Paul's imagination of the body is more fragile, more piecemeal. In chapter 5 it is a flimsy tent compared with God's sturdier building (v. 1). But also in Second Corinthians, Christ's power to recreate, to render the body new, is claimed emphatically. As if conjuring the terracotta votives at the sanctuary for Asklepios in his mind, in Second Corinthians Paul likewise writes, "But we have this treasure in clay jars, so that it may be made clear that this extraordinary power belongs to God and does not come from us" (2 Cor. 4:7).[86] That Paul merges here, however briefly or subtly, with clay objects beneath his feet resonates in a material key with the psychodynamics that Benny Liew has observed relative to Paul in the Corinthian exchange: "The diasporic Paul is not just a subject of loss of melancholia who mourns his various losses without end, he himself is also a lost object of Greco-Roman imperialism."[87]

Wholeness nearly always brings with it the fear of puncture, the xenophobic anxiety of wounding from outside. But there is connection in disjoint, in failures to translate properly. The aesthetics (if not quite the ideology) of the cult of Asklepios might be taken as a diasporic counterpoint to Paul, especially in its resonances with Edwards's understanding of *décalage*. This could point toward some explanations of the success of the cult in this period: Asklepios is the son of a life-giving and death-dealing god whose main form of restoration (itself a disquieting notion) was gathering broken parts together. These devotees form a social body that knows that the connections between members is one built from pain, not coherent, but still vital, and a testament to the ambivalence of the ties that bind.

"We are afflicted in every way," Paul writes, "but not crushed; perplexed but not driven to despair; persecuted but not forsaken; struck down, but not destroyed, always carrying in the body the death of Jesus, so that the life of Jesus may also be made visible in our bodies" (2 Cor. 4:7–10). The ruined Jesus as a magnet for diasporic self-understanding and sociality suggests that forms of collectivity gather around figures not just incidentally or out of their expediency, but because of their expressive power, their experiential resonance: Christ is a figure for colonial wreckage and the possibilities that attend it.

Collectives often emerge out of rubble, not because they "survive" or because they triumph over destruction. Collectives emerge out of rubble because the very foundations of social life are built with the materials of what's past—and "what's past" is already eroded at least by time, if not by other means. New cities are constructed awkwardly over old ones, the cornerstone of one building becoming the marginalia of another, or vice versa. People inhabit the very places laid waste by themselves or others. They do so preoccupied, often without knowing, by what's underground. Collectives are not "anchored" in the past, in other words. They are rearranging its debris, and arranging themselves in the process.

HISTORIES UNWRITTEN IN STONE

The Frustrations of
Memorialization

Herodotus of Halikarnassos here presents his research so that human events do not fade with time.

HISTORIES 1.1.1

What does it mean to defend the dead?

CHRISTINA SHARPE, IN THE WAKE: ON BLACKNESS AND BEING

Two epigraphs representing two attempts to reckon with disappearance, with considerable time and distance between them. In the first, at the Western historical tradition's ostensible beginning, we find not just an account of military victory and the commandeering of political autonomy—the victory of the Greeks in the Persian Wars. We also find a naming of that work "history" (*historiē*, or "inquiry") as a form of memorialization of great achievements of the dead, their *erga*, which might also be translated "monuments." In the second, we find a response to the normalized effacement of Black deaths, from the spectacular to the mundane, deaths that are mandatory to the inception and function of the nation and its rendition of justice. We find a claim staked on postmortem care, or "wake work," as witness to the contradictions of Black existence in the afterlife of slavery. Both contend, albeit in distinct ways, with how to represent sovereignty's other: the Persians in the former, the Black "bad" citizen or noncitizen in the latter.

But both position themselves as agents in the quandary of what does and does not remain.

In this chapter, I reflect on the ways practices of memorialization attempt to reckon with the effects of political ruination. Memorialization might be understood as an attempt to build a legacy, and it might be understood as marking an event or a life, fortifying against its disappearance. In any case, memorialization means speaking for and about something or someone that has passed, an attempt to generate meaning, often narrative meaning, around it or them. But I'm especially absorbed here with the ways memorialization can also periodically carry out elegiac work for forms of sovereignty, writ large and small. That is, in its attempts to sustain, mark, and/or narrate a life, memorialization often subtly registers the costs and calamities of political dominion.

Memorialization as a practice holds and registers frustration. The relentlessness and strange turns of time, the inability of sovereignty actually to offer what it promises, and other factors intervene in any sense of memorial resolution. In what follows, I cull forms of ancient and contemporary memorialization that, in seeking to care for the dead, or to protect them in some way against the strains of decay, cannot capture the life they long to capture. While perspectivally distinct and politically divergent, this collection of memorials largely struggles with the promises, limits, and consequences of sovereignty, sometimes against their own designs. Importantly, they are frustrated not just by the refusal of the past to be or stay past, but also by an inability to manage the terms of disappearance and survival.

Compatible with the previous chapter, here too I speak to sovereignty and ruination, and the ways that the personal and the monumental touch. I reflect on the ways the ephemerality of life is redressed in the concrete form of writing, and the ways writing both is and is not satisfying for the project of remembrance. But what's more, in this chapter I want to recast what we think inscriptions record, and what we think it is possible to touch, to see, when we deal with inscriptions, those privileged objects of study in the material culture of the ancient Mediterranean.

Writing and memorialization often coincide: this is perhaps because writing creates a sense of agency and power for its writer, and takes on an air of material durability—if in different ways and to different extents in the ancient and modern worlds. Ancient epigraphy then, as especially tied to questions of agency, power, and material duration, becomes a signal instance through which we might consider memorialization and the designs of political dominance as they are bound to the perils of disappearance and decay.

But as we will see, there are clearly forms other than writing that memorialization might take, and the frustrations of memorialization, as well as those of survival, often materialize in less ostentatious ways and places.

THE WRITING ON THE WALL

In that very same hour fingers, as though of a human hand, came forth and wrote on the wall of his house, and on the plaster opposite the light, facing King Baltasar. And he saw a hand writing, and his appearance changed, and foreboding pressed him.

DANIEL 5:5[1]

In the book of Daniel, not one but two foreign kings are tormented by the foretelling of their downfall. Nebuchadnezzar of Babylon is plagued with dreams of which he fears the meaning. But Baltasar of Chaldea is in the middle of a feast for a thousand when a disembodied hand appears scrawling something on the wall—something he apparently cannot read. In both cases, Daniel is conscripted into the role of interpreter, delivering the terrible news of the kings' undoing. Upon these experiences, both kings, otherwise secure in their dominion, sense something terrible is about befall them. But the power of the dreams, and of the writing, is a visceral one: they frighten even before their meaning has been discerned.

While dreams are a familiar vehicle for delivering predictions, the image of the disembodied hand and the writing on the wall is more obscure (however cliché it has become). The words read: "Mane, it is numbered; Phares, it is taken away; Thekel, it is established." It certainly creates an eerie moment in the narrative, and as John Collins notes, "The sudden transformation of the king from arrogant luxury to physical dissolution has a comic effect."[2] That is to say that Baltasar begins to fall apart as the words are written, as if in the very act of their writing his fate has been sealed.

This image—the detached hand, the words on the plaster, the instantaneous deterioration of the king, the anticipation of disaster and loss of power—is a text of the Hellenistic, not Roman period. But I want to suggest that it offers us a trace, an associative thread, for helping us better understand what has been called the "epigraphic culture" of the Augustan age through the end of the second century.[3] Tied closely to monuments, memorialization, and thus to questions of posterity and death, the coincidence of the rise of epigraphy and monumental inscriptions with the most robust extended moment of the Roman empire has piqued quite a bit of scholarly interest.[4] Why does epigraphy carry such traction in the first two centuries of the Roman imperial period?

What do we make of the psychosocial forces behind the impulse to carve letter and line into stone, and how might we view epigraphic culture as part of a fabric of other cultural impulses and forces?[5] Greg Woolf, in a discussion on monumental writing from Roman propaganda to tomb-stones, notices not only that perhaps seventy percent of inscriptions were epitaphs, but that monumentalization and epigraphy had strong overlaps, suggesting that funerary and nonfunerary monuments were often preoccu-pied with the same things—preserving reputation and honor: "The eternity of monuments guaranteed not lasting things, but rather momentary events of lasting significance."[6] Inscriptions are indeed a "special kind of monu-ment,"[7] Woolf argues, one "representing the contingent as permanent and the contestable as fixed."[8]

One repeated impulse of epigraphic culture in the Roman Mediterra-nean more generally is the inscription of names as a mode of location, as a way of marking and fixing one's place in ritual, in a particular set of relation-ships, or in the cosmic order.[9] Woolf attributes this impulse not to universal existential angst but rather to the complex social scene of the Mediterra-nean at this time, which included both hopes for and anxieties about social mobility: an especially high density of inscriptions occurred in militarized and urbanized areas, which were the most itinerant. As Woolf writes, "These monuments stress stability and success, operating ideologically to deny or disguise insecurities engendered by the pace and nature of social upheavals, and omitting to record disappointed hopes and realized fears."[10]

Roman imperial propaganda was most obviously concerned with ques-tions of posterity and the demonstration of honor. But this obsessive mark-ing and longing for permanence were ironized both by the tendency for emperors to rededicate or restore monuments and write their names over others—a practice criticized by writers like Cassius Dio, for instance[11]— and by literature that undercut, recontextualized, and even satirized such inscriptions and their aspirations.[12]

For Freud, monuments and symptoms have affinities. Both are "mne-mic symbols," visible signs of loss, and monuments seek to "soften the loss by building structures within the context of the activity of mourning."[13] There are psychic and affective subtexts to epigraphic culture, and perhaps it is not so much that the "disappointed hopes and realized fears" are omitted from monumental writing as that they subtend it. Epigraphic culture plays into not only aspirations for sovereignty, but longings and losses around it as well. Angelos Chaniotis, writing on "affective epigraphy" in the Hellenistic Mediterranean, examines a number of decrees that recollect military threats and (ostensibly) collective decisions about how to respond to such threats, as well as some posthumous and biographical honorary decrees for those who died with loyalty to their cause and to their homeland.[14] He begins his article by comparing the Themistocles decree from the fourth century BCE, which describes the fifth-century decision by the Athenian assembly to abandon the city in the face of the invasion by the Persians, with a decree from Aphrodisias which, four centuries later, claims loyalty to the Romans against the threat of Mithridates VI. "Without explicitly referring to emotions," he writes, "both decrees nevertheless allude to emotions. The Themistocles decree refers to the hope that the gods will help; to the love of freedom; and it alludes to courage. Similarly the Aphrodisian decree alludes to courage, trust, and faith; it alludes to the concord among the entire population; and above all it refers to the gratitude felt by the Aphrodisians toward the Romans, the 'saviors and benefactors.'"[15] In addition to the more expected or obligatory language of courage and loyalty in these inscriptions, however, Chaniotis observes the affective undercurrents of these decrees. He also notes that explicit mentions of fear regularly accompany claims to autonomy and freedom.[16]

Such testaments to audacity and allegiance in the face of military threat often occur long after these threats have passed; thus these decrees use the language of the past to model courage against fear and goad observers into a similar loyalty.[17] But we might also notice that a landscape peppered with these inscriptions presented constant reminders about battles lost, the shakiness—even long-term impossibility—of complete political autonomy, and the price of belonging. The fluidity of time in these inscriptions, in which one sees oneself in past events that seek to shape future allegiances and self-understandings, also creates a sense of already being "in history," so to speak: one's present loyalties and fears belong to the realm of the immortalized, and the entity to which one belongs is already slated for defeat.

Even outside of the language of cosmic eventfulness and military achievements, so many inscriptions exhibit a surprising level of tumult within the formality and convention. No simple testimony to the virtues or good names of the dead, grave inscriptions sometimes served to hold a place for the not yet dead, often accompanied by a threat that anyone who inappropriately buried a body in that spot would need to pay a fine. One example from a Judean grave in Phrygia:

> The grave and the burial ground beneath it together with the base and the place belong to Aurelia Glykonis daughter of Ammianos, and her husband Marcus Aurelius Alexandros Theophilos, also known as Aphelias, both Judeans. They will be buried in it, but it is not lawful for anyone else to be buried in it. If this is violated, the guilty one will pay a fine of one thousand denarii to the people of the Judeans. A copy of the inscription was stored in the archives.[18]

The glorious recognition and sense of position (meaning both status and location) that memorialization offered were not only unreliable but liable to appropriation and theft. And the consolations of memorialization were weak at best: grave inscriptions often archive sadnesses both subtle and dire at untimely deaths. This is illustrated by a grave near Rome, which commemorates not just a girl, but the meaninglessness and grief experienced by her family:

> A nine-year-old girl entering her tenth year, who also perceives the pointless distress of my parents, I, Julia, daughter of my sweet father, Quintillius Elpidephoros, lie here, inhabiting the final, tear-soaked gift of my father . . .[19]

Epitaphs recounted not just the accomplishments or importance of the person for whom they were written, but also, on occasion, their losses or minor failures, as in this mid-second-century grave inscription from Pontus:

> It was now my thirteenth year. My father named me Aemilianus. Geminos, a man of the nobility, brought me up. In the presence of burning incense (or: burnt offerings), I led the band of revelers mystically in the rite for the triennial god Euios (i.e. Dionysos). I was also revered in the gymnasia and experienced in wrestling, javelin-throwing, kick-boxing, discus-throwing, circular racing (or: using a hoop), jumping, and all rhythmic ball playing, each of which my foster-father taught me. I won with a satyr play (or: satyr dance) at Kyzikos and Pergamon. At Kyzikos, I myself won the crown, but at Pergamon cruel fate carried off the crown. Misfortune withered my body on Dorian soil, but Geminos my foster-

father, carrying my bones to my homeland, placed them into a stone chest
which was adorned with eternal crowns.[20]

This inscription is especially evocative—the withered body, the bones being
brought to his homeland, the "eternal crowns," not to mention the use of the
first person. A striking number of funerary inscriptions mention, like this
one, fate and/or homeland, and it is not uncommon for funerary inscriptions to describe bones being taken back to one's designated homeland or,
for example, to mark out common graves for people who claimed the same
homeland.[21]

Inscriptions such as these delicately entwine an abstract, melancholy
sense of the inevitability of death with the shock of, the outrage against,
its incomprehensible reality. They sometimes attempt to work out the puz-
zles and contradictions of the body—its near-simultaneous strength and
vulnerability, its vitality and breakdowns—exhibited most distinctly in the
withering of the accomplished athlete.

But the regular mentions of homeland in grave inscriptions suggest
they are more than simply waxing on universal human mortality. Threaded
into the language of accomplishment and disease, glory and fate, are not
only allusions to divestment or a sense of displacement, but a subtle mourning for, perhaps even an indictment of, the aspirations of sovereign power—
national, imperial, personal. In both an admission that political ascendency
is only ever built on destruction, and a gesture toward diasporic collectivity,
decomposing parts are rendered into enlivened social wholes.[22] Sovereignty's costs are counted and its conceits reclaimed in and through the materiality of death and in the gathering of bones in graves.

LIVING ON: THE GOSPEL OF MARK AND
THE FRUSTRATIONS OF TIME

———————

"Epigraphic culture" then was full of vexations—stabs at permanence and
legacy were overturned by the simple replacement of a name, and burial
places were subject to dispossession. The Gospel of Mark, to repeat, is likely
written in the wake of the war and thus also the loss of most hope or sense
of Judean political autonomy. The gospel, a gospel "in ruins" so to speak,
registers these frustrations and dramatizes them, and does so in the form of
a somber and wry reflection on sovereignty and memorialization.[23]

Mark is framed by an implicit reference to sovereignty, a reference that also occurs inscribed in stone: "This is the beginning of the good news . . ." The phrase occurs in the Priene calendar inscription, which celebrates the birth of the emperor Augustus, who is hailed as savior and bringer of peace, as the dawning of an era.[24] The "good news" in the case of the Priene inscription refers specifically to the reign of Augustus as a new cosmic order. The Priene inscription — as a *calendar* inscription — is not only a form of memorialization of accomplishments or *erga*. It seeks to structure, or restructure, time along the lines of Roman historical achievement, rendering it in cosmic terms. Mark includes another instance of epigraphy as memorialization, one that also includes a reference to sovereignty. At the scene of Jesus's crucifixion, we find words written above his head on the cross: "And the inscription, which identified his crime, read, 'the king of the Judeans'" (Mark 15:26). It is an eerie counterpoint to Mark's implicit referent at the beginning of the gospel, given the association in Mark between Jesus's death and the destruction of the temple, a moment symbolic of Judea's reckoning with its own collapsed hopes for political autonomy.

Memorialization hopes to organize time — emblematized by the Priene calendar inscription — but Mark struggles with time and an ongoing sense of suspense. Mark 13, discussed in the previous chapter, tells the story of waiting for the end of everything: "Tell us when this will be, and what will be the sign when all of this is drawing to its close?" (13:4), Peter, James, John, and Andrew ask Jesus, after he predicts the destruction of the temple in Jerusalem. Jesus answers with a long description of chaos, violence, and natural disaster. Families will be torn apart, nations will war, there will be earthquakes and famine, all culminating in the disintegration and darkness of the cosmos.

The original question of "when," however, is not answered directly. "Not yet," Jesus says. Then he adds that no one knows, only the Father (13:32). Be on your watch, though, he warns them. You don't want to be caught unaware. This entire chapter, the "little apocalypse," is wracked with questions of time: not just when will all this disaster happen, but how long will it last? Oh, not too long, Jesus says. God will be merciful to his chosen people so he will limit the days of suffering, and he will gather his people together from the ends of the world. However, this passage was written in a present different from the one presumed by its characters, as scholarship has long noted. The present or the near past is made to seem inevitable, predictable, an obvious development, at least to some knowing souls.

There would seem to be an inherent teleology in this literary mechanism

—the world has long been leading up to this climactic moment. Indeed this phenomenon often coincides with what has been termed "apocalyptic" literature—literature that envisions, broadly speaking, cataclysmic resolution to the world's woes. The true state of the world and the ends to which it will return are revealed. In fact, for a vision of the end of the world, the whole passage ends up coming off as oddly reassuring. Not only will there be restoration at this end—Israel will be gathered together from the ends of the earth—but it will come at exactly the right time (whatever that time turns out to be). "Learn the lesson taught by the fig tree," Jesus waxes. "As soon as its branches are full of sap and it is bursting into leaf, you know that summer is near" (13:28).

This apparently teleological bent doesn't quite win the day in Mark 13, however. The question of "how long" until they all die, and Jesus's vague and vexing reply, suggest both a sense of doomed inevitability and a terrifying lack of resolution in the extended moment in which Mark is composed, a lack for which a definitive course of history would seem to compensate. Jesus knows what, and how, but as far as "when" goes, he really knows only that the time will be right. "Learn the lesson of the fig tree." Yet earlier in the story Jesus cursed and withered a fig tree, that exemplar of propitious timing, for not giving fruit even though (as the story says) "it was not the season for figs" (11:12–14). Was the suspense of waiting too much to bear?

Mark 13 archives a survivor's frustration, the frustration of not only having lived through too much, but having to go on afterward.[25] Notably, much of Mark is written in what is called the "historical present"—a past event narrated in the present tense.[26] The practically emphatic use of the historical present in Mark paired with the temporal suspense of Mark 13 not only illustrates a fluidity between past and present—the queerness of time. It also represents a juncture in which the apparent queerness of time meets the demands of story. It is the problem of *history*, in fact. To write history—to by necessity relegate some things to the past—is to long for something to be over, to impose an ending upon it, even as we attest to its continuing pressure on us.

As a narrative, Mark garbles beginnings, middles, and endings. It's worth noticing that this vision of the end in the Gospel of Mark erupts in the middle of the story. After the end of the world, the story goes on, upending expectations of any resolution at all, let alone "at the right time." In fact, the rest of the Gospel of Mark echoes Mark 13 in both its building toward dramatic resolution and its withholding of one. Jesus dies in a climactic fashion, but not only is this the penultimate chapter of the book (the story pressing on beyond that ending), but what is supposed to be the moment of his recognition is undermined.[27] What's more, the final chapter hardly ties up loose ends: Jesus isn't "resurrected" per se, he's "raised," the text says ambiguously, and he's notoriously absent.[28] The women who have gone to the tomb "don't tell anyone" and run away scared, leaving readers with at the very least a lot of questions, if not an overriding sense of dissatisfaction.[29] Jesus outruns death only to be poised between resurrection and forgetting. He can be neither grieved nor celebrated.

The Gospel of Mark includes several such moments of frustrated memorializing. When Jesus is anointed in Bethany (cf. 14:3–9), it is by a woman whose act is criticized by the disciples for its wastefulness, but hailed by Jesus for its prescience in preparing his body for burial. "Wherever the good news is proclaimed in the whole world," he says in a dramatic gesture, "what she has done will be told in remembrance of her" (14:9). Not only is the woman's act a kind of anticipatory grieving, but Jesus's words subtly undercut what would be a more expected insistence at the moment, to commemorate Jesus. That is to say that Mark undercuts the very thing, according to the noble death tradition, that makes a martyr's death meaningful— the memory of the martyr carried on by those who follow after him.[30] Mark gives that weighted remembrance to a woman *without a name*, no less, in a painful irony.[31] The woman knows Jesus will die, but "Mark" (regularly an omniscient narrator) doesn't know her name.

HISTORIES WRITTEN ELSEWHERE: THE "VISCERAL ARCHIVE"

In what later became a landmark feminist historiographical project for the history of early Christianity, Elisabeth Schüssler Fiorenza's *In Memory of Her* takes its name and inspiration from this moment in the Gospel of Mark. Indeed, it seeks redress for the very frustrations that Mark registers. Her book, which found its ethos, terms, and historical picture replicated amongst generation after generation of feminist scholars, crystallized hopes and disappointments bound up in the writing of ancient Christian history. Repeatedly confronted with the silence of ancient literature, its refusal to yield and supply what she wants and needs from it, Schüssler Fiorenza constructs a method, a feminist hermeneutic, and suggests an "imaginative reconstruction of historical reality."[32] She lays claim to her work as fan-

tasy in a certain respect, even while her work relies on a referential continuity between ancient and modern women that goes unscrutinized.[33] Her
work reckons with the scraps and remains of that which patriarchal and
androcentric (in her language) histories have destroyed, thus questioning
what historians name as evidence and how they manage it. In elaborating
her feminist historiographical method, in her stabilizing of the category of
"woman" across time, Schüssler Fiorenza moves between grief, frustration,
and a subtly crafted fantasy of the feminist historian as sovereign subject.
She is the doer of justice, a justice that takes the form of history, once the
record has been straightened out.

Schüssler Fiorenza forces me to pause on my own hopes for "doing
justice" with history, as I overturn stones, literal and proverbial, to register
nondominant experiences from a long-gone elsewhere. How, and to what
extent, can history do justice? What kind of justice would be sufficient for
differential death and disappearance? And where does this particular fantasy of doing justice get us, other than (perhaps) out of living with our frustration?

If absence has its frustrations, continual presence—survival—
frustrates no less. And not all attempts at memorialization foreclose frustration. Sharpe's *In the Wake*, quoted earlier, grapples not only with forms of
presence and absence but, much more explicitly, with the impossibilities of
closure. "I wasn't there when my sister died" is the first sentence in Sharpe's
book, and the entirety of her work reckons with forces and factors that
suspend attempts to account for lives and deaths: bad or biased archives,
disrupted relationships, inept police reports, the vicissitudes of individual
psyches, and more. The normalization of Black deaths means not only that
they go on without remark, but that even the conditions and circumstances
of death barely register. They are, as Sharpe describes, "the weather." Sharpe,
though, curiously begins not quite with the absence of information around
her sister's death, but with her own absence from the scene of her sister's
death. Sharpe herself is not there. Where she is: at an academic conference,
finishing her "first attempt at the work that became this book"—a book
called *In the Wake*. In her work trying to mark the many forms of Black
death as they are indebted to slavery, to be present to the ongoing life of
slavery, she is interrupted by a death for which she is not present.[34]

Sharpe's book does not seek resolution to the problem of Black social
and political negation in which Blackness is rendered sub- or nonhuman—
the undertow of U.S. sovereignty. She opposes the logic of monuments and
memorials that would seek to contain histories of slavery, to situate them

solely in the past and thus transcend them.[35] She "looks instead to current quotidian disasters in order to ask what, if anything, survives this insistent Black exclusion, this ontological negation, and how do literature, performance, and visual culture observe and mediate this un/survival."[36] She addresses forms of expression that "depict aesthetically the impossibility of such resolutions by representing the paradoxes of Blackness within and after the legacies of slavery's denial of Black humanity."[37] Sharpe is driven by the "gaps and unanswered questions," the unknowable pieces, weighing heavily on those left to deal with Black deaths, individual and collective.[38] And yet the power of the wake is, for Sharpe, the "power of and in sitting with someone as they die, the important work of sitting (together) in the pain and sorrow of death as a way of marking, remembering, and celebrating a life."[39] Wake work means remembering and marking the lives and deaths of others, but it also means contending with, living with not against, the continual frustration of absence, erasure, negation.

Like Mark, Sharpe continually reveals the ways in which linear time is undone. It is undone specifically in the paradoxes of Blackness. Blackness is "in and out of place and time."[40] Given Sharpe's elaboration of the slave ship as grounding metaphor and condition for thinking through Black life and death, she associates this interruption in linear time with not just stopping (stop and frisk), but holding (the belly of the ship), and being in the middle (the Middle Passage).

In one chapter, Sharpe describes a discussion between her friend and her friend's son, in which her friend's son asks for a bulletproof shirt. "She promises him that they will protect him, that they will keep him safe. She does this knowing before, and as, and after, she writes this, that there is a limit to what she can do to protect him; that there is no safe space."[41] Sharpe poses, "What kind of mother/ing is it if one must always be prepared with knowledge of the possibility of the violent and quotidian death of one's child?"[42] In the wake, motherhood involves a kind of anticipatory grieving, a hauntedness not just by the past, but by the future. And indeed Black death is the guarantor of the nation's future, what is deemed necessary to the continuity of national sovereignty and the freedom of those citizens deemed worth protecting, or those who are in a position of being deemed citizens at all. Sharpe's sense of continuity then is not only that the present is a continuation of the past, but that the pushing forward of the past means deep precarity for some to ensure the sustenance and prerogatives of others.

Simone Browne's reading of the conditions and layout of the slave ship *Brooks* in her book *Dark Matters* likewise finds the slave ship to be both figuratively and materially significant for understanding the contradictions of Blackness and the foundations of U.S. sovereignty. Browne complicates Foucault's singularly influential take on surveillance in *Discipline and Punish* by demonstrating the ways in which the population production and management tactics attending the transatlantic slave trade are critical to the history of surveillance, and thus to the way in which U.S. sovereignty articulates itself at present. The slave ship is then paradoxically the form of documentation that disappears from our histories of documentation. It is that which has not been seen even in histories that critique the visual field.

So I'd like to settle on the belly (of the ship), the middle (passage), the place that holds the objectified, commodified — consumed — bodies of slaves. If the slave ship is an archive, in the sense that it both holds histories and produces history, it is certainly a "visceral" one.[43] Its effects, and affects, reverberate in the body, even as they regularly disappear from other forms of documentary history. The slave ship and the national/imperial sovereignty it helped birth into being prompt us to attend to objects that live inside and to reconsider what counts as history. What happens to history when we consider what lives in the belly?

In antiquity (no less than the present), the belly was a major preoccupation. One example: a great many magical gems used for healing referenced the belly and ailments or diseases associated with it. "Belly" of course references not only the stomach but the digestive and even reproductive systems (especially the uterus) together. As Véronique Dasen notes, "*Stomachos* is constructed with *stoma*, the mouth, and can describe other organs with an opening, such as the uterus, the bladder, the esophagus and the larynx. The range of 'stomachic' diseases is thus very large."[44] With a kind of offhanded curiosity, though, she wonders, "Why do so many gems insist on diseases originating in the belly?" She concludes: "Certainly, partly because food poisoning and intestinal parasites were not rare. Just as in modern nations the doings of one's bowels are widespread, almost obsessive, concerns, so the *stomachos* and its ailments became a sort of '*maladie de société*' in Roman antiquity."[45]

Perhaps the most well-known case of digestive misery is Aelius Aristides, whose famous "hypochondria" (as it is often described) sends him repeatedly to the Asklepieion. Dasen observes a more material component for the ancient obsession with the stomach but doesn't offer any more speculation or resolution. She does note the unique characterizations that the stomach takes on in ancient literature, however. It has a kind of autonomy ("independent will"), but at the same time is not associated with virtue, and certainly not with self-possession. The stomach *undoes* self-possession; it has "strong needs" and is "the seat of uncontrolled emotions, usually negative." One *feels things* in the gut; one gets a *visceral sense*—a sense that has an ambiguous relationship to, is perhaps at odds with, the rational subject.

Maladie de société is a felicitous choice of phrase, since it holds together in a literal way something of both the pathological and the social realms. We might take seriously the physiological vagueness implied in recourse to the "belly" or "stomach" (likewise, the bowels or the guts), and the strong affective valences associated with that region, to suggest that as a social malady, these stomachaches register something more than "simply" a malfunctioning of organs. And yet they are also not "psychosomatic" in the sense of either being "made up" or relieved through an individual psychological catharsis. They compose a visceral archive, a nonconscious account of social forces as they converge on, and implicate, individuals.

These gems emerge on a whole landscape of frustrated memorialization. Like ruins, they are where flesh meets stone, where body becomes object. But what does it mean when the organs associated with digestion, sustenance, and reproduction "speak"? What are they saying? The amulets and gems Dasen describes might offer some suggestions. One of the themes in the engravings and images on these objects is the "agonistic" notion of disease common to the ancient world, in which one has been invaded, even "assaulted" by an outside force (not always a demon).[46] Indeed, Dasen notes the prevalence of Ares/Mars or other figures associated with war; diseases are often "visualized as a bound or defeated enemy."[47] What's more, the disease is often represented as wild (*agrios*) or bestial (*theriodes*), a creature "disrupting the civilized order."[48] This is compatible with medical literature in which "[l]ike an animal, a severe disease is devouring, *phagedaina*, and eats the flesh."[49]

These gems require that we hold the psychic, physiological, and sociopolitical (as well as the material) together. In her book *Depression: A Public Feeling*, Ann Cvetkovich redescribes depression as a social symptom, doing so against the grain of the pathologizing and medicalizing discourses that understand depression as a chemical and individual problem. She treats the thick contemporary American landscape of depression as intimately tied up with the numbness, emptiness, and numerous daily violences incurred by late capitalism and, significantly, the histories of colonization and slavery that undergird American existence. In one chapter, Cvetkovich hones in on diasporic sadnesses that (overlapping with histories of slavery and colonization) emanate from geographic displacement. She addresses African dia-

sporic sadnesses in the work of Octavia Butler, Saidiya Hartman, and Jacqui Alexander, giving specific attention to the distinct strategies each writer
takes in her attempt to heal. Cvetkovich notices that, in some instances,
these strategies for healing are negotiations of sovereignty, particularly on
antinationalist or nonnationalist terms.[50] In this body of work "the psychic
is also a domain for sovereignty and one that is intimately connected to
questions of land rights, governmentality, and political transformation."[51]

Cvetkovich's reading of Jacqui Alexander is particularly striking, in
that she notices in Alexander's concertedly spiritual account of healing a
recourse to the connectedness of all living things, the African notion of
ase, a shared life force. Cvetkovich sees this as a direct if implicit response
to biopower and biopolitical systems. And it seems this might be related to
a certain gut-level chafing against the world's very specific and differentiated cruelties. In fact, while depression is a condition or state that involves
lots of different kinds of feelings (anger, helplessness, pain, melancholy,
numbness), depression is only one way in which one registers this terrifying entanglement of the life and sustainability of some with the suffering
and deaths of others.

Importantly, Cvetkovich puts these accounts of African diasporic
depression alongside those of writers such as Sharon O'Brien and Jeffrey
Smith, who write on their histories in working class families in Boston and
Appalachia, respectively, to produce a picture of diasporic depression that
crosses racial lines. It is a depression tied not just to geography and disloca-
tion but to the breakdown of aspirations of upward mobility, a response to
the thinness and chimerical nature of the American Dream. While maintaining sensitivity to the distinct differentials in the ways that racism plays out
on the bodies and psyches of people of color, Cvetkovich seeks an alternate
picture of the American psychosocial landscape in which "we are all living
in an environment steeped with racialized violence: the land we walk on is
stolen, the labor that produced the things we use is underpaid and exploit-
ed, the neighborhoods we live in are either segregated or gentrifying."[52]

The healing gems present us with a compatible instance in which ancient people express conflict, discomfort, and/or melancholy around the imperially structured "web of life." The representation of disease as war, for instance, in which the "enemy" is bound and defeated—contained, put under
control—is of course an installation of fairly predictable ideology, and standard disease etiology, in which the individual and/or social body fends off
invaders. It naturalizes defeat of an enemy other as wellness and equilibri-
um, and imagines the body as, in its most ideal state, bounded with borders

secured. Attempting to process relationships between war and civilization, the creaturely and the human, these healing gems express, if sometimes only subliminally, the ways in which one's own life, prosperity, or sustenance might mean, or even require, the intensified vulnerability of another.

This felt ecology of violence might reframe the trope of the destroyed and consumed body that appears in the associations of Christ's crucified body with bread and wine, the story of Perpetua the lactating martyr, or more pointedly, in the letters of Ignatius of Antioch. Although whether Ignatius himself ever existed is debatable,[53] these letters offer an extended meditation on colonial consumption, expressing a wish to die as a desire to become "food for beasts," wheat ground for the "pure bread of Christ" (Rom. 4.1). A few lines later, the soldiers attending Ignatius are likened to "wild beasts . . . who become worse when treated well" (Rom. 5.1). This not only insults them by calling them animals but makes a kind of subtle commentary on the political "food chain."[54] "I have no pleasure in the food that perishes nor in the pleasures of this life," Ignatius writes. "I desire the bread of God, which is the flesh of Jesus Christ, from the seed of David; and for drink I desire his blood, which is imperishable love" (Rom. 7.3). Rather than propagating a Christian theology or constraining a set of ritual meanings, the letter echoes back darkly a relatively mundane notion: life in this world is death, and death nonetheless promises vitality.[55]

In fact the Roman arena, the scene of Ignatius's impending death, has already been described by scholars in ecological terms, and even with some biopolitical (or necropolitical) subtexts.[56] The theatrical dimension of the arena, in which mythical and historical battles are reenacted, criminals are executed and animals devour the condemned, offers up for consideration — through "consumption" by spectators — the ways in which power orchestrates the terms of life and death at large, and how the social body feeds and sustains itself with the bodies of certain, often criminalized, populations. Ancient discourse on the arena is full of latent recognitions that the people who die there die "like animals," and that the arena is a place in which "civilization" both depends on the dehumanization of certain populations and itself comes dangerously close to devolving into "animalistic" states.[57] The boundaries of civilization in the arena especially are understood through the category of the animal and terms of consumption, visual or literal.

The appeal to sacrifice in these letters as a way of understanding death, too, might be read ecologically. While sacrifice itself has various meanings and practices associated with it,[58] as part of material economies and expressions of cultural distinctness, it was also simply a mode of production of food. As a mode of production of food, however, it likely already contained ample space for reflections about the interimplication of life/sustenance and death, especially on a grand scale. In combination with the "for you" formulation of noble death mythologies, such a notion of a death being a "sacrifice" or "ransom" amplifies the sense that one's living is entwined with another's dying.

Ignatius's letters are likewise steeped in worries about agency and memorialization. "All the pleasures of the world, and all the kingdoms of this earth, shall profit me nothing. It is better to die in Christ Jesus than to reign over the ends of the earth" (Rom. 6.1). If, as Cvetkovich suggests, renegotiations of sovereignty sometimes happen in attempts to heal, the renegotiation in Ignatius's letters occurs through an imagination of his death as voluntary and virtuous. In figuring his death as "for you," the letters anxiously bind Ignatius to the inherent memorialization of noble death traditions. If these letters truly belong to a historical Ignatius, the letters themselves might be understood as a significant piece of Ignatius's own attempt at self-recovery: he renders himself a "word," attempting to preserve himself through language as redress for his physical disintegration.[59]

In describing Ignatius's death as a sacrifice "for you," though, Ignatius's letters partake of the same economies and cultural politics of life and death from which their subject wishes to sublimely absent himself in the first place. Christ's death promises vitality for those who can die in heroic subjection, rendering senseless violence cosmically meaningful. But so does the politics of ruination, as that which is destroyed or eaten is absorbed into the social body for its "greater good." That is to say that Ignatius's letters do not refuse the politics of ruination as much as simply registering those politics in a different key, telling their own story of anticipatory grieving. Ignatius is cast in an intimate and sorrowful ecology in which the life and prosperity of the social body depend on a set of sinister and consumptive interrelations.

Ignatius, as he appears through the letters, is a figure who circumscribes his own death as best he can, trying to place himself into history, even as he knows, or maybe because he knows, he will enter the visceral archive. And the visceral archive holds, among other things, the pains and conundrums of historical accounts. Ignatius, Mark, Sharpe, and others—including, notably, those others of us spending so many hours writing about violence and pain and ruin—seek recourse for asymmetrical violence through writing, and witness in different ways to what little recourse there is. One problem is that we don't always know exactly what we're captive to: our relationships to forms of loss or ruin are often multiple, incongruous and confusing, appearing sometimes as, for instance, a feeling in the pit of the stomach, a vague notion that something doesn't "feel right." We are captive not just to ecologies of ruin, but to fantasies of agency and power. What happens when our forms of remedy—in this case, our fantasies of agency in the form of writing and memorialization—fail to provide what they promise? What is going on when they seem to succeed?

Memorialization, particularly when enacted through the medium of writing, is an attempt at recovery of and from sovereign power. But the visceral archive is where history as a sovereign project is undone, not to mention where the ongoingness of the dead materializes. As such, the visceral archive logs a continuity that will only ever outdo us, holding the trace of an ache we cannot seem to name.

4

TERTULLIAN OF CARTHAGE AND THE MATERIALITY OF POWER

COAUTHORED WITH CARLY DANIEL-HUGHES

As the letters of Ignatius remind us, it would be hard to speak for long about memorialization and ruin without stumbling into the stories of the martyrs. If martyrdom in the history of Christianity was long understood as a history of persecution and faith witness, scholarship of the past few decades has demonstrated that Christian persecution was largely fictionalized, but socially useful: it has recast martyrological literature as part of a discourse of Christian identity production, and even *central* to the production of a Christian identity (and then orthodoxy) in late antiquity. In this more recent scholarship, martyrdom literature has been an object of intense interest, investment, and imaginative (historical) elaboration, and not just because of its appeal to graphic violence. It is also because it houses some of the most unsettling claims endemic in the longer history of Christianity—innocence and exceptionalism.

The work in this and the next chapter specifically reads martyrological texts against the grain of their modern reception, asking what *else* we see when the object of our inquiry is not the privileged (and, for the most part, historically unviable) object of Christian identity, but rather the lost object of ethnic peoplehood. Alongside and part of that reorientation, these chapters too offer their own expansions and reconfigurations of what it means to direct attention to materiality and material culture. The next chapter cuts across the language/materiality divide by treating martyrs' last words as material culture—that is, as culture that materializes through the voice and in the body. This present chapter springs from the way physical objects, specifically those objects disseminated by the Romans to express their power, cultivate elaborate fantasy lives. However, it lingers more fully on the way supposedly insubstantial fantasy lives are themselves evidence for describing the texture and force of imperial power, and the ways these fantasies likewise end up being the essential material out of which real populations are born.

Tertullian of Carthage, the third-century writer often catalogued as an "early church father," is the route to the reconfigurations in this chapter. His writings are an expression of the fantasy life of power in Roman North Africa and beyond. Tertullian paints gothic melodramas in which Christians come into violent confrontation with Roman officials. He exhibits fascination with stark relations of domination and submission, and an ultimate trust in power to demonstrate the truth of who one really is. Tertullian has also been of interest almost exclusively to scholars of early Christianity. But grounded in (and relativized by) the colonial matters of Roman Carthage, Tertullian's writings actually don't speak to anything particularly or distinctly "Christian." Tertullian's Christians, it turns out, are fantastically summoned, too. But Tertullian's writings do offer a whiff of an uncanny landscape, one bathed in the fantastical imaginations that Roman power ignited through its curious combinations of distance and presence. Likewise, Tertullian provides a glimpse into the productive and haunting power of preoccupations with juridical scenes, one for which the eventual production of a Christian population is not incidental.

TOUCHING THE DIVINE

The aspect of erotic transference that I will address here has to do with the analyst as the bestower of recognition—the one who knows, or could know, the patient. To be known or recognized is immediately to experience the other's power. . . . The other becomes the person who can give or withhold recognition, who can see what is hidden, can reach, conceivably even violate, the 'core' of the self.

JESSICA BENJAMIN, "WHAT ANGEL WOULD HEAR ME?"

In the analytic scene, transference is projection of the qualities or thoughts the patient imagines the analyst possesses. In writing about the erotics of transference, Jessica Benjamin draws a parallel between the power of the analyst, as experienced by the patient, and the power of the divine (in this case, the figure of the angel). The potential of the analyst to *truly see* the patient produces both awe and threat in the patient, a fear of annihilation. This godlike power, erotic at its core, is of course idealized, wishful, and a consequence of the mystery surrounding the analyst in the analytic space. It produces both admiration and submission.[1] The patient knows little, if anything, about the analyst aside from the way in which they present themselves in that space. But the gaze, the receptive ear, in combination with the particular physicality of the analyst, affords just enough specificity to give flight to fantasies of omnipotence.

Mystery produces power. The smile without words, the message unanswered, a late arrival unexplained: it is the absence of detail — or, perhaps, the presence of only a few key details — that sets entire imaginative worlds of terror and potential in motion. Nothing commands our fierce attention like speculation, and nothing elicits our speculation like the fragmentary.

The Roman empire has long held a central place in the modern European and American imaginations: its breadth, its grandeur, its accomplishments, and, more recently, its severity. Our distance from Rome, our sometimes fragmentary sense of its conditions and machinations, enables these imaginations, as modern people fill gaps in knowledge with projections, fears, a sense of nostalgia — and more. But the Roman empire, as a specific governing power, was no less of a mystery and preoccupation amongst some of its constituencies, and likewise inspired fantasies about its dominance over the Mediterranean in its own moment.

The Romans were in some ways ubiquitous, in that evidence for their dominance could be seen everywhere. Yet Roman rulers themselves were rarely if ever seen — untouchable. Indeed Roman rule might itself be characterized as, in part, a fantastical project cultivated through material objects. To name two examples, paper and stone (documents and statuary): Roman rule often meant the rulers themselves stood back and gave a lot of tokens of themselves away, whether via paper or body-objects for consumption.

Bureaucracy and documentation, which proliferated with expansion of the empire, was how Roman ideology managed to slink into the minds of its subjects.[2] Roman bureaucracy not only managed the sometimes significant distance between Roman authorities or administrators and provincials, but also shaped literary, historical, and legal imaginations.[3] What's more, ritual participation in Roman bureaucratic documentation (property records, the census, death registrations, poll taxes) concretized and reassured what might have otherwise been an amorphous sense of belonging to an almost incomprehensibly large and far-flung entity.[4]

This sense of unity and coherence of the empire was also generated through the depiction of the emperor's divine body as symbolic of the social body—a body dispersed across the empire in friezes and statues that depict the hypermasculine Roman rulers, often against the subjected and feminized bodies of those they conquered. It's now a universal assumption that Roman rulers leaned heavily on visual propaganda to communicate their status and authority to their vast constituency, and the physical body of the emperor occupies a special place within this propaganda.[5] Roman depictions of the emperor as military victor and patriarch were not simply forms of intimidation and expressions of dominance over those he conquered, but rather over time managed to sweep populations up into an imagined whole, bound through Roman benevolence as much as conquest.[6]

But these astonishing visuals, as well as the libraries, baths, roads, aqueducts, and colosseums for which Rome has now become so famous, were a primary point of contact between most of the population in the ancient Mediterranean, especially those in the provinces, and those who ostensibly ruled them. One simply did not encounter—and did not expect to encounter—Roman governors, let alone Roman emperors.[7] In most places across the Roman Mediterranean, client rulers and Roman legions were the primary or even sole forms of Roman bodily presence that one confronted, and these were obviously mediated or delegated ones. In North Africa, contact with any direct form of Roman administration could be sparse or nonexistent. Images of the emperor, like the documents that issued forth from him, was as close as one could get. The proclaimed divinity of emperors is possible only because of their physical remove, which both heightens their power and requires more imaginative energy to conceive.[8]

The strong and smooth bodies of the emperors, their raw and frightening power elegantly scored into marble, corroborated, if only intermittently, in legions, monuments, and arenas, took on a life of their own. That life was often highly eroticized. There was widespread ancient enchantment with the bodies, sex lives, and objects of affection of Roman emperors, from the standardized stories of emperors "poaching" the wives of Roman elites, to the same-sex romances of Hadrian and Antinous and Nero and Sporus.[9] Caroline Vout argues that the historical value of these stories is not in their verifiability but rather exactly in their "gossip" value—the fact that ancient historians and the larger public alike devoted so much thought to these stories and figures in the first place. Vout hopes to "open up a world that sees the display of imperial power not as force, or written decrees, but as a series of stimuli (stories written by Suetonius, statues erected throughout the empire) to make subjects imagine what it might be like to be, or be with, the emperor; a world where responses to the emperor are neither embassies nor revolts, but personal feelings, flights of fantasy, and gossip."[10]

The gears of Roman power turned in the minds of its subjects. And Roman power often came in the form of the promise of recognition,[11] *even if that recognition was internal to the subjects themselves*. If documents installed a sense of being seen from afar, the rituals and ceremonies associated with the imperial cult were an eternal preparation for being seen, a performative anticipation of it: the honorary activities (e.g., festivals, sacrifices) associated with the imperial cult were hardly performed for the direct recognition of emperors as such, especially since emperors hardly visited, going decades or even a century without an appearance in some provinces.[12] These rituals were rather modes of self-representation for provincial people, symbolic systems crafted for, as Price puts it, "making sense of an otherwise incomprehensible intrusion of authority into their world."[13] Price's description of the work of these rituals bears striking resemblance to the work of fantasy: the psyche representing the world and the self to itself—an attempt to make sense of relationships, feelings, and contradictions in the self and the world.

Once again, in theories of the psyche, fantasy is not antithetical to reality. It is the knitting of a reality, one that is under constant revision as it encounters new information or its own limits. So what difference might it make to mind this contrast between the presence by proxy and the distinctive physical *absence* of actual Roman rulers from the lives of so many of those they ruled? How does one think about specifically *Roman* violence and what is "real" about it, given the steep and elaborate fantasy life of power that the Romans cultivated? This latter question cannot be answered universally or unequivocally, of course, and it has pressed heavily on scholarship on martyrological literature as it has become clear that any sort of historical persecution of Christians was mostly fabricated. This is even while scholarship has emphasized that the literature that falls under the heading of "early Christianity" struggles with violence as a significant part of its critical and creative work.[14]

And in fact the question is not "whether" or "how much" violence there was. Rather the question is *what kinds* of violence are we looking for?[15] Provincial subjects seemed to live with a lot of physical brutality, for instance, but the overwhelming bulk of this brutality was at the "micro" or local level, only occasionally actually adjudicated and inflicted by authority figures— also largely local elites—working within Roman legal arrangements.[16] To what extent are these local elites imagined by those they governed to be Roman?, one might ask. And when we speak of specifically Roman violence, we might ask in tandem, how do certain more ambiguous or diffuse forms of pain and felt violation get expressed in the minds of those who suffer it? There are ambiguities inherent in colonial imposition—that is, less acutely or obviously repressive or oppressive forms of divestment such as cultural appropriation, resource redistribution, loss of traditions, and altered self-understandings. How might these experiences create a longing to communicate the urgency of such conditions and effects in terms that would more readily be recognized as "violence"? Another question we might ask, one that goes beyond Roman history: When are we entering the fantasy life of power conjured by the authors we read, and how might we do some "reality testing," as it were?

TERTULLIAN AS WRITER AND
ROMAN COLONIAL SUBJECT

Magistrates of the Roman Empire, seated as you are before the eyes of all, in almost the highest position in the state to pronounce judgment: if you are not allowed to conduct an open and public examination and inquiry as to what the real truth is with regard to the Christians; if, as happened latterly in the Proconsul's secretariat, hatred of this group has all too effectively blocked its defense—then let the truth reach your ears by the private and quiet avenue of literature.

TERTULLIAN, APOLOGY 1.1[17]

The picture of Tertullian of Carthage that lives in the contemporary scholarly imagination is not only of an avid proponent of martyrdom but of a writer who argues for his own fully worked out theology of martyrdom, and who thus falls on an obvious doctrinal trajectory within the clear (by his time) social phenomenon of Christianity. In this traditional picture, his brooding fixation on power and its inversion is a function both of the ways in which Christians figured themselves in relationship to Rome, and of the extremity of Roman cruelty (to Christians, or in general). His opponents are real, and the stakes are high for him and his interlocutors as they carve out social roles and ideologies for Christians as they confront the challenges of Roman targeting and subjection.[18]

But one might entertain a different picture of Tertullian: a lonely figure in a library, occupying a world of literary and antiquarian fascination, who has had little real interaction (or even acquaintance) with Roman authorities. He is someone with florid fantasies about Roman power and its possibilities; a regular colonial subject, flustered by the accruing ethnic histories and local politics that swept Roman Carthage in his time; part of a wider cultural landscape of captivation with juridical scenes; someone who has no real-life opponents. He writes into the void—into the ample gap between narratives of Roman power and its material actualities—even while there is nothing or no one there to receive his words. The notion that Tertullian is speaking for anyone or anything other than himself, let alone a group of Christians, is little more than a scholarly elaboration of Tertullian's own fantasy life.

In fact, other forms of belonging are threaded through Tertullian's material circumstances. Roman Carthage is a city built over the remains of the older Punic city, with its massive forum resting on the Byrsa where that city's acropolis once stood.[19] Scraps and traces of other, older histories were discernible in the province: in the Libyan, Punic, Greek (and perhaps Hebrew)[20] languages people spoke, in their names and those of their towns and cities, in the foods they ate, the clothing they wore, and the gods they venerated.[21] Rome did not immediately displace the cultural elements of its conquered peoples, and Rome's arrival meant the arrival of other populations, including Judean settlers and Greek-speaking communities from other parts of the Mediterranean, such as Alexandria, as well.[22] It is no surprise then that in such a colonial ambiance Tertullian trades on his complex ethnic/national identity as a Roman, African, and Carthaginian throughout his writing.

In Africa, Rome's arrival meant the promise of upward mobility through new social and economic arrangements—the most expansive taking place in the first through third centuries.[23] In Tertullian's lifetime, Carthage became one of the richest cities in the empire and the capital of Rome's province Africa Proconsularis.[24] As with all colonies, Carthage was shaped by Roman institutions and civic structures: civic councils, fora, baths, amphitheaters, temples.[25] But the province itself contained only a few "Roman" cities (military veteran colonies), and the remainder of the towns were Punic and Libyan in origin. The management of these African cities was not the task of relocated colonists from Rome, but rather the job of locals.[26] The administrative machinery of the empire demanded a whole lot of buy-in from provincial elites. These people not only populated the various, and

most important, offices in the running of these regions but also were responsible for applying the law in most cases, as we will see. The rich cache
of inscriptions from Roman North Africa testifies to the African origins of
civic and military officials operating in this region.[27] These local elites were
Latinized by virtue of circumstance and the promise of wealth. This cultural
exchange also meant that over time Rome was dominated by a new class of
Africans in its highest echelons of prestige and power.[28]

With the promise of upward mobility, however, Roman colonialism
also brought the disruptions of resettlement and the threat that local histories would be lost or forgotten. The Romans regularly rewrote geography
and narratives of peoplehood, and the fear of Roman erasure of these local
histories was coupled with new forms of civic and national allegiances—
ones that were mutable and uncertain, if not completely rife with conflict.[29]
In this landscape, Tertullian appears as an agitated figure, a foundering
voice: "Why is it," Tertullian wonders, "that we who are considered enemies
are refused the name of Romans?" (*Apol.* 36.1).[30] In *De pallio*, the treatise
in which he deals most graphically with the disappointments of colonial
rule, Tertullian bemoans the upheavals of the Severan dynasty, including
the founding of new towns and the migration and disenfranchising of various people:

> How much of the world has been changed in this period? How many
> towns have been produced or enlarged or refounded by the triple virtue
> of the current government? . . . how many census lists have been tran-
> scribed, how many peoples cleaned up, how many orders given their
> former splendour, how many barbarians excluded? (*De pall.* 2.7)[31]

Such a wasp's nest of social perplexity and colonial sentiment is, perhaps obviously, not incidental to Tertullian's obsessions with guilt and
innocence, justice and truth. Tertullian's apologetic works are an exercise
in making sense of the looming threat of Roman violence. He catalogues
incidents of violence against his "Christians" in *Ad nationes*, *Apologeticum*,
and *Ad Scapulam* (a purported letter to the proconsul of the province), as
well as in the opening of *De corona militis*. He organizes and rationalizes
Roman state discipline, sorting out its logic, often revealing it to be bungled
or misguided, then using his conclusions to demonstrate that Rome fails
to deliver on its own claims to possess mercy and arbitrate justice. Cries of
innocence, misunderstanding, confusion in procedure, and misreading of
"evidence" populate Tertullian's apologetics (e.g., *Apol.* 44.2–3). His asser-

tion, in other words, is not that Roman juridical procedures *cannot* bring justice, but rather that they *do* not do so.

Tertullian seems unwilling—or perhaps unable—to forgo the possibility that properly adjudicated Roman law can exonerate the falsely accused: it *can* produce innocence and truth. "Now," he charges, "I should like the most scrupulous guardians and avengers of laws and institutions of our forefathers to answer whether they have been faithful to all of them . . . or caused *any necessary and appropriate matters of discipline to be forgotten?*" (*Apol.* 6.1).[32] In the wake of botched justice, of misapplied discipline and law, Tertullian in the *Apologeticum* stages his own trial in a literary form. What this move reveals is an abiding attachment to scenes of discipline and judgment—one that extends well beyond his apologetic works—and this attachment resonates with the fraught and stormy space Tertullian occupies as a colonial subject.

FANTASIES AND ROMAN POWER

The sex lives of the emperors were hardly the only fodder for ancient fantasies. Scenes of law and justice were also settings in which fears, desires, contradictions, and idealizations around power got elaborated, in part because of the wild inconsistency in the application of the law (and perhaps in the laws themselves) and the inscrutability of juridical procedures. But it was also because of the changing colonial landscape of the Mediterranean.

Trial and courtroom scenes are key features of what scholars describe as Christian martyrological literature. However, literary scenes of arrest, interrogation, and trial are not limited to this literature; they are not exclusively "Christian" preoccupations.[33] Ari Bryen argues that the *Acta Alexandrinorum*, literature that recounts scenes of arrest and trial in which Alexandrian citizens confront Roman emperors, like Christian martyrological sources,[34] reflect the concerns of provincial subjects with a legal system that operated arbitrarily. These narratives challenge a system in which judgment was a matter of aesthetics, wherein determinations of guilt or innocence were, according to Bryen, "bound up with the state's claim to be able to tell, by looking, who is decent and who is criminal."[35] While Roman law proceeded by means of aesthetics, it did so alongside assertions that justice was based on rationality—an ideal that was circulated on monuments as well as on inscriptions and papyrological records.[36] In response, martyrological texts and the *Acta Alexandrinorum* register this conflict, and they imagine an arrest or a trial in the way provincial subjects wished Roman justice operated.[37] Thus we often find scenes in which the accused party engages in an eloquent and dramatic speech in an effort to expose officials' charges as an unreasonable disregard for "procedure." Such narratives aim to circumscribe the juridical power of local officials, to subject them to bureaucracy.[38] In other words, they stage a fantasy in which Roman-style trials reveal truth and the workings of justice (even if in an inverted way).[39] They establish innocence.

Trial scenes are also a central feature of the Greek novels, and the novels seem to exhibit a captivation with legal procedure, as Saundra Schwartz has observed.[40] "The theater of law loomed large in the imaginations of the novels' authors and audiences,"[41] Schwartz writes. These standardized narratives both fictionalize and aim for a certain historical verisimilitude,[42] and the novels exist, she writes, "somewhere in the gray area between historiography and poetry, between truth and lies."[43] Which is to say they are a form of fantasy.

One facet of these scenes in the novels is their tendency to render conflicts in starkly dichotomized terms, with the reader always assured of who is guilty and who is innocent—though the verdicts rarely reflect this truth, upping the dramatic ante.[44] Schwartz notices that in the novels, disciplinary scenes are indeed quite dramatic: "Modes of punishment are always painful and spectacular: crucifixion, burning at the stake, precipitation, and torture. . . . The more spectacular the punishment decreed, the greater the pathos of the wrongly punished defendant."[45] Exoneration then often occurs through supernatural or divine means.[46] The revelation of the real and true identity of the protagonist is indeed a constant in the novels, whether as the vindicated accused, or as the hero disguised as the slave.[47] The reader, like the gods, knows the truth.

The justice offered (or rather promised) by the gods—and the idea of their constant scrutiny—was itself a source of fantastical imagination in the ancient Mediterranean. Obviously ancient people evoked the gods under a whole range of inexplicable or opaque circumstances in ways that implied justice or retribution. But even beyond this generalized notion of divine comeuppance, people of antiquity also regularly imagined that the gods adjudicated more local crimes and disputes. Describing a cluster of "confession inscriptions" that declare a person's offense and the due penalty issued by a god in Asia Minor from the first through third century, Angelos Chaniotis has shown how sanctuaries, priests, and oracles provided a means of procuring justice alongside official Roman channels.[48] These inscriptions record confessions not of transgressions directly related to cultic life (e.g., purity violations), but of crimes that have little to do with cultic life itself— property violations, adultery, injury, murder. These inscriptions imagine the gods giving future recompense, or they imagine that a current ailment, loss, or other condition is the direct result of divine justice (in which case sometimes the crime is known or presumed, and sometimes it is not). While Chaniotis is careful to note that such inscriptions don't necessarily mean that Roman channels for law and justice were not pursued as well under these circumstances, he does observe the ways these inscriptions mark the limits and ambiguities of Roman juridical procedures, procedures that (perhaps obviously) could not back up their own bombastic rhetoric of truth and justice.[49] More generally, Chaniotis notes the inherent comfort of the long-running notion that the gods could see crimes and violations: that one couldn't fully "get away" with one's crimes, and that the gods would enact revenge on or discipline violators, if sometimes only after death, "reduced the frustration of the just."[50]

In a fourth and very different study of ancient preoccupations with law and justice, Benjamin Kelly examines papyri from Roman Egypt that document legal petitions and litigation processes.[51] Kelly illustrates the ways in which official juridical processes and procedures offered rare, incomplete, or no resolution on actual claims. Nonetheless and simultaneously, however, they offered important venues for articulations of ideology and social relationships. In fact, Kelly notes, the legal system "did not contribute much to 'legal control'" in any direct sense.[52] Rather these settings and procedures culled interest and investment—in Roman Egypt, and potentially elsewhere—with the effect of "informal social control," perpetuating state ideology through means that were almost incidental to the success or failure of these scenes to deliver on their promises.[53] At the same time, local people leveraged petitions for all kinds of purposes and minor conflicts, so that the Roman legal system was hardly much of a system at all. Legal systems are, Kelly writes, "ramshackle collections of institutions, practices, and discourses, used by large numbers of individuals and groups to enact their strategies."[54]

Among the social services performed by the legal "system," petitions and litigations tended to confirm and consolidate status and forms of belonging. Like funerary inscriptions, petitions were a key place in which one received recognition for and sometimes instrumentalized one's own status or group affiliation. Thus simply the act of engaging the legal system sharpened and focalized socially overdetermined modes of self-understanding.[55]

Kelly's reading of the social function of Roman legal processes is ideological-critical, showing how these processes transmitted Roman ideology.[56] However, in the same way Vout approaches images of the emperor— not as straightforward renditions of ideals but rather as stages for dynamic collective fantasy lives, so too one might say that these juridical settings provided a stage in which one got to imagine and even act out fantasies about power. These stages worked out one's relationship to authority, one's status, one's agency—sometimes with material effects, and sometimes without them.

While these examples offer genre-specific and geographically specific case studies, together they provide a glimpse into the ways in which the bombastic Roman rhetoric and propaganda on law and justice, combined with the arbitrariness and/or mystery of ancient juridical processes and the absence of Roman rulers themselves, got worked out in the minds of Roman subjects in and across provinces. These studies gesture toward a cluster of more widespread conundrums that ancient people worked out through fantasy. Trial narratives, petitions (or participation in Roman bureaucracy more generally), confessions to the gods, and images of omnipresent Roman emperors negotiated the promise of power to disambiguate the ambiguous: to arbitrate questions of right and wrong, to offer a sense of reparation or fairness, as well as (not insignificantly) to see and tell you who you "really" are.

Again, fantasy involves both the internalization of certain dimensions of external reality for use, and at the same time a negotiation of external reality. Likewise, fantasy often works to consolidate and produce a stable identity where there is none.[57] Just as in the novels and confessional inscriptions, Tertullian, too, imagines a god who doles out real justice. For his falsely accused, exoneration occurs through supernatural or divine means. Working out the asymmetries and uncertainties—if not outright mystery—of Roman law and justice, Tertullian creates his own crisp and relentless moral landscape. And despite his critique of the Roman authorities, he nonetheless expresses a deep faith in juridical scenes to reveal certain kinds of truth.

Quite apart from his imagined moral landscape, Tertullian's material landscape is a hazy and haunted one, one in which ethnic upheaval and colonial confusion, more than Roman imperial authorities, reign. His fantastical elaborations of juridical scenes, which depict ultimate powers and innocent victims, are only one iteration of these compatible and perhaps common fascinations in the Roman Mediterranean. These fascinations, at least in Tertullian's case, are especially poignant amidst the specific ambiguities of belonging, the affections and disaffections, that attended colonial life under the Romans.

MINDING THE GAP

What does Tertullian even know about Roman juridical processes and authorities? What does he know about "Christians" and their encounters with Roman legal systems? And how does he know it?

The enactment of justice in Africa Proconsularis, as in all the colonies, was a variegated, uneven, and mostly local exercise. The emperor certainly hoped (and managed in varying degrees) to stay out of the fray of local disputes, and he relied on governors and the will of provincial communities under the guidance of their elected magistrates to work out their difficulties.[58] Magistrates were local people, representatives of Rome in some sense, but not imported ones. Governors on the other hand were (generally) appointed by the emperor, outsiders to the regions that they managed.[59] Their roles were mainly advisory. The mundane execution of justice was usually the work of local chief magistrates.[60] Policing was largely localized, with civic officials providing for social order.[61] The governor was to adjudicate serious cases like those dealing with large sums of money or offenses for which conviction entailed public dishonor (*infamia*) for the one charged (violence, fraud, or theft) or capital punishment—that is, in theory. Some evidence suggests that local magistrates did on occasion condemn their own citizens to death.[62] In other words, the case had to be worth the governor's time and effort; it had to be important enough to garner his attention and to demand the display of imperial power in the province. All told, the governor was not a dominating figure in the lives of colonial subjects. He was not someone with whom citizens of the colony would regularly come into contact. He had a small staff with which to carry out his work in the province, perhaps a few hundred people, including his family and slaves.[63]

Imperial presence might have been more readily felt in Roman Africa in the vicinity of Roman legions, whose job it was to aid the governor in bringing "peace" to his territory. Yet in Tertullian's lifetime, there was only one, stationed in Lambesis, west of Carthage, and like other provincial institutions, it was composed largely of Romanized Africans.[64] In other words, what Tertullian knew of the Roman empire was felt in unexceptional bureaucracy. Rome appeared in the names and layout of towns, in the infusion of the Latin language into the landscape. It was felt in the tax structure, zoning of cities, names of civic officials, cultic festivals and calendars, civic structures (the forum, amphitheater, baths).[65] The names and images of governors and emperors on coins, in inscriptions, and in marble reminded one that Rome was in charge.

This context implies that what Tertullian knows of Roman justice is a product of his investigations, his impulses, ones that lead him to the library. Like any number of Roman educated elites, Tertullian was a collector of books, and he used these materials to construct his arguments.[66] His writings are evidence of his curatorial passions. One encounters in them excerpts stitched together, whether from classical authors, such as Cicero, Pliny the Elder, Soranus, or Seneca, or from what we now call "early Christian" writings, such as Justin Martyr, Irenaeus, sayings of the Phrygian prophets, the writings of Marcion, or various scriptures.[67] Tertullian, like many literary elites of his day, had developed a potent fantasy life.

Trained in rhetoric, Tertullian honed his imaginative capacities in an effort to persuade and capture a small audience for himself. If historians have laid aside images of Tertullian as a cleric or established leader of a Christian community, they have supplanted it with an image of Tertullian as a member of a Christ-assembly and a self-authorized philosopher.[68] Part of his literary persona demanded the ability to invent opponents—in colorful and compelling ways—against which he might hone his rhetorical craft and entertain those who would commission and collect his various treatises. Tertullian was, in short, a constructor of literary fictions, and ones that were suited to his historical moment, but in an affective register. The goal was to establish his social capital, to connect to his readers through their love of a well-crafted argument, their claims to a literary pedigree, their notions of scandal, or their sense of disaffection from and attraction to Rome. He brought his readers imaginaries of gruesome enemies and dimwitted opponents, such as "virgins" who concealed pregnancies, opponents who conjured a Christ with no real body,[69] and Romans officials readily swayed by the slightest whims of an ignorant public to murder guiltless Christians.

But what should we make of those latter moments? Tertullian knows of the martyr Perpetua and her companions' deaths in the arena. But what strikes him as memorable is not her death; it is her visions. That is, she is familiar to him from a written source, one that he uses to argue for his vision of the self as corporate unity of soul and body as it pertains to the afterlife (*De an.* 55.5).[70] In *De corona militis*, he does mention an incident in a military camp where a "Christian" soldier rejects the laurel crown and finds himself imprisoned. This incident, it seems, is the stuff of local gossip (*De cor.* 1.4).[71] Even his letter *Ad martyras*, while seemingly written to imprisoned Christians, features heroic examples of martyrs, none of whom are Christians but rather historical and literary figures who were hostile to Rome.[72] One would be hard pressed to find specific events in and around Carthage that would serve as Tertullian's rhetorical impetus to defend Christians. What's remarkable about Tertullian's *Apologeticum*, in fact, is that it draws evidence for Romans' unfair attacks on Christians from sources collected from earlier times and other places—crucially Tacitus's *Annals* and the correspondence between Pliny and Trajan.[73] In *Ad nationes*, a work that precedes the *Apologeticum*, Tertullian likewise tackles rumors that come from outside and elsewhere, such as Tacitus's notion that the Judean God is represented by the head of an ass (*Ad nat.* 1.14). Literary sources are so critical to Tertullian's apologetics that they might even be understood, at least in part, as *replies* to Pliny and Tacitus.[74] Attention to his sources reveals that Tertullian constructs the attacks and insults directed against Christians from *writings*. But he can conjure criticisms of Rome from literary sources as well. In *Ad nationes* his representation of Roman gods and cultic practice rings as bookish: it is a sustained engagement with the antiquarian writings of Varro.[75]

Tertullian's rhetorical practice suggests a complicated relationship between his writing and the social conditions of life in Carthage. But it's also worth attending to the ways that trials and tortures feature in it. Tertullian's penchant for Roman-style juridical scenes was noted even by his earliest Christian readers. The fourth-century writer Eusebius of Caesarea, who undertook his own imaginative history of Christianity, for instance, circulated the notion that Tertullian was trained as a Roman lawyer (*Historia ecclesiastica* 2.4). Without accepting Eusebius's claim as true, one might notice that Tertullian deploys forensic rhetoric and that legal imagery and concepts infuse his writings. That legal themes and stylistics figure so strongly in his work has been attributed to his training as a rhetorician, which necessarily included instruction in legal argumentation.[76] But this perhaps does not fully account for Tertullian's beguiled fascination with discipline and judgment: he routinely inhabits the voice of court orator, turning any number of potential opponents and allies into witnesses from whom he can extract the truth: Roman magistrates, Marcion, and even the soul itself: "I call to our aid new testimony, even better known than all literature, more discussed than all doctrine . . . : Stand forth, then, O soul," Tertullian chimes in the *De testimonio animae*.[77] Attracted to moments of revelation of the truth in the form of a trial, Tertullian muses on the efficacious power of torture and punishment to reveal it. "Cutting, burning, stretching" bring "useful pain," in that it portends one's very salvation (*Scorp.* 5.6).[78] God uses punitive measures when he needs to: "And it will be permissible for God to administer eternal life *through fires and swords and anything sharp*" (*Scorp.* 5.7).[79] But curiously, the unmistakable brutality of Tertullian's God is not, as in the case of Roman juridical processes and figures, a matter of misapplication of justice, but rather a matter of misperception: "The one who does not understand believes God to be cruel" (*Scorp.* 7.5).[80]

Tertullian's god operates like an emperor,[81] pursuing order through the discipline of the spirit. At the heart of Tertullian's theological imaginary is a god whose juridical gaze has an expansive reach. There is not a minute in daily life when that juridical gaze can be avoided, Tertullian warns. There were no private moments before a mirror, in a dressing chamber, at the theater. That penetrating gaze calculated the sum of a Christian's action, measured it against order and truth. God would save and damn accordingly. While that fact might inspire fear, it provided a great deal of assurance for Tertullian. For if God only ever acted in accordance with reason, then he staved off an even greater existential threat: a capricious sort of justice, sometimes clemency, sometimes punishment.[82] Yet the enactment of justice in the empire was, in fact, a rather unpredictable and nonsystematic affair, even as the emperor was imagined "as an ever present protector."[83] This fact animated Tertullian's fantasy of a perfectly and consistently punitive god. Moreover, it is worth noting that this god (one who is always watching, always present) portends comfort to Tertullian, a colonial subject, conditioned by Roman propaganda to understand the emperor in much the same way. The emperor too was to be understood as present in the life of the colony, in the actions of its magistrates, in its festivities and games. One had to always look for signs of imperial presence. One should know that it was in fact there.

Tertullian's vision of final judgment itself proceeds in the form of a great tribunal, over which his god presides dispensing perfect and total justice, which includes salvation and damnation. Most graphic are the comments that close his *De spectaculis*, a gripping scene in which Tertullian casts his audience as a witness to god's own judgment in the form of an arena show:

> How vast a spectacle then! What excites my admiration? What my laughter? From where does my joy come? Or my exaltation? — as I see so many

illustrious kings, whose reception into the heavens was announced, groaning now in the lowest darkness with great Jove himself, and those, too, who bore witness to their exaltation; governors of provinces, too, who persecuted the name of the Lord, in fires more fierce than those with which in the days of their pride they rage against the Christians. (*De spect.* 30.3)

Across Tertullian's writings we find the arena, the trial, the prison, the agonies of military triumph and athletic contest stealthily inserting themselves into his vision of justice. Tertullian seems, in short, incapable of conceiving justice outside of Roman disciplinary frames.

Vulnerability and violence gnaw at Tertullian. The questions that attend these preoccupations of his, though, tend to circulate around Tertullian's own cast of what it means to be Christian — that is, the content of Christian identity, according to Tertullian — and, not unrelated, Tertullian's own ideological position relative to Roman power. Tertullian's writings bespeak ambivalence to Roman discipline, and that ambivalence has pressed his interpreters into guessing on which "side" of Roman imperialism and its cultural norms (subversion or resistance) Tertullian and his Christians predominantly fall. Perhaps, as it has been argued, he revalues low-status figures (slave, prisoner, athlete, gladiator), or reorients social values from courage and dignity to humility and shame.[84]

But what might we make of Tertullian's Christians and his extended defense of "the name"? In the *Apologeticum*, Tertullian mounts an argument demonstrating Christians' innocence. They are, he argues, well-meaning, mild-mannered, morally upright citizens who simply gather for modest dinners and pose no threat to the state. Their practices are banal, their philosophical views familiar, and their morality is exceptional. They are, in short, much better subjects than others populating the empire. They are a model association, and even their dogged monotheism and disdain for idolatry make them a society of philosophers without repute (*Apol.* 46.8–47.10). On the one hand, this might seem to be a rhetorical strategy: directed to Roman officials, Tertullian's arguments are in fact designed to guide group insiders toward a more congenial mode of self-representation so as to protect them against the threat of state violence. Or such a treatise might be seen as a form of pedagogy, aimed to instruct insiders about how to behave and why they abstain from civic festivities — instruction, in other words, in what makes them distinctive. But such readings raise problems if they presume that behind such rhetoric lies a community (however motley) that Tertullian wants to preserve, or for whom he wishes to speak. Instead, Tertullian's specific defense of "the name" witnesses to both the ways in which such juridical settings articulated affiliations—producing criminals and populations, among other things—and the way the material distance from these juridical settings could magnify and further entrench them in the ancient imagination.

"CHRISTIANS" AND "MARTYRS" AS
ATTACHMENTS TO JURIDICAL SCENES

Well, then, if it is simply the name that is hated, what guilt can attach to names?

TERTULLIAN, APOLOGY 3.5

We are from your own ranks: Christians are made, not born!

TERTULLIAN, APOLOGY 18.4

[T]he ancient martyrs transform shame into the source of an oddly pure identity politics.

VIRGINIA BURRUS, SAVING SHAME

Tertullian is engrossed with Roman authorities, the theater of justice they would seem to command, and the place of "Christians" within that theater. Tertullian's *Apologeticum* immediately begins with questions of truth—specifically, with truth within juridical scenes. Truth is a tricky figure, however, a "stranger on earth" (*peregrinam in terris, Apol.* 1.2), and telling the truth—*confession*—has its ironies, at least for those charged as Christians: "When others are charged with the same crimes as we, they are given full liberty to answer the charge and to cross-question" (2.2).[85] Christians are ostensibly brought to court for the name—they are "haled" before magistrates, Tertullian remarks: "one thing is only what they [magistrates] wait for ... the confession of the name Christian" (2.3),[86] but they are tortured to deny the name that is the very source of their guilt. Thus for Tertullian, truth seems to reside elsewhere than in such juridical scenes, even while he implicitly acknowledges the ways such scenes produce kinds of truth. Indeed it turns out that Tertullian's own writings become the stage for more reliable scenes of truth and justice, with Tertullian's god presiding.

Tertullian has baffled scholars for seeming to show an "unnatural desire for confrontation with the political system and its resultant persecutions."[87] His *Apologeticum* is fully consumed not just with truth and justice, but with questions of guilt and exoneration, specifically around the behavior of those called "Christians." Not incidentally, Tertullian is also fully invested in the commitment and virility of martyrs. But rather than a crucial figure in the propagation of martyrological discourse, a discourse that has most recently been understood as a series of constructions of Christian identity pivoting ontologically on suffering, innocent victimhood, masculinized heroism, or subversive resistance,[88] Tertullian might have more to offer relative to the ways juridical scenes worked out specifically colonial desires and fears.

Tertullian's record of Roman offenses against the Christians is full of his literary embellishments of scenes from elsewhere (in some other place, in some gossip overheard, or found in a scroll). And it seems that the community of Christians as such for Tertullian to preserve or defend materializes largely, perhaps only, in his imagination, as well. In Tertullian's writings everything about Christians is a matter of dispute: what Christians should eat, wear, do for fun; what they do when they convene, read and study; what they consider a sign of membership; how they organize their gatherings; how they understand dreams and visions; how make a living, conduct their households; not to mention what theological views they hold precious or how they should respond to Roman violence. One could say that Tertullian presents one image to outsiders in the *Apologeticum*, which is a defense after all, and feels free to open up messy disputes that define his community in the other treatises, in which he tries to take the lead in inter- or intracommunal power struggles. But Tertullian's treatises suggest a more complex set of social dynamics and fluid associations that marked life in Roman Carthage.[89] Éric Rebillard, for instance, has shown that Tertullian's treatises suggest that those affiliating with Christian groups did not understand their participation in the absolute terms that Tertullian implies they should. Rebillard concludes that partaking in a Christ assembly did not prohibit people from involvement in civic life (observing civic festivals, attending naming ceremonies, holding civic office, etc.), or from holding other kinds of group affiliations.[90]

Rebillard raises another set of questions that provoke some rethinking: despite the field's generalized preoccupation with (certain forms of) evidence and data, there is no epigraphic or archaeological data for Christians at all from Tertullian's lifetime.[91] When Christ assemblies gathered (daily in the morning, and weekly in the evening, for a meal, Tertullian argues in *Apol.* 29:16–19), they occupied buildings that were indistinguishable from the meeting places of other associations, likely domestic dwellings. Those attending Christ assemblies were not distinguished by unique names, or by the language they spoke. Tertullian himself wrote in both Latin and Greek. They occupied a variety of social and economic positions. Rebillard's work coheres well with the work on Greco-Roman associations more generally, in which any given group in the ancient world that fits the broad mold of "associations" could have contained multiple and overlapping affiliations— family, profession, cult, neighborhood, or ethnic.[92] While the scholarship on Greco-Roman associations largely deals in the literature and epigraphy of the first century BC through the second century CE, it has continually pressed for pictures of Christ groups as thoroughly ordinary in their sociality,[93] and even for the people using Christ rhetoric, and perhaps even more for people interested in Jesus but not using the moniker "Christ," it is far from obvious that Christ would be considered the specific "glue" that holds them together.

The earliest uses of *christianus* (a Latinized Greek word)—1 Peter, Acts of the Apostles, the Pliny-Trajan correspondence, and the letters of Ignatius—largely coalesce in the very small circle of early-second-century Asia Minor; and these sources associate the term not with a universal constituency and/or obvious theological content, but rather with juridical contexts.[94] They suggest not a self-designation but a term that was the product of local gossip and deployments of ethnicizing language, coined only from this circulating rhetoric about Christ rather than distinct or exclusive affiliation. If this is true for Asia Minor in the second century, we can also entertain this possibility for the landscape of Tertullian in the third century. At the very least, it unsettles the certainty of "the name" in Tertullian's time.

It is perhaps only with time and in eventual confrontations with actual Roman authorities that this rhetoric *produced* a population—the making of delinquents.[95] This is not to say that "Christians" *were* delinquents. While both the disciplinary associations with "Christian" and the mixed sociality of so-called "Christ groups" have led to idealized fantasies of Christians as especially subversive or exceptionally queer,[96] it seems instead that a certain fabricated delinquency attends "Christians" because that is part of the mechanism that produced the name in the first place. *This* history, available in literary fragments through which Tertullian is sorting, is what ignites Tertullian's fantastical imaginations of Christian guilt and innocence.

"Christian" of course does become a self-designation eventually, and it seems that Tertullian might help us explain why: the colonial condition implies intensified social-experiential ambiguities. It is precisely the proclaimed, and thus also often imagined, power of such juridical scenes to produce truth—the truth of who you "really" are—that makes them so completely captivating.

Tertullian is not alone in associating the term "Christian" with juridical scenes, and certainly not in associating being "Christian" with violence and suffering, as Acts, 1 Peter, and Ignatius attest. But the pained attachment to juridical scenes in Tertullian helps us understand not only the transition from "Christian" as slanderous and practically empty epithet to positively claimed self-descriptor. It also helps us understand how it is that "Christian" self-understanding becomes so thoroughly entrenched in suffering.[97] Justin Martyr's apologetic speeches, for instance, which elaborate specific content for the term Christian, cannot be detached from their juridical framing and respective addresses to the Roman Senate and the emperor. It is perhaps not a surprise then that "martyrdom" becomes so crucial for differentiating and/or claiming authenticity of one's "Christianness" for Justin (and likewise for Tertullian). Interestingly, Justin begins his *First Apology* by saying he presents it on behalf of "all those nations unjustly hated and wantonly abused" (*Apol.* 1), himself being only one, concertedly placing his apologetics in a rather ordinary topography of juridical targeting and population production (what gets dubbed "persecution"). Likewise, the *Acts of the Scillitan Martyrs* seems hardly more than a rendition of attachment to the site of wounding, to the juridical grid, as one after another in a series of accusations and coercions by the authorities results in the statement "I am a Christian."

Again, this is not to say that those claiming relationship to the term "Christian" had *more experience* with juridical contexts—in Tertullian's case it would seem to be quite the opposite. It is rather to say that the term Christian is, at least at first and for a long time, inseparable from these juridical scenes. The term derives its initial content then not from shared practices or beliefs or values, as scholarship has long presumed, but from the elaborate fantasy life around and deep attachments to juridical scenes inspired by the contradictions of Roman colonial conditions and Roman articulations of power.

These associations between the term Christian, truth, and the various violences of juridical scenes are not limited to what have been classed as martyr texts. Two of the merely three instances of "Christian" in the New

Testament occur in the Acts of the Apostles, for example, and it is not incidental that the Acts of the Apostles echoes Greek novels. The difficult nature of the category of "martyrdom literature" is in part due to the fact that there are so many trial/punishment scenes in ancient "Christian" literature.[98] In fact, it would seem that in light of the simultaneously standardized and highly ornamented nature of "martyr" stories and the absence of real evidence suggesting communities of Christians even into the third century, both the term "Christian" and what has classically been termed martyrdom literature might be understood better under the more general cultural rubric of *attachments to juridical scenes*, attachments that culled investments and catalyzed imaginations across genres and geographies in the Roman Mediterranean.

Tertullian, like the "Christians" and "martyrs" he traces in ink, might be seen as witnessing less to a delineated social phenomenon than to something richer, more complicated, but also subterranean: the wildly productive potential of these fantasies of power. They echo and amplify a cultural flutter, represent a collective curiosity in concentrated form. Martyr stories archive other, adjacent colonial experiences, too, as I will discuss in the next chapter. But in the middle of colonial disarray, when one is unsure of where and to whom one belongs, or how to imagine those at the helm, it's not hard to see the appeal of a transparent moral world, with violences that are more easily verified, and thus more easily claimed. It's not hard to see the allures of the notion that one could, against the odds, get closure and recompense, however eventual, for pain or injury; or better yet, that one could be truly known, seen, thus made plain to oneself by the powers that be, and rendered guiltless before their eyes.[99]

THE PERILS OF TRANSLATION

Martyrs' Last Words and the Cultural Materiality of Speech

In what respect, therefore, can the passion of a Franco-Maghrebian martyr testify to this universal destiny which assigns us to a single language while prohibiting us from appropriating it, given that such an interdiction is linked to the very essence of language . . . ?

JACQUES DERRIDA, MONOLINGUISM OF THE OTHER

The tensions between the linguistic turn and the material turn(s) would seem to suggest a contrast between words and things, speech and substance. But the most central theories of the linguistic turn evince a thick, if sometimes also unwieldy, set of alliances between language and the body.[1] Case in point: Jacques Derrida, a hugely influential figure in the literary movement of deconstruction (he himself coined the term) and what was only later termed the linguistic turn, has been read extensively for his universalizing theory of language as slippery and profuse, rendering meanings that always elude. And yet, as we will find, this theory is, at least in one central text, strapped to both physical injury and cultural specificity.

For Derrida, one cannot "have" language, one cannot "grasp" meanings; texts are always and essentially unresolved, founded on an "irreducible" complexity and absence, a deferral of meaning that he calls *différance*.[2] In *Monolinguism of the Other*, Derrida waxes on the multiplicity of language—no language is ever "one." He offers an extensive account of the divestment constitutive of speaking, a basic alienation of the speaking subject in, and through, language: language is in fact an original condition of estrangement.[3]

But as original as this estrangement might be (preceding, as it does, the subject), in his calling up of the martyr, Derrida seals speech to bodily peril. What is also striking about this book is that his ground for theorizing the fundamental divestment in speaking is his particular experience as an Algerian Jew, for whom French is simultaneously the only language and a language that cannot be fully owned: "I have only one language; it is not mine."[4] He is, he contends, *disowned* by the French language, and his disjoint within it is revealed in things like his accent and intonation.[5] But his condition is not exclusive, he notes, and indeed "mastery" of the colonial language by those for whom that language would seem to be more original is an illusion.[6]

Derrida continually oscillates in this book between general postulations about language and the particularity of his experience as an Algerian Jew and uncertain citizen of France:[7]

> All culture is originarily colonial. Every culture institutes itself through the unilateral imposition of some 'politics' of language. Mastery begins, as we know, through the power of naming, of imposing and legitimating appellations. . . . The question here is not to efface the arrogant specificity or the traumatizing brutality of what is called the modern colonial war in the 'strictest definition' of the expression, at the very moment of military conquest, or when a symbolic conquest prolongs the war by other means. On the contrary. . . . But once again, it reveals the colonial structure of any culture in an exemplary way. *It testifies to it in martyrdom, and 'vividly.'*[8]

Derrida emphasizes that he does not wish to lose the extremity of French colonial violence, but neither does he wish to make it exceptional. He repeatedly stresses the physical violence connected to this colonized condition within language, using the word "martyr" or "martyrdom," and even sometimes "passion," to characterize his relationship to the French language. But his "passion" involves *both* a passiveness or subjection, *and* a kind of aggressive devotion. His condition is a kind of surrender, but not as much an "acceptance of defeat by an enemy" as "an affirmative, binding gesture of submitting to the force of an inexorable, impersonal other."[9] He describes, for example, his encounter with French literary culture as captivation—an uncertain combination of love and capture:

I seemed to be harpooned by French philosophy and literature, the one and the other, the one or the other: wooden or metallic darts [*flèches*], a penetrating body of enviable, formidable, sentences which it was necessary to appropriate, domesticate, or coax [*amadouer*], that is to say, love by setting them on fire.[10]

The "martyr" for Derrida is someone who "suffers and testifies," more deeply implicating language and speech with violence.[11] But the testimony that this martyr gives is of a "universal" structure: the (colonial) subject in language. To speak is to have been injured, and thus to testify to and about that injury.

Derrida's association between speaking dominant languages and martyrdom is a loaded one for sure, but it is not presented as historical. He's evoking the associations of martyrdom (violence and confession) strategically—and ironically, given the associations of martyrdom with Christianity, the religion of the very colonial culture inhabiting him. But what if we take Derrida's associations seriously as a kind of historical proposition? What if we read Derrida "backward," and against the universalizing move Derrida and those following him make:[12] what if martyr stories are, at least in part, staging scenes of cultural and colonial divestment?

I would like to take cues from Derrida's predominant concern with language and to extend the questions of colonialism, diaspora, and attachments to disciplinary scenes that emerged with reference to Tertullian in the previous chapter. I would like to ask after the associations in so-called "martyr" stories and linked juridical scenes between imperial disciplinary violence and speaking.[13] I want to suggest that one of the functions these stories have is to reflect on the fraught place of language within colonial experience.[14] What do these figures say as they are about to die, and what might it mean? I also want to use these intractable tensions between cultural specificity and universal subjectivity, speech and physical violence, to remind us that dominant languages and frames of legibility are how things materialize, how they *become material*. That is to say that I want to place acts of translation, especially cultural acts of translation and translations into dominant languages, in the realm of "material culture." Finally, taking up again the question of language, dominant grids, and representation of nondominant experiences from the first chapter, I want to use these tensions to ask about the traces left behind in the act of translation itself and to represent some of the experiential subtexts of translation, namely, its psychic tolls.

Most scholarship has read the speeches and confessions of martyrs as part of the larger literary task of constructing identity as innocent victim or masculinized hero, and/or claiming that identity as an inversion of power, or a subject made through suffering.[15] The notion that martyr stories might (fantastically) construct an identity, even sometimes a Christian one, is obviously not wrong. But Derrida pushes us to consider other dimensions of these stories. At least as interesting as the production of identity within the juridical scene, and not unrelated to it, is what desires, attachments, pains, and conundrums are being recorded between the lines in such stories of heroic deaths, specifically around the experience of speaking as a colonial subject and the perils and inescapable expenses of entering dominant cultural "languages." While on one hand such stories are fantastical imaginations of power, on the other, as in Tertullian's writings, these stories still *do document something*, and what they document is neither literal nor incidental to the content of these narratives. In fact, it is their generic quality that makes them richly available as archives and as dramatizations of other, more generalizable experiences, ones that disappear in the dark shadow cast by the story of a Christian phenomenon.

Likewise, so much scholarship has critiqued the ideological implications of such texts and their repurposing, and rightly so, since the legacy of the trope of the innocent victim has been a volatile and even toxic one. But there is a way to give the possible ideological problems of such stories of victimization and persecution their weight *and* keep them in play as a witness to other, less immediately discernible things.

THE GRIEF OF SPEAKING IN
THE GOSPEL OF MARK

When they bring you to trial and hand you over, do not worry beforehand about what you are to say; but say whatever is given you at that time, for it is not you who speak, but the holy spirit.

GOSPEL OF MARK 13:9–13

At noon darkness came over the whole land until three in the afternoon. And at three o'clock Jesus cried out in a loud voice, "Eloi, Eloi, lema sabachthani?" which is translated, "My God, my God, why have you for-

saken me?" Some of the bystanders who heard it said, "Look, he is calling Elijah!"

GOSPEL OF MARK 15:33–35

In the Gospel of Mark, speaking is often fraught. One of the gospel's prin-
cipal themes, secrecy, suggests high stakes around speaking. Jesus is always
talking in parables that are meant to confound and confuse outsiders, speaking so that they may "listen, but never quite understand," but then needs to
explain himself even to those who should ostensibly get it (4:1–13). Almost
from the beginning of the story, some word starts to spread about Jesus and
he gets nervous:[16] "Don't tell anyone," Jesus repeatedly warns those who
witness his acts of healing.[17] Even while spreading the word about the kingdom of God is one of the central tasks of Jesus and the disciples,[18] there is
ambivalence about the speaking of that good news: the gospel famously
ends with the first, and apparently only, witnesses to the empty tomb running away afraid and telling no one what they saw there. This abrupt ending
impairs the characterization of the story as "good news" but then problema-
tizes the story as an account (if they didn't tell anyone, how does the author
hear about it?). It is on this landscape of problems with speaking—indeed
problems that circulate around speaking and witness—that the two pas-
sages above appear.

   In the first passage, some kind of "trial" is referenced,[19] and the one
under trial is left speechless, perhaps doesn't know what to say. Someone or something else will have to speak for them. In the second passage,
Jesus's last words on the cross are a quotation from Psalm 22 in Aramaic; or
rather, Mark renders the phrase in Greek transliterated Aramaic, further explaining in Greek to its audience what the phrase means. Then, in the next
verse, some onlookers *misunderstand* Jesus—they think he is calling out to
Elijah—and they taunt him for it. Why does the Gospel of Mark use Aramaic at this moment? What does one make of the Greek transliteration of
the Aramaic? To make things even more complicated, it turns out that the
phrase is a Hebraicized Aramaic one rendered in Greek transliteration,[20]
and the bystanders misunderstand Jesus. Did they mishear him, or do they
perhaps not understand Aramaic (even while they seem to know who Elijah
is)? Finally, how might one think about these two scenes together?

   Scholarly explanations for the Aramaic in this scene, and in the Gospel
of Mark at large, have hovered around questions of textual, historical, and/
or cultural authenticity. For example, one highly traditional reading suggests

that Mark was originally written in Aramaic.[21] Some have suggested that the gospel was composed for bilingual followers who are translating for the benefit of a Greek-speaking audience.[22] Another possible reading is that the use of the Aramaic trades on the exotic appeal of Judean culture in almost a fetishized fashion to a Greek audience, for example.[23] Each potential explanation produces different tensions between translation and authenticity, and the subtext in each case is the question of how fully or authentically Judean Mark or Mark's audience might be (which is inextricably tied to the question of Mark as a "Christian" text). Jesus has with few exceptions been speaking Greek in the rest of the gospel. Does the fact that the writer clarifies the meaning of the Aramaic (for non-Aramaic speakers) suggest perhaps a non-Judean audience? Is the fact that the Aramaic is a Greek transliteration representative of a hybrid identity on the part of the writer? Does this gospel point to a transition away from Judean belonging and toward a Greek or gentile constituency? A Greek-speaking/Judean spectrum is usually presumed, with Mark falling somewhere in between, and the earliest tradition (Jesus or an earlier version of Mark) is more closely aligned with Aramaic and thus Judean belonging.

Yet, as we've seen, Mark is a gospel steeped in questions of Judean belonging. Jesus's death within it occurs in an ominous and tangled scene: Jesus has just been given a crown of thorns, and the words "King of the Judeans" have been inscribed over his head, in a painful satire of Judean aspirations of sovereignty. At the climactic moment of Jesus's death, the temple veil is torn in two, a detail from the sack of the temple by the Romans, also given by Josephus (*Jewish Wars* 6.5.3). Jesus is being crucified under the auspices of a Roman centurion, and as he dies he quotes scripture in Greek-transliterated Aramaic (with a little Hebrew mixed in) about being abandoned by his god, and the defeat of Judea is referenced. Then the Roman centurion speaks something that only God or spirits spoke or knew in other parts of the gospel: the identification of Jesus as God's son. Specifically, the centurion's words seem to echo God's words at Jesus's baptism and the transfiguration (1:11, 9:7). God's voice, it seems, is ventriloquized through the mouth of the Roman soldier. Or differently said, in this moment of naming, the voice of God and the voice of the torturer become one.[24]

Given the broad resonances of the term "son of God," which in Hebrew literature could mean a king or simply anyone belonging to Israel, and also given the exemplary rather than singular status of Hebrew figures and figures in the noble death tradition,[25] it seems that Jesus is a representative figure, one through whom aspirations and losses of Judean sovereignty get reflected and considered. But in its representativeness, this scene registers a kind of signal or symbolic moment in which state disciplinary violence yields both questions about belonging ("Why did you abandon me?") and an interpellated ethnic specificity, as he appeals to his "native tongue." In other words, while this moment is full of questions about God's sovereignty and Judea's place relative to it, it also seems that it is at the very moment when Jesus is most given over to the colonial power that he is most authentically Judean.

Despite Mark's constant reliance on irony as a literary strategy, this is not simply irony. It is rather a poetic capture of colonial and/or diasporic subjectivity at large, in which cultural authenticity, itself a form of sovereignty, and its terms of articulation are not in tension with colonial experience, but rather produced by it. Building in part on Derrida's experiential and culturally specific framing of language in *Monolinguism of the Other*, Rey Chow has offered something of a phenomenology of the "nonnative speaker." Chow notices, among other things, that Derrida expresses no nostalgia for an apparently more "original" language, but still expresses dis-ease at his inability to fully authenticate himself within the French language—a dis-ease he can only ever express in French. The totalizing nature of dominant languages means that even "original" or "native" languages appear within their frame, a cultural distinctiveness produced in and by colonial interpellation: "*Toi, le Juif-d'Algerie!*"[26]

Appeals to cultural authenticity, especially by nondominant populations, are nearly always a function of colonial constraint.[27] Not only does the notion of the "authentic" minority subject support a fantasy that someone could be untouched, unadulterated by the colonial encounter (a fantasy appealing to people on all sides of the colonial relation), but the content of that authenticity is always caught up in colonial representations of what counts as *real belonging*.[28]

As a poetic capture of experience, though, this scene seems to register or archive something more than the contradictions of cultural authentication. Not only are colonial/diasporic self-understandings always already spoken in the dominant language, but that speaking, not insignificantly, coincides (in Mark and in Derrida) with physical pain: translation is affliction. Mark places alongside the extremity of government torture and execution the more minor pains and frustrations of communication. Jesus is crying out, and part of his humiliation is that people can't understand him or, perhaps, they are mocking his accent ("Look, he's calling Elijah!").

Why pair the extremity of torture with more everyday pains of speaking? Both Mark and Derrida's texts are imbued with more than the inherent ideological violence of language imposition or the conflicts in colonial subjectivity. Significantly, Chow connects "languaging" to racialization, to the embodiment of race and the injuries that constitute it. This racialization is in part the result of being hailed in the classic Althusserian sense[29] as other, a process that both deeply wounds and naturalizes itself on the surface of the skin—what she calls the "epidermalization of naming and calling."[30] But Chow also notices the way languages themselves register with a racial charge. She quotes Frantz Fanon: "The Negro of the Antilles will be proportionately whiter—that is, he will come closer to being a real human being—in direct relation to his mastery of the French language."[31] This is what Chow calls "biosemiotics." Not only is it that "language possession is translated into and receives its value as skin color."[32] It is also that language means the appearance and legibility of the subject, but *only at the price of injury*, a recruitment into the dominant language or grid that is simultaneously an "amputation."[33]

The use of Aramaic throughout the Gospel of Mark echoes this association between injury, authenticity, and speech: each instance of Aramaic accompanies a moment of physical instability—illness, exorcism, resurrection, healing, as well as the place and moment of Jesus's execution.[34] Each use is a transliteration, and each time the author of Mark translates for the reader. The use of Aramaic along the lines of *both* illness and healing resonates with Derrida's and Chow's notion of the "prosthetic" dimension of coloniality: it incurs injury even as it enables. But two of these instances of Aramaic are also associatively rich with questions of speaking and mouths. In Mark 5:35–43, Jesus has just healed the daughter of a synagogue leader, explaining that she is not dead, simply sleeping, and tells her "*Talitha koum*" ("Little girl, get up"). Jesus's immediate next words are that no one should know about this, and he tells her family to give her something to eat. A few chapters later, Jesus heals a deaf man with a speech impediment, first by putting his fingers in his ears, and then he "spat and touched his tongue" (7:33). Looking up to the sky, he "sighed" and said, "*Ephphatha*," or "Be opened" (v. 34). The text then says that immediately the man's ears were opened and his "tongue was released, and he spoke plainly" (v. 35). As in earlier episodes, Jesus warns the crowd to tell no one, but "the more he ordered them, the more zealously they proclaimed it" (v. 36).

Healing is politically charged as a symbolic act of power in ancient culture, but the political charge in these scenes extends beyond the illustration of Jesus's power (or its limits). Read as a phenomenology of colonial life or an archive of colonial grief, the latter scene might easily ring with questions of cultural legibility: a man is tongue-tied, calling forth the many instances in which, for instance, nonwhite English speakers are asked incessantly to repeat themselves or speak more "clearly." It is the deployment of Aramaic that makes the man understandable: appeals to cultural authenticity are the antidote to illegibility. Immediately after, however, speech is out of control: the more people are told to be quiet, the more they talk. Jesus's Aramaic instruction, "Be opened," seems to have opened a kind of Pandora's box: what might get said? Ambiguous dangers attend speaking, even while (as the women running from the tomb also painfully show) *not* speaking also has its problems.

The instruction to feed the little girl in the earlier story ties speaking to eating. These are not only two activities of the mouth, but two activities that are culturally loaded. Chow connects these two forms of orality in her work, as well, through the trope of the "consumption" of culture. Just as language might be understood as "prosthetic," joining its inherent injuries to its capacities, food and eating provide their own complex opportunities for agency. She observes the way food and eating are evoked specifically in the work of Chinese writers Leung Ping-Kwan and Ma Kwok-Ming, and she elaborates more broadly on the idea that if one "imbibes" culture, it makes sense that literal consumption would be a site of cultural investment.[35] Aramaic in Mark seems to offer a "taste," or lend the aura, of something culturally familiar, whether or not Mark's readers actually speak Aramaic — perhaps the way hearing Polish spoken reminds me of my grandmother, even though she spoke only a handful of Polish phrases. (In this way, exoticism and familiarity are not mutually exclusive.)

But more to the point, questions of what you take in and what comes out (consumption and expression) are a matter of a certain anxiety for Mark. "Do you not see that what goes into a person from outside cannot defile, since it enters not the heart but the stomach, and goes out into the sewer?" Jesus says (7:18–19), responding to the Pharisees' accusation that his disciples hadn't washed their hands before eating. "He thus declared all foods clean," adds the author reassuringly. Mark's Jesus is making both a scatological joke and an admonishment about intentions and behaviors. "For it is from within, from the heart, that evil thoughts come," Jesus says, offering a classic list of sins. "All these evil things come forth and defile a person"(7:21–23). Not incidentally, the debate is framed as one about "tradition" (*paradosin*, vv. 5, 13) — what is essentially a synonym, or even euphemism, for cultural authenticity.

That is, in the matters of "tradition" and cultural production, you are not what you eat, but you are the shit that comes out of you, at least according to Mark. This negotiation of cultural purity is both disillusioned and strangely idealized: the closest to purity one can get is in *intention*, as if everything else is impossibly alloyed. It is significant, then, that what so often "comes out" of Jesus are words in his "native tongue," or at least words struggling to be so, the sounds and intonations of which are expressed through the prism of Greek. The *intention* of his speaking is pure. This is even while Jesus is also periodically exorcising colonial forces from others: "Get out of him!" he yells to the demon "Legion" who, among other torments, *speaks through* the man he is possessing (5:1–20).

But again this knot of speaking and cultural purity and authenticity is so often tied into scenes of physical anguish. This is no wonder since the Greek term for torture or torment (*basanos*) also (and more originally) meant "touchstone"—that which tested purity and differentiated the good/true from the bad/false. As classicist Page duBois has demonstrated so graphically in her book *Torture and Truth*,

> The Greeks first use the literal meaning for *basanos* of 'touchstone,' then metaphorize it to connote a test, then reconcretize, rematerialize it to mean once again a physical testing in torture. . . . The slave on the rack waits like the metal, pure or alloyed, to be tested. . . . The test assumes that its result will be truth.[36]

DuBois notices a certain fantasy in these ancient associations with torture: truth is not just possible, it is accessible, and can be revealed through the body of another. Truth is hidden, it is a *secret*, waiting to be discovered, extracted, and the instrument of that extraction is violence. That is to say that secrecy also represents *a desire for disambiguation*. The oft-noted "secrecy motif" of the Gospel of Mark, which plays itself out most often around these scenes of bodily precarity, has almost entirely been treated theologically as about "who Jesus really is," meaning his identity as an exclusive figure, which finally gets "revealed" by the centurion at Jesus's crucifixion. But perhaps it simply reflects a broader network of associations and resonates more with the pains of the production of identity and authenticity at large—not to mention the perils of speaking *at all* as a colonial/diasporic subject. One's language, always prosthetic and constantly, maddeningly misunderstood, instantly "reveals" one as the true cultural other, the "ethnic" subject who is made so through the discipline of the state.

In these scenes in Mark, the terms of cultural authenticity and the terrible means of truth production are staged again and again. Truth, including the truth of who one is, is ever shadowed by the means of its extraction. But even as what actually gets said under duress is ambiguous and speaking is perpetually fraught, the desire for purity, for authenticity, for clarity—in other words, the *attachment to the terms of legibility*—also seems to infuse Mark no less than it infuses the much later Tertullian. The assurance "Don't worry about what you will say, the holy spirit will speak for you" suggests that truth, secret even to its bearer, will make its way out somehow, even as the "good news" remains unspoken.

BEARING TRADITION: APOLOGY AND THE PERILS OF TRANSLATION

> But you God will speedily overtake, since you are cutting out the tongue that sang songs of praise to him.
>
> 4 MACCABEES 10:21

Mark is not the only text in which a "martyr" has recourse to a native language at their death. In fact, in the Martyrdom of the Holy Apostle Paul in Rome, Paul's final words are a prayer recited in Hebrew (5:27). Even more chillingly, in a Latin expansion of the earlier Greek story, Pseudo-Linus offers the following detail of Paul's decapitation: "After [his head] had been severed from the body, it called out the name of the Lord Jesus Christ in Hebrew in a clear voice" (16:46).[37]

In 4 Maccabees, too, the mother of seven sons who are tortured and die at the hands of King Antiochus offers her encouragement to them "in the Hebrew tongue," and the detail that her speech occurs in Hebrew is mentioned twice (12:7, 16:15–16). Curiously, perhaps, the mother is the only figure to speak in Hebrew in 4 Maccabees. She is not the only figure who testifies to the grief of speaking or the perils of translation, though. Eleazar's torture and death in the first part of the book is framed not only by his Stoic endurance, but by his apologetic speech that describes Hebrew law as fully reasoned philosophy (*philosophia*). Both his endurance and his apology constitute moves toward legibility—an act of cultural translation.

Eleazar's story is directly preceded by the cultural assimilations of the temple's high priest, Jason (appointed by Antiochus).[38] Then, as Antiochus drags a group of Hebrews in to choose between eating unclean food and dying, he singles out Eleazar, who is "of priestly stock, expert in the Law and advanced in age, and known to many of the tyrant's entourage for his philosophy" (5:4–5). Antiochus mocks Eleazar for Hebrew cultural curiosities, saying that his devotion (*threskeia*) makes him "anything but a philosopher":

> "Why should you abhor eating the excellent meat of this animal which nature has freely bestowed upon us? Surely it is sheer folly not to enjoy harmless pleasure, and it is wrong to spurn nature's good gifts. But in my judgment it will be greater folly still if you indulge in idle conceits about truth and continue to defy me to your own cost in suffering. Will you not awaken from your preposterous philosophy, abandon your nonsensical calculations, assume a frame of mind to match your years, and accept the true philosophy of your expediency?" (4 Macc. 5:9–13)

The terms of legibility have been set: "philosophy" is the frame of reference offered by the Hellenistic ruler and his world. The text describes the grid on which Hebrew piety and culture must be placed, as either a "reasonable" and "true" philosophy or a "preposterous" one full of folly, but a philosophy no less. In what follows, Eleazar's speech and virtue answer that call in spades: he endures violence and death with steely will, illustrating how thoroughly Hebrew law inculcates one in the arts of wisdom and self-control. But in demonstrating how deeply reasoned and worthy of philosophical devotion Hebrew law is, 4 Maccabees affirms the grid.

This move to render Hebrew law understandable by translating it into the terms of Hellenistic philosophy is echoed in writers such as Philo and Josephus, and it is illustrative of broader social impulses issuing from the fourth century BCE on, but becoming distinct during the Roman imperial period, when 4 Maccabees was composed. Steven Mason comments on the scene between Antiochus and Eleazar as part of 4 Maccabees' rhetorical strategy for its first-century CE context: "By repeatedly preferring to call Judaism a *threskeia*, [Antiochus] links it with superstition, in which taboos are observed through fear (cf. 5:13)."[39] While being associated with *philosophia* hardly meant immunity from Roman suspicions,[40] it was certainly better than a charge of "superstition."[41]

While 4 Maccabees doesn't "invent" Hebrew law and piety as a philosophy, or offer a historical account of that cultural translation, it does capture the *dynamics* of cultural legibility within dominant culture and the production of subjects, ethnically specific ones, within disciplinary machinery. Scholarship has puzzled about 4 Maccabees' consonance with Christian martyrdom accounts, as well as its concerted "Greekness." But similar to considerations of Mark's Aramaic lines, these questions carry the subtext of 4 Maccabees as a "culturally mixed" text, somehow not quite as "purely Judean" as perhaps some others. Indeed 4 Maccabees seems to be at the very crux of questions of what constitutes "truly Jewish" literary/cultural production.[42]

To reiterate, however, Chow, Derrida, and recent theorizing around diaspora at large demonstrate that there is no such thing as an authenticity unmarked by colonial relations,[43] that the very diagnosis of something as "more" or "less" authentically Judean is a reproduction of colonial/diasporic discourse. The overt rhetorical strategy of cultural translation of 4 Maccabees, alongside its dogged insistence on cultural purity, and even nationalism, makes it a target for these questions. But it is not anomalous or strange—it is *exemplary* of diasporic/colonial collectivity. Neither does 4 Maccabees' consonance with Christian texts, to my mind, jeopardize its emphatically and "authentically" Judean status since, as I have argued, so many of what we now consider Christian texts are doing the very same thing.[44]

But more than a poetic capture of a colonial dynamic, 4 Maccabees archives the costs and agonies of translation: Eleazar's belabored translation does not spare him pain, of course, it *coincides* with pain. Likewise later in the text, the third of the seven sons to die under Antiochus has his tongue cut out, a form of torture both graphic and symbolic. "But you God will overtake, who cut out the tongue that sang songs of praise to him" (10:21). The mother's speech makes sure to offer an explanation of what that endurance, what those deaths, yield:

> "My children, noble is the struggle, and since you have been summoned to it to bear witness for our nation, fight zealously for our ancestral Law. Shameful were it indeed that this old man should endure agonies for piety's sake, while you young men were terrified of torments. Remember that it is for God's sake that you were given a share in the world and the benefit of life, and accordingly you owe it to God to endure all hardship for his sake, for whom our Father Abraham ventured boldly to sacrifice his son Isaac, father of our nation; and Isaac, seeing his father's hand, with knife in it, fall down against him, did not flinch." (4 Macc. 16:16–21)

Speaking "in the Hebrew tongue," this unnamed mother tells whoever is listening that the deaths of her anonymous sons translate into a *nation*.[45]

Curiously, the text makes sure to note—not just note, but fully play out—what the mother of seven murdered sons *might* have said instead, and what she might have said is a fierce lament, nearly as long as the speech she makes to rationalize their collective suffering. As many have observed, through her resolute refusal to be given over to her grief and vulnerability, the mother in 4 Maccabees becomes a model of masculine virtue and impenetrability—a theme played out in other stories of martyred women.[46] But it seems that the dramatization of what she *could have said* functions not just to highlight her fortitude, but also to actually *express* that grief.[47] For all its desire to fortify against helplessness, 4 Maccabees, allows (obliges?) the reader to sit for a long time, line after line, with the uselessness of the mother's loss.

The mother makes reference to the book of Daniel, a text not only portraying miraculous survival under tyrannical violence but caught up in its own dense symbolics on the arts and perils of translation: one might recall that Daniel manages to ascend through foreign administrations because of his ability to interpret dreams and, not incidentally, translate the "writing on the wall" to King Baltasar– a phrase in Hebrew that predicts the end of his rule (Daniel 5:5–6). While Daniel survives, his survival becomes increasingly incredible, and the association between translation and precarity stands nonetheless. Similarly, the fact that Eleazar is the name of a priest in the *Letter of Aristeas* is no small detail, since the *Letter of Aristeas* is a narrative imagination of the translation of the Hebrew Law into Greek, a deal made by the King of Egypt in exchange for the return of Hebrew slaves. The exchange value of slaves for the Greek translation suggests the cost, in corporeal terms, of such cultural labor. Here, too, we find a thick web of associations, as one of the primary sources for the *Letter of Aristeas* is Josephus. Perhaps as a result of his own ambivalent survival (and perhaps his own work of translation), Josephus identifies strongly with the figure of Daniel.[48] He in fact describes his work in the preface of the *Antiquities of the Jews* with a heart-rending exhaustion: "[B]ut in the process of time, as usually happens to such as undertake great things, I grew weary and went on slowly, it being a large subject, and a difficult thing to translate our history into a foreign, and to us unaccustomed language."

Translation is both enabling and disfiguring. Cultural survival, which is inevitably cultural production, occurs only at the price of loss of bodily integrity. The torture and death of the martyrs in 4 Maccabees surely testifies to this. But the emphatic "willingness" of martyrs in this story to die testifies to something else: it signals a devotion not just to their "philosophy" but to the very disciplinary scene that renders them comprehensible at great expense, a rapt devotion to the grid on which they have been pinned.

Jesus's death in the Gospel of Mark does not bespeak willingness to die—quite the contrary, Jesus expresses ambivalent and hesitating submission and a sense of abandonment. But it does illustrate with striking and visceral detail the ways in which disciplinary or juridical scenes might produce *both* crises about belonging *and* cultural recognition and distinctiveness in one and the same move. The production of the truth of who one really is within disciplinary scenes is a constitutive feature of the noble death tradition. Typically, violence reveals the true character, the virtue, of the hero/heroine, as well as the veracity of the cause for which they die. This is no less present in the texts composing the classical canon of martyrological literature, of course, but many of these texts layer additional truths into the scene. Not unlike the alignment of God's voice with that of the centurion in Mark, in many of these stories God's cosmic truth aligns with the discipline of the state, giving the juridical scene an absolute and existential value. In Peter's final speech in the Martyrdom of the Holy Apostle Peter, for example, one finds an emphasis on God's truth being revealed in violent death:

> After coming to the cross and standing beside it, [Peter] began to say, 'Oh, name of the cross, a mystery completely hidden. Oh, grace inexpressible, spoken in the name of the cross. Oh, unspoken and inseparable love, which cannot be revealed through unclean lips. I am compelled to begin revealing it and making it known to you, oh person, whoever you are, until the end of my imprisonment here. I will not conceal the mystery of the cross, which for a long time has been closed up and hidden in my soul. Do not let that which is visible be for you the name of the cross, oh you who hope in Christ, for it is something other than what is visible in you.' (*Martyrdom of the Holy Apostle Peter* 8)[49]

Here inscrutability is fetishized as mystery, and just as in Mark 13, the truth buried in that "mystery" is not necessarily accessible to the one that bears it.[50]

In the letters of Ignatius, one finds an even more theological ontologizing of state power and even more spellbound attachment to the disciplinary scene. His letters—especially, and not insignificantly, his letter to the Romans—suggest an elaborate, almost erotic fantasy life about the mo and meaning of his death, as Ignatius wishes to become part of the imperial "food chain." Recall that he begs his audience, "Allow me to be bread for the wild beasts" (Rom. 4.1), wishing to be completely destroyed and dissolved (Rom. 4.2) in that most spectacular disciplinary theater of the arena. He insists there are no pleasures in this life but imagines deep pleasure in the food and drink of Christ's flesh and blood.[51] Danger and possibility, pain and pleasure attend the activities of the mouth: in fusing himself with Christ, not only is his death a feast, but in being eaten, he gets to eat.

What Ignatius will ostensibly become at the moment of his death is no small thing: he is described as not only becoming a disciple of Christ, "attaining" Christ but, not insignificantly, becoming a "Christian."[52] Yet Ignatius's transformation is always depicted as "in process": it is not fully achieved until his death in the arena. In fact, the term Christian in Ignatius's letters is mostly subjunctive or aspirational: he not only hopes to be "called" (*legomai*) a Christian, but hopes to be "found" (*euretho*) one.[53] That is to say, Ignatius does not die for being a Christian; he rather fantasizes *fulfilling his interpellation*, suggesting a captivity to the grid that makes him not just consumable, but legible.[54]

THE UNTRANSLATABILITY OF GRIEF

I have argued here that these texts are stories of cultural divestment, colonial and juridical attachments, and the knotty politics and feelings around speaking as a diasporic and colonial subject—the cultural materiality of speech. However, I don't necessarily want to claim that all martyrdom or noble death literature is entertaining these colonial and diasporic questions—even if I am convinced that such questions are part of what gave these texts purchase. My point is rather that interpretations of "martyr" texts have been overdetermined by questions of identity construction. Christian identity then becomes the only perceived social and cultural investment these texts evince. Reading these texts for traces of colonial experiences, among other things, allows us to both expand and refine our senses of what such stories of empire and violent death, of apology within juridical scenes, might be evidence of, and what they might be accomplishing for their writers and readers.

Circling back to Derrida, we can and should pause for a long moment on the colonial particularity of the grief, the longing for truth, the devotion to frames of cultural legibility—even ones that terrify or impale you—

archived in these stories. The traction of such stories has overshadowed that particularity, not unlike Derrida's (and his readers') own persistent stretching toward more generalizable conditions. Along with the increasing attraction to "Christian" and "Christianity," respectively, came a certain loss of culturally and colonially specific meanings. Again, we need to read against that grain. But we must do this even while noticing that the power of these stories has been precisely that their graphic severity and standardization worked as cathartic overstatement; or, better said, as fantasy, they provide a capaciousness into which one can almost seamlessly slide. They give expression to, among other things, one's own desires to become who one "truly is" against the inherent dispossessions of sociopolitical life and mortality in general. They chart the ways that part of what is so injurious about being hurt is one's ongoing, but perhaps not necessary, dependence on that hurt for understanding who one is. These stories have had an alarming prolixity over time—alarming because grief, or any experience, involves its own untranslatability, and such stories provide an ambivalent grid through which so many have made, and continue to make, their own lives and pains legible. But their prolixity only further testifies to their efficacy as archives—not to mention that their unbridled ability to speak, to say more or differently than the speaker might intend, is ever haunted by the sense that there is some other language, long gone, being murmured in the background.

PENETRATION AND ITS DISCONTENTS

Agency, Touch, and
Objects of Desire

I want to return to Pygmalion and his woman-statue. I want to come back to his fantasy, his *tactile* fantasy, in which she awakens at his touch, in which she occupies an uncertain space between object and subject, between Pygmalion's mind and her physical autonomy, between passive recipient and active agent.[1] That space, that touch, introduces uncertainty (however brief) into their initially dramatic differences in status.

In what follows, I take issue with what is the predominant and by now almost exclusive template for describing sexuality and erotic life in antiquity: the penetration grid, in which all sexual pairs are figured as active, penetrating subject and passive, penetrated object. As Pygmalion's story, with its structural misogyny, so forcefully shows, power and violence were deeply knit into erotic life in the ancient world. But even this story hints that sexuality was more complicated: even the most intractable-seeming roles don't *always* hold up, and erotic touch can often accompany the breakdown, if fleeting, of expected positions. The Acts of Paul and Thecla, as I read it, suggests an alternate framework for describing sexuality and eroticism in antiquity, one that takes its epistemology not from the wounding violation of penetration, but rather from the ambiguities of touch.

The Acts of Paul and Thecla shares in ancient culture-wide attachments to juridical scenes. Just as in the Greek novels (the form this story takes), The Acts of Paul and Thecla depicts multiple moments of confrontation with figures and scenes associated with the law. And like other literature collected under the category of martyrdom, the Acts of Paul and Thecla locates the term "Christian" in those disciplinary scenes. But unlike the protagonists of the "martyr" texts with which this text is typically associated, the central character, Thecla, does not die a violent death. Indeed, she evades injury at every turn and skirts the power of the law. The power of the law is forceful but not ultimate in this story. In this story of resilience, a vulnerable body remains intact, impenetrable, despite the dangers that follow her at every turn. Hinting at her potential objectification, at one point (and in some manuscripts), Thecla even turns into an object, a rock, to protect herself from an experience of sexual violence. The story enables a renegotiation of danger and power that brings (generally foreclosed) resilience to the fore.

Like the "martyr" texts I have discussed, the Acts of Paul and Thecla offers us an archive of experiences around and below certain grids of legibility. In this case, it is erotic experiences. Because the Acts of Paul and Thecla has often been placed in martyrological and ascetic trajectories, though, most scholars have suggested its take on sexuality is either one tied to violation and trauma on some level, or one absenting sexuality completely.[2] By contrast, I find in the Acts of Paul and Thecla forms of eroticism that widen our aperture for ancient sexuality. Again, Thecla's story importantly offers some readjustments to ruling contemporary theories that imagine penetrative wounding as the exclusive model for sex and relationality more generally.

I attend first and primarily to historians' portraits of ancient erotic life and linked social relations, and then intervene in and refine these portraits more directly through ancient literature. Alongside this literature, I leverage the work of Luce Irigaray and some theoretical work on affect to draw a portrait of erotic life and relationality that might present an alternative (and not a mutually exclusive one) to penetration. But I also include here some of my own resonant experiences in order to draw out ways of imagining erotic life and relational encounters that neither ignore traumatic or traumatized implications, nor let them reign.

GENDER AND DESIRE IN HISTORY

Ancient constructions of sexuality, it has generally been thought, hinged not on the gender of the person with whom one had sex, but rather on what position one occupied in the sexual act: penetrator or penetrated. Indeed penetration and concomitant notions of active and passive structured not only ancient senses of selfhood, but also, by metonymic implication, social relations at large.[3]

The singular reliance on the penetration paradigm is not a tendency displayed only by classicists or early Christian historians. So many of the reigning or most often elaborated portraits of sexuality and erotic life propagated by the overlapping fields of philosophy, psychoanalysis, and queer theory—Freud, Lacan, Georges Bataille, Leo Bersani, Julia Kristeva, Emmanuel Levinas, to name a few—figure *erotic life itself* through or as penetration. Indeed penetration, either the word or its implicit figurations, has been so thoroughly naturalized onto sexual topography, and even relational encounters at large, that it seems almost counterintuitive to articulate other ways to theorize sex, interrelationality, and erotic life. But penetration is a very particular construction of the body and subjectivity, one in which the boundaries of the body or self are heavily articulated only to be punctured, and, as I'd like to press, one that problematically constructs both bodies and selves in terms of surface/depth binaries.[4]

This is not to say penetration is a "bad" or wrong way to figure sex or interrelation, especially given all the compelling literature that is engendered by that figuration. (I have myself relied heavily on this paradigm.) But I find myself, well, *dissatisfied* with it of late, especially as a way of understanding the total organization of social relations and erotic experience in both the ancient world and the contemporary one. Penetration as a concept has acquired its own disciplinary power, and it is, after all, only one way to figure sex/relationality, one that consistently brings traumatic experience with it. If all sex, or even all relationality, is figured as traumatic, I wonder what kind of room such reductive and flattening universalization leaves for what I would even risk to say all of us experience as a contradictory, even lavish, and affectively variegated field? It would seem that understanding eros itself as wound additionally and not insignificantly takes some of the edge off experiences that more directly include violence and injury.

Historically speaking, the penetration grid with its hierarchically organized active/passive binaries is limited because of its exclusive focus on frames of legibility. If what any grid does is make everything but itself difficult to register, it is vital to theorize ways to account for erotic life off or under the grid; to attempt to account for, in some fashion, experiences that don't make for any easy emplotment or that fall just below the official register.

The question is not just historically compelling for me, though. It is also personally compelling: I've found penetration as a primary figuration for encounters between people especially reductive, frankly, since having gone through Eye Movement Desensitization and Reprocessing (EMDR) as a form of trauma therapy. EMDR is a form of psychotherapy in which one recounts and reassociates traumatic memories, usually while being guided through hypnosis-style side-to-side eye movements by the therapist. One of the major benefits of that work has been a new ability to roam the world *without* a sense of imminent injury; to fumble my way through a vivid landscape of relational experiences that don't collapse easily (or even at all) into trauma or its twin in extremity, *jouissance*. What I want, what my experience demands, are some new and perhaps warmer concepts that accommodate the pushes and pulls, the more minor and intriguing, and sometimes uncomfortable, impressions and touches that shape erotic life and relationships at large—and do so without a sense of ontological shattering.[5]

The penetration grid and its attendant assumptions have proceeded largely from K. J. Dover's *Greek Homosexuality* and the similar but theoretically much more sophisticated thesis in Foucault's work on the history of sexuality. Foucault argues that the notion of an identity based on "sexual orientation," so to speak, was an invention of the modern (specifically, bourgeois) culture—"homosexuality" particularly being coined in the nineteenth century.[6] Sexuality for Foucault was a politically flexible category for self-understanding—a "technology" of culture, as it were, that has a history.[7] Won by this argument, authors of studies of sexuality in the ancient Greek and Roman worlds have focused largely on questions of power and dominance at both individual and collective levels. David Halperin's work on classical Athens in *One Hundred Years of Homosexuality*, for example, emphasizes that there was no concept of a "sexuality" per se as an essential or ontological feature of one's character, only a set of behaviors and tastes that rather illustrated or fortified one's social position: "Not only is sex in classical Athens not intrinsically relational or collaborative in character; it is, further, a deeply polarizing experience: it effectively divides, classifies, and distributes its participants into distinct and radically opposed categories."[8] Notably, these opposed categories are hierarchical. Halperin and others emphasize that these ancient attitudes toward and imaginations of sex, linked to notions of masculinity and femininity, coincided with discourses of social stratification and conquest: the ideal body was a masculinized body, not only impenetrable/invulnerable, but actively dominating/violating other bodies/peoples.

Halperin's book has been particularly influential in the field of early Christian studies for the specific historical traction it gave to Foucault's broader mission. While there have been some rather hot contestations of this model, ancient sexuality is rarely (if ever) described without recourse to an ideological paradigm in which penetration reigns supreme.[9] Penetration with its assumed relationship to the active/passive binary is the over-determining model, not only for erotic experience, but again for *all social relations*, though it is also occasionally opposed via idealized notions of nonhierarchical mutuality, as I'll discuss in more detail.

Those who contest the Dover/Foucault/Halperin model of penetrative and active/passive relations have often expressed worry about the profound level of violence it implies. James Davidson and T. K. Hubbard, for instance, have objected not only to the stark picture of relationships painted by the active/passive binary (what Davidson calls the "zero-sum model"),[10] but also to the hesitance to claim homosexuality as such in the ancient world — and these two pieces are not unrelated.[11] If one is to claim "homosexuality" as such in the ancient world, one would, for both ethical and political reasons, perhaps want to untangle it a bit from the violence of ancient social-sexual relations. Hubbard writes:

> Although Halperin's essay aims to liberate us from what he regards as the nineteenth-century intellectual construct of 'homosexuality,' his formulation of Greek sexuality is itself firmly rooted in the even more modern intellectual constructs of victimization theory and child molestation. . . . It equally loses sight of the notion, commonly articulated by the poets, that the lover is the yoked horse whose reins the beautiful boy controls at will. Those who have actually been in love with attractive men or women twenty years younger than themselves know where the true power in the relationship resides.[12]

Interestingly, Hubbard explicitly criticizes the "reductionist fallacies" and phallocentrism of the active/passive model but does so only to reveal a troubling ignorance around how power and status differentials might affect erotic relations.[13]

Many (though not all) of the more direct contestations of the Dover/Foucault/Halperin genealogy have followed various kinds of identitarian logic. In her critique of Halperin, Bernadette Brooten's *Love between Women* observes how female eroticism was both noted and eclipsed by ancient male writers in part for its occasional and stubborn inability to be assimilated into active/passive binaries.[14] While Brooten recognizes differences between contemporary understandings of sexuality and understandings of sex and love in ancient Greek and Roman cultures, she challenges Halperin's claim that sexual orientation as a sustained and critical dimension of one's character or personality is only a modern phenomenon.[15] Brooten captures an entire landscape of erotic relations between women in the Greek and Roman periods in order to culturally situate and relativize responses to them in certain kinds of Christian literature. Not insignificantly, she thus implicitly casts "early Christianity" as only a negative or backhanded resource for the forms of eroticism in which she is interested. One of Brooten's primary arguments is that the Christian polemic about the "unnaturalness" of erotic relationships between women was tied into their transgression of gendered norms — the notion not only that women should always be passive partners or objects in sex, but that any given sexual pair involves a penetrating/penetrated opposition.[16] She finds that the ancient discourse on "female homoeroticism" expressed worry about these transgressions — both the possibility of a woman's being the active partner, and perhaps the possibility that there was no way to place sex between women on the penetration grid. But like Davidson and Hubbard, Brooten struggles with the severe and reductionist picture of active/passive relations and the related reluctance to think about homosexuality as such in Halperin et al.[17] Brooten, Davidson, and Hubbard thus want not only a more definitive picture of same-sex object choice in the ancient world, but a friendlier picture of erotic possibilities within those same-sex relations.

Page duBois's *Sappho Is Burning* launches a different critique of Foucault. She does not hunt for ancient homosexuality, or even necessarily for a sanguine picture of female homoeroticism. She objects to the historicization of lesbian identity in Sappho, in fact, even while she finds in Sappho a figure who is vastly underresourced in histories of sexuality beyond her place in lesbian genealogies. For example, according to duBois, Sappho is "unthinkable" for Foucault because she is an actively desiring woman who does not fit any prescribed social roles.[18] DuBois indeed wonders whether any erotic behavior between women would have even registered as sex or sexual to male writers in the ancient world.[19] Yet Sappho herself is not quite "off the grid" of legible pleasures since her desire fits with the dominant active/passive figuration. Likewise, while duBois critiques the (lesbian) identitarian model for Sappho, she still describes Sappho's desire as compelling largely because of the gender of her object choice.

It is hardly surprising that gender takes up so much space in discussions of ancient sexuality. The relationship between gender and sexuality is intricate and inextricable, in theory and in practice. But as Brooke Holmes has argued, gender has dominated discussions of sexuality in antiquity, especially as homosexuality and heterosexuality as usable concepts have met their limits.[20] Gender, in other words, is the primary object of our study in discussion of ancient sexuality, overshadowing the fact that (as Holmes notes) erotic life was itself a matter of deep interest and importance to people in antiquity.[21] I would even go so far as to say that the centrality of gender and object choice in these discussions inadvertently ontologizes gender, rather than, say, imagining gender as (among other things) a language through which erotic experience is expressed. This is not to make some kind of naïve or retro claim that language isn't productive, or doesn't have its violences, but rather to underline how the language of gender is as often a sticky and elastic web with which one toys as it is a cage in which one uncomfortably knocks around. Think, for instance, of the way one's partner's masculinity and/or femininity, playfully exaggerated or ostentatiously countered, can intensify the charge of an erotic moment—a moment that I would venture to say is only rarely if ever "about" gender in a central way, even if gender is its structural pretext.

It also seems that over time, and over the course of the many condensations of his work, some subtler dimensions of Halperin's readings have gotten lost. In fact, in *One Hundred Years of Homosexuality*, Halperin not only offers a broad reorientation to sex and sexuality in classical antiquity, but also examines the friendships between ancient hero-pals, prostitution's relationship to democracy in classical Athens, and how the female figure of Diotima participates in male erotic ideals in Plato's *Symposium*. In this essay, Halperin is interested in the *representation* of experience, rather than reconstruction of real experiences—as his Foucauldian genealogy suggests. So Halperin's tenacious focus is the cultural machinery and political ideology of sex in a given era.

What's interesting about so much of Halperin's book, however, is that it hardly paints the flatly gloomy ideological picture of sexual-social life he first sets out (and which so much scholarship has assimilated), where, he implies, *no* relationships, *no* gendered identities are configured without some form of penetrative domination.[22] In fact, Halperin's book suggests a much more colorful and tensive ancient topography for sexuality, desire, and even power than the penetration grid would let on. For instance, Halperin reads the relationship between Achilles and Patroclus in Homer's *Iliad* in relationship to two pairs of hero-warrior-friends in other ancient near eastern texts—the Epic of Gilgamesh and the books of Samuel. What he finds is a kind of affiliation, a friendship with a "high pitch of feeling," that takes on both "fraternal and conjugal" shades, but that fits into neither modern categories of (homo)sexuality, nor classical active/passive dogma.[23] As Halperin also admits, later Greeks who read the Homeric epic were apparently somewhat befuddled by the relationship, since it didn't quite fit the pederastic expectations of same-sex love.

Halperin takes this befuddlement, this attempt to "map their own sexual categories onto the Homeric text," as proof for the changing attitudes and constructions of sexuality even within a single culture.[24] But in a later essay, "Why Is Diotima a Woman?," he concludes that Plato's notion of eros (at least in the *Symposium*) actually departs from the active/passive binary in important ways, drawing up a notion of erotic relation that is "not hierarchical, but reciprocal; it is not acquisitive but creative."[25] Significantly, though, Halperin's reading of "reciprocal" and "creative" eros in Plato doesn't allow for too many egalitarian fantasies. Plato is still of course referring to pederastic relations, ones in which boys/students are elevated, or nurtured in some sense, into a sublime love of high ideas through a kind of intoxication with the teacher.[26] As Halperin notes, both the student and the teacher here are described as active and desiring.

The point is not to uncritically accept Plato's rendition of eros in this obviously pederastic scenario. But one should notice that it's not necessarily self-interest or justification that leads Plato to this account of eros, since it departs from the active/passive social ideology of the day. It indeed ascribes a kind of idealized or stereotypical "femininity" to student/teacher relations, which means the student is not necessarily a passive object but exhibits a kind of feminine responsiveness.

In Plato's vision of erotic relations between teacher and student, sex might occur, and power relations are, obviously, not absent. But it is also importantly not a dominating use of another as an object, a use of another solely for one's own pleasure (which, again, wouldn't be terribly problematic for ancient people, but rather an assertively masculine virtue). Whether or not Plato's vision of eros was experienced by students this way—perhaps some did and some didn't experience it as such—changes neither the obvious power dynamics of the relationship, nor the legitimacy of mutual desire (if only imagined). In other words, the vision of eros that Plato sets forth, whether or not it actually applies to the relationships he suggests it does, witnesses to an erotic relation that puts power and reciprocity in tensive combination.

Halperin notes that by choosing or inventing the figure of Diotima, the prophetess who teaches about eros in the dialogue, Plato not only figures eros in feminine terms, but predictably signals femininity as that through which men negotiate male relationships and understand themselves.[27] Halperin is almost excessively cautious about inferring women's experience or subjectivity from Plato's account. While I don't wish to surface anything like an essentialized "women's experience" from ancient literature, it does seem that "femininity," in this case and in others, may represent, and even archive, something like *nondominant experiences*. After all, it's clear that "woman" and "the feminine" already have a difficult and not always clear relationship to representation, since, as Julia Kristeva and Luce Irigaray have argued, they have often been posed as a "problem" for representation, as representation's other, that which mysteriously eludes the symbolic order.[28] Diotima's gender in the representational economy, then, is not just a "projection by men of their own experience . . . for internal consumption,"[29] but may also be a kind of ventriloquized legitimacy for that which does not fit comfortably within masculinized symbolics of experience such as the active/passive binary. What if Diotima gives space, however circumscribed, for felt experiences otherwise seemingly foreclosed in the social-sexual hierarchy?

Plato's idealized notion of eros would also seem to dissociate sex from penetration in some sense. That is to say that while sex is implied, it is not the goal of interaction, nor is it coextensive with straightforward domination. Instead the goal of "the act" for Plato seems to be admiring affection and apprehension of the Forms (ideal, invisible images of the existent world); the act for Plato has a different valence from the wounding infiltration implied by the term "penetration."

This reconsideration of Halperin's reading of eros in Plato poses the question of what kind of erotic/social relations, both in the ancient world and in the contemporary one, might we suddenly notice when not doubling down on identitarian attachments. What might we see when not caught in the obsessive if also sometimes pleasurable return to traumatized/traumatizing penetration? (And what is trauma if not obsessive return?)

ARCHIVES OF EROTIC EXPERIENCE

Paralleling ancient historians' debates on penetration, contemporary theory has centered on (and struggled with) penetration as a predominant representation of erotic experience and relationality at large. Here too gender often claims a primary and calcified place. In *This Sex Which Is Not One*,

Luce Irigaray provides a well-known takedown of the symbolics of penetration especially in Freudian thought. "Female sexuality has always been conceptualized on the basis of masculine parameters," she writes. "Thus the opposition between 'masculine' clitoral activity and 'feminine' vaginal passivity, an opposition which Freud—and many others—saw as stages, or alternatives, in the development of a sexually 'normal' woman, seems rather too clearly required by the practice of male sexuality."[30] Irigaray suggests that this "masculine sexuality" constructs the vagina as a "hole-envelope" in which "her lot is that of 'lack,'"[31] and she goes on to describe heterosexual genital sex as an "interruption" of woman's autoeroticism:

> This autoeroticism is disrupted by a violent break-in: the brutal separation of two-lips by a violating penis, an intrusion that distracts and deflects the woman from this 'self-caressing' she needs if she is not to incur the disappearance of her own pleasure in sexual relations. . . . Will woman not be left with the impossible alternative between a defensive virginity, fiercely turned in upon itself, and a body open to penetration that no longer knows, in this 'hole' that constitutes its sex, the pleasure of its own touch?[32]

Hetero genital sex is an essentially violent act for Irigaray, either in its barging in on female autoeroticism, or in the male aim to "appropriate for himself the mystery of this womb where he had been conceived."[33] She uses phrases like "forced entry," as well as the phallic cliché of the sword, and thus observes and plays with the violent implications of penetration as a figuration. But since Irigaray opposes the act itself more than its figuration, Irigaray's critique of the symbolics of penetration actually renaturalizes those symbolics onto bodies. In Irigaray's barely mitigated gender and biological essentialisms, acts remain stuck in the dominant symbolic economy, rather than open to the adjudication and reassignment of meaning.[34]

The association of sex with injury implicit in penetration is more complicated and dynamic than Irigaray's critique lets on. Because implicit in the term "penetration" is the association of sex with injury, it is particularly productive ground for resignifications and affective reassociations of both sex and injury. For instance, in *Is the Rectum a Grave?* Leo Bersani's description of penetration as a way of reading sex offers an interruption to the happy, harmonious, life-affirming image sex has absorbed in heteronormative, marriage-obsessed culture. Drawing constructively from Freudian theory, and specifically the death drive, Bersani argues that sex is not only inextricable from the exercise of power, but injurious at its core. He argues that both the pull and the fear of sex are its radically self-shattering potential, which is emblematized in being penetrated.[35]

Ann Cvetkovich rightly observes that Bersani's counter to sex positivity and heteronormativity contains its own essentialism, and she likewise notices that his framework "only seems counterintuitive (or 'queer') if it is assumed that everyone really wants to be 'masculine' and on top or that the trauma of penetration must necessarily be negative."[36] Likewise, Cvetkovich comments on the provocative and famous first line of Bersani's essay, "There is a big secret about sex: most people don't like it."[37] She writes, "Bersani's counterintuitive premise that people don't like to have sex is less startling in the case of women, for whom the dangers and discomforts of sexuality (whether pregnancy, rape, or an inability to attend to their own pleasure) have been all too readily apparent."[38]

Cvetkovich's critique of Bersani paves the way for her own project in *An Archive of Feelings: Trauma, Sexuality, and Lesbian Public Cultures* which, in part, mines the queer productivities of trauma. In her chapter "Trauma and Touch: Butch-Femme Sexualities," she suggests that "femme accounts of receptivity avoid a redemptive reading of sex, insisting on the fear, pain, and difficulty that can block the way to and be conjured up by making oneself physically and emotionally vulnerable or receptive."[39] She suggests that "[w]hat is required instead is a sex positivity that can embrace negativity, including trauma," which refuses a collapse into experiential resolution, romanticization, or fantasies of perfectly nonhierarchical relations by holding a place for shame and perversion.[40] Cvetkovich is not uninterested in the metaphorics of penetration, but rather sees such metaphorics, constructed as they are, as having poignant variation.[41] But because Cvetkovich intervenes in the eventfulness of trauma that is so heavily inscribed in theoretical literature, and because she seeks more mundane, less spectacular/fetishized accounts of psychic and bodily injury and their reverberations, she is also generally cued into a wider range of experiences that coalesce around erotic life than pain or self-shattering jouissance.[42]

Cvetkovich and Bersani demonstrate how penetration has been extraordinarily productive for queer discourse in working out injury and pain, as well as (not insignificantly) interrupting normative imaginations about what sex is and does, but that doesn't mean it needs to be the only or predominant way of understanding sex or subjectivity. We need not dispense with penetration as metaphor or its clear associations with trauma, but we do need to notice the ways those associations have commanded and overwhelmed our portraits of erotic life. As Cvetkovich notes, sex positivity and sex negativity need not exclude one another. Opposing them, I think, would blot out the mixed and minor dramas of most of our daily experiences of sex specifically and erotic life in general: the frustrations, the awkwardness, the suspense and delight, for instance, or the comforts and discomforts, the neuroses, the little hungers, and the sighs of relief that often arrive together. Further, and following Irigaray, whatever the act or the gender of the actors that penetration describes, it still carries in it a phallic economy, a figuration of bodies or selves as *encased* that need not be mapped onto every sexual or relational encounter.

Cvetkovich, aligning with others theorizing affect, sees trauma not as exactly puncturing boundaried selves, but as constructing boundaries *through violation.* The sense of having been injured crystallizes a sense of a "wound," and so it *produces hard boundaries through hypersensitization,* which is quite a different picture.[43] But the very fact that touch, an encounter with the "surface" of the skin, can be a violation refuses such dichotomization. Likewise the skin, laden as it is with nerves and wired so directly into one's most seemingly internal self, could hardly be so easily relegated to "surface." What happens when touch is not wounding, though — when contact, an impression, neither sits ineffectually on the surface, nor cuts to the bone? What about the pique of curiosity, the shiver, the hint, the turn away in distaste? What about the chafe, the ache, the rub?

Indeed while the ancient term *kinaidos,* describing a man who desires to be penetrated, has taken most of the attention among nondominant forms of ancient erotic life,[44] I find myself much more interested in the two slanderous terms associated with women having sex with other women in the ancient world: *tribas* and *frictrix/fricatrix*—both terms that derive etymologically from the verb "to rub."[45] While writers regularly ascribed penetration and masculinized active positioning to those designated as *tribades* or *frictrices,* we might note that the term "rub" figures pleasure and relationships, not to mention the topography of the body, quite differently: as something like the interplay of two electrified fields. In the etymology one finds at least an imagination, perhaps even an experientially driven one, that rather than surface/depth, one could (at least sometimes) be all surface. In this scenario, agency is not necessarily or automatically conferred anywhere. One might place this etymological richness alongside Irigaray's alternative to penetration, her "geography of feminine pleasure,"[46] which is concertedly plural and diffuse: nonteleological. Strikingly illustrated in the image of two lips rubbing together, it moves away from the concept of lack (the "hole-envelope") as well as from the monotheistic and solid power of the phallus, and toward doubleness and liquification—a kind of "stickiness" that softens or blurs boundaries rather than crystallizing them.[47]

Irigaray too roots herself firmly in identitarian investments, as she conjures a quintessentially feminine/female form of relationality. So while I don't follow her literalization of biological metaphors, I do find myself intrigued by the notion of the rub—or shall we say *friction*—as an alternative and supplementary figuration to penetration. Somewhat against Irigaray (and Brooten), it seems that friction doesn't actually specify very much in terms of agency/power relations or gender. Unlike penetration, friction quite capaciously entertains a whole suite of possible variations on agency and power, and need not at all be confined to representations of the female body. Friction is ambiguous along all sorts of lines, since it automatically installs neither "good" nor "bad" experiences (i.e., one can be rubbed the wrong way, too).

In fact, while both Brooten and Irigaray impute a kind of lesbian and/or feminine resistance against penetration to the figures and figurations in their work, it is exactly because of penetration's implicitly poor mapping of the penetrated person as receptive cavity and because of its constitutive relation to trauma that it feels like a disappointing reduction/generalization of erotic life in general, and sex in particular (including, say, heterosexual genital sex). In other words, to associate any and every form of sex or encounter with "penetration" is both to overdetermine and perhaps to fail to describe the experience, namely, by associating it with ruinous invasion. By contrast, describing contact with others in a more generalized or abstract way as friction invites some compelling possibilities. But I'm less interested in any grand theory of eros or of contact with the Other (a solidified, phallic concept itself) than with carving out space for specific kinds of contact that appear off the grid.

The Acts of Paul and Thecla might be a kind of productive wedge into the history of ancient sexuality, as well as contemporary considerations of erotic/eroticized relations. It is an enthralling interlocutor in questions of ancient erotic life: an unusual piece of literature, but not an exceptional one; an archive of erotic experiences that, when read closely, might cue us into a set of feelings and relations that don't ordinarily appear in distractingly dramatic, or spectacularly troubling, pictures of ancient sexuality.[48]

Threaded through modern accounts of ancient women's sexuality one finds constant articulations (subliminal or explicit) of longing to *make contact* with ancient women "themselves," if not specifically lesbian women.

Gathering these scholars alongside Hubbard and Davidson's critiques of Foucault, one might even describe it more generally as a longing for one's own experience to be situated, recognized somewhere in ancient litera-ture—a longing to bridge the past and present via identity.[49] I obviously don't negate the possibilities of real, tangible contact with past figures. But perhaps that contact is not on identitarian terms. And again, what if we entertain these ancient discourses on women and desire as not about women or their erotic lives per se? Rather what if, somewhat in the vein of Diotima, we treat them as still preserving *some kind* of erotic experience, particularly experience that challenges phallocentric mapping? Indeed in the gendering of a set of experiences as belonging to women in some fash-ion, one does preserve them—albeit ambivalently, since the very gendering of these experiences circumscribes their potential for recognition.

Since so much of the scholarly literature on ancient sexuality is char-acterized by claimed subjective investments in the writing of a history of sexuality—inherent in debates about historians' own desire and the contem-porary stakes around identity—I too am planting myself in this debate in a concertedly subjective fashion. I do so less with identitarian investments than with loosely defined experiential ones. I also do so by intertwining Thecla's story with some (apparently) compatible experiences of my own. I don't doubt that I find Thecla appealing or her experience resonant with mine because she is a woman; I just don't see gender as the determinative node of our connection, especially since the gender of a literary character, one who potentially ventriloquizes or registers desires of men, is always a dicey matter. I entwine her story with mine to echo and amplify the person-alized stakes of the debate on writing the history of ancient sexuality. More pointedly, however, I do so to offer one very particularized instance in which eros as only or primarily wounding fails to do justice to the full breadth and dimension of lived experience—the ways grids discipline and overdeter-mine our understanding of what even strikes us as erotic in the first place.

NEITHER MARRIAGE NOR DEATH
(OTHER LOVE STORIES)

The Acts of Paul and Thecla, a second-century tale of a young woman whose encounter with the words of the apostle Paul impel her to flout social, sexual, and gendered conventions and then venture out as a teacher, has attracted

considerable scholarly and popular attention throughout its long history.⁵⁰
And while readers have recognized the author's interest in negotiating erotic
life, the text's association with asceticism (generally understood as sexual
renunciation and thus the cultivation of an un- or antierotic life) has meant
that it has been underappreciated in histories of sexuality, particularly those
on the Greco-Roman era.⁵¹

In the story, the young woman (Thecla) overhears the apostle Paul
expounding on the "word of Christ," which in this case includes statements
on ascetic virtues, resurrection, and compassion. Enamored with his message and longing for the life of which Paul speaks, Thecla cannot tear herself away from the window where she sits, listening to the sound of Paul's
voice (the text mentions that she has not yet seen him in person), even as the
man she's contracted to marry comes to visit. "Where is my Thecla?" he asks.
Theocleia, her mother, replies, "I have a strange story to tell you. Indeed for
three days and nights Thecla has not risen from the window--either to eat
or drink--but gazes as if looking upon some enjoyable sight. In this way she
clings to a strange man who teaches deceptive and cunning words." She continues by explaining that Paul's words are so appealing to the local young
women that he is a threat to the city. "My daughter, like a spider in the window, is also bound to his words, held sway by new desire and fearful emotions. For the maiden fixates on the things he says and is captivated." Both
"loving her and also fearing her passion," Thecla's fiancé, Thamyris, goes to
her and asks, "What is the emotion that binds you in passion? Turn toward
your Thamyris and be ashamed." Her mother asks, "Child, why do you look
down and sit like this, answering nothing but acting like a mad person?"
Both Thecla's mother and her fiancé weep and grieve for the captivated Thecla as if she has died, yet she remains rapt in her attention to Paul's words.

Later in the story, Thamyris plots to have Paul arrested and brought to
court. Thecla follows Paul to the prison just to hear him speak more about
"freedom in God," a notion that emboldens her and even moves her to kiss
Paul's chains. At the trial, Paul is slandered as a "magician," and Thecla is
called to testify about why she will not marry Thamyris. Upon her refusal to
respond, her mother cries, "Burn the lawless one! Burn the one who refuses
to be a bride in the middle of the theater so that all the women taught by
this man will be afraid!"

There follows a series of attempts to execute and harm Thecla, none
of which succeed. Although she is stripped and on the pyre, ready to be
burned, the fire mysteriously "did not touch her." God compassionately puts
out the fire with a terrible storm. Even though many die during the storm,

Thecla survives. In another scene, Thecla manages to evade an imminent sexual assault from a man on the street, and she reverses the shame caused to her by his actions by tearing off his cloak and crown and throwing them to the ground. For her "crime" of dishonoring the man, the governor sentences her to death by wild animals in the arena. This attempt to kill her also fails, as Thecla is defended by the lioness sent to devour her. In another strange turn, Thecla is saved from a pool of killer seals by a lightning strike, which kills the animals but not her. Once again, she is preserved from both harm and shame: "And surrounding her was a cloud of fire so that neither the wild animals could touch her nor could she be seen naked."

Thecla's adoration of Paul is continually directed at his words rather than at the man himself (and the text specifies that Paul is rather unattractive).[52] Meanwhile, Paul seems ambivalent about Thecla's attachment: he witnesses Thecla's near sexual assault but does nothing. Indeed, the man attempts to persuade Paul to "give" Thecla to him, but Paul demurs, saying, "I do not know the woman of whom you speak, nor is she mine." But Thecla's world is also populated with surprising allies, generally female ones: the lioness who defends her in the arena, as well as scores of women in the stands attempting to distract the animals from killing her by throwing in flowers and spices. In this same scene, a queen named Tryphaena walks Thecla to the site of her execution and confides to her that she loves Thecla like her own deceased daughter. She mourns Thecla's fate, pleading to God to help her.

Though not twenty years of age, Thecla hardly crumbles in the face of these dangers. She refuses to testify against Paul in court at her own peril, and she deflects shame upon the man who seeks to shame her through assault. She also boldly baptizes herself (after Paul puts off her request), makes confident petitions to God for her own rescue, and at one point stitches and dons men's clothing so that she can find Paul and report her self-baptism. She never marries, and even Paul, who would seem to be central to the text, disappears from the story. The text closes by charting Thecla's long and productive life as a teacher and healer.[53]

This harrowing and often hilarious story is written in the style of the Greek romance novel, a popular narrative form that is characterized by the adventures of a couple who must face danger, death, separation, and threats to the woman's body and/or sexual reputation as obstacles to being together. The novels tend to be characterized by violence emanating from every direction--strangers, animals, pirates, bandits, local authorities--and by a climax involving the civic ceremony of marriage.[54] While much of the plot of these stories revolves around the near unraveling of civil society, the final scenes in which the couple finally comes together again, if a bit battered, in a glorious civic union reassure the reader of civic coherence.[55]

The various "Acts" placed in the Christian tradition are elaborations of this form, with some key variations. Among these variations, these Acts often culminate in violent death—that is, martyrdom.[56] Martyrological texts, especially those narratives that center upon women, are not unlike Greek novels in that penetration and a kind of "immunity" from penetration are predominant themes. Virginia Burrus has amplified and tracked this theme in early Christian literature most cogently.[57] In her article "Word and Flesh: The Bodies and Sexuality of Ascetic Women," for instance, she describes, among other things, the distinct and highly sexualized investment later male writers had in such impervious female bodies, writing that "imagined physical enclosure or intactness of the female virgins' sexual organs functioned symbolically in the rhetoric of the fourth century to reinforce social and ideological boundaries."[58] But Burrus significantly notes that in texts that describe women's ascetic behaviors, including the Acts of Paul and Thecla, what one sees is not a timidity or indifference toward erotic life, as much as a renegotiation of it. She writes, "If sexual asceticism entails successful resistance to male control, this in turn liberates the women's sexual energies, albeit in 'sublimated' forms; for the women are now free to direct their eros toward the pursuit of knowledge and spiritual growth as well as the formation of new relationships."[59]

Burrus (like Halperin) is careful to remark that she is not trying to reconstruct anything like "women's experience," at least not in any limited way.[60] But both here and in some of her other work, Burrus accounts for alternate forms of eroticism, thus expanding the archive of what counts as erotic. Most notably, in her later book *The Sex Lives of Saints*, Burrus rereads hagiographical literature for such forms of eroticism (or rather "countereroticism") that refuse social-sexual convention.[61] So much of what Burrus excavates in this retelling of the history of sexuality via "early Christian" literature, however, still circulates around not only pain and death, but in general a certain extremity of experience. Drawing from Elaine Scarry's work on torture, Georges Bataille's assimilation of desire to death, as well as Jean-Luc Nancy's equation of love and touch with wounding, she writes, "When *jouissance* is understood as a 'mode of ascesis,' the ascetic emerges into view as an erotically *joyful* 'body in pain,' disclosing suffering as the vehicle of the ongoing unmaking and remaking of worlds."[62] "Ancient hagiography," she writes, "participates in such a self-mortifying *jouissance*, such a divinely

erotic joy, in which the performative 'death' of the self becomes the sancti-
fying matrix of life's renewal."[63]

Similarly, in "Word and Flesh" Burrus places Thecla alongside the
stories of female ascetic martyrs, whose stories include them evading sexual
penetration and shame, but not the sexualized, penetrating wound of murder and death. But the Acts of Paul and Thecla differentiates itself from the
martyr acts, since she thwarts the traumatic conclusion of execution, in
addition to the happy resolution of marriage. Thecla continually fends off
traumatic injury of all kinds, even managing to deflect the shame that would
perforate her confidence. In the meantime, she finds a set of pleasures in her
own fearless speech and gestures: rapt delight in the words of others; comfort in a cosmic force that thinks kindly of her; and sustaining, surprising
connections to others, animal and human, in the world around her. Burrus
sees in ancient literature a masochistic erotic self-annihilation as an alternative to the reproductive and marital framing of sex (not unlike Bersani's
theorizing of sex toward the death drive). But if Thecla is not a martyr, it
seems to me that the Acts of Paul and Thecla's erotics instead *bypasses* the
death/marriage binary.

When I read Thecla's story, I cannot help but install myself at nearly
nineteen, still a girl, having had a fragmenting episode of sexual violence
that occurred a couple of weeks after my mother inexplicably left my father,
with whom I ardently identified (and still do). Within a few months of these
traumas, and in the disoriented and vacated state induced by them, I had a
lucky encounter with a charismatic, consistent, adoring, and deeply harm-
less person whom I smilingly finessed into cohabitation almost immediately, and for twenty years following. The twenty years were many things,
too many to recount in any single narrative, or even five, but among those
many things, they were structured by a steady refrain of experiments in autonomy and returns to traumatized attachment. That sweet and companion-
able marriage, in other words, tethered me enough to alight on adventures
in quasi-independence that I would have felt too frightened and too small to
approach otherwise. Another way of putting it is that he held me in my fear
response long and tightly enough for both my fear and the marriage itself to
burn out. Or another: the marriage made possible my healing, even as my
healing stripped our relationship of its most powerful motor.

The safe structure of this relationship, formed in the grid of the law
which rendered our lively sexualities winsomely and invariably hetero, had
many experiential subtexts for me, ones that echo the more difficult moments of Thecla's story: the hot lightning strikes of shame; a constant feeling

of danger, narrowly escaped; the mystifying and devastating sense of being sold out by the same person who secured me to this world (which could easily happen again). These senses stood alongside a number of people and moments and things that gave or taught me pleasure—and also resonate, all too precisely sometimes, with Thecla's story. Just to name a few: dream-like immersions in books and ideas; regular and wild cathexes in teachers who only sometimes wanted to claim me back; minor if ostentatious exhibitionisms and the thrills of occasionally flouting tradition; a set of affectionate, captivating, and only rarely definitively sexual creative/intellectual affiliations with men and with women; and an imaginative life that regularly aligned with a sense of omnipotence. Subtending all of these was a sense of growing intellectual mastery that gave me a language for the dark and sharpened world in which I lived.

One could easily point to the continuities these experiences and encounters had with my childhood before the traumatic eventfulness of my nineteenth year: I lived as an ordinary girl in a mysterious and magical world, accompanied by companions of all sorts, on whom I endlessly crushed with only half a thought toward mutuality, and with music, poetry, and some big and generally benign cosmic force as our ambience. So these later pleasures are actually not best understood as direct addresses to traumatic experience, even as they did deliver relief from trauma's consummations. They are rather diaphanously, if also ineluctably, tied to trauma, mostly by virtue of time and their inhering in the life of a single person. And these experiences were also not without their discomforts, or disjoints in agency: miscommunications and disheartening rejections; inability to get what I wanted, or being on the receiving end of more than what I wanted; the incomplete satisfactions of daydreams, or the too-fast dissipation of interpersonal chemistry and other disappointments; anger, frustration, boredom, melancholy, longing. But that is the abundance and ambivalence of friction, the currents and points of contact that sustain and fail but do not break us.

AN EROTICS OF THE MUNDANE

We might consider the Acts of Paul and Thecla's erotics expansively—focusing less narrowly on Thecla's gender and even more traditional notions of the objects of her desire, and attending more closely to her heightened sensual/sensory experiences, the moments of flush that pepper the story.

When we do so, what emerges is an archive of pleasures in which traumatic, "penetrative" relations don't win the day, even as it accounts for the existence and dangers of those relations. The plotting of enjoyable and frictive moments and encounters alongside of them in the Acts of Paul and Thecla is instructive for what we historians (and others) might miss in our overattention to the grid of legible pleasures, or our relentless hunt for absolute figurations of power or their subversion. Where on the grid might we place the warm connection between the queen Tryphaena and Thecla, as surrogate mother and daughter? Where might we place, say, Thecla's cavalier excitement in stripping and pitching the crown of her would-be offender? Her affiliations with the observing women who, throwing their petals in the arena, help save her? Or her adoration of Paul's words and chains, her exhilarating and passionate plunge into a set of ideas, and a life, that seem absurd to her mother and the man to whom she is obligated? Her love of risk? Of course I worry that these delights, not uncomplicated ones, might be characterized as not quite fully erotic, or worse, as "adolescent," not least because of Thecla's literal adolescence.[64] But that only reiterates the necessity for accounting for them. Rendering these as "adolescent" or less full pleasures would likewise place these experiences on a grid—a developmental (and thus teleological) one, in which such pleasures are "outgrown" in the name of other, more "sophisticated" ones.

Thecla's erotic experiences are not exactly without wounding, since violence, danger, and power infuse the story. And as I have shown, those forms of violence and danger and power are not completely distinct from her various pleasures. More generally, there is no life without wounding or the impingements of the grid, and there are no scenarios so perfect that they are without differences in power and agency. What I seek is not a romanticism in which trauma evaporates, nor do I want to hold out via theory any kind of promise that certain forms of eroticism could be a model for relations at large, or could completely shield one from injury, just as Thecla is shielded again and again. In fact, we might think of her pleasures as perhaps an electric excitement at a sense of her own resilience, rather than a form of insulation. Likewise, Thecla's pleasures happen within, against, and across all kinds of status differentials, including gender, but they do not easily, or even ever, condense into the straightforward hierarchical active/passive binary that penetration stages. The goal here is, among other things, to interject into history and theory the relatively obvious, if vastly underplayed, recognition not only that pleasures of all kinds are ambivalently knit into relations of power and status rather than being determined by or occurring despite them, but also that pleasure can happen without disfigurement, and that resilience is as real as injury.[65]

It is worth piecing together in the domains of both history and theory a fuller and more daily account of eros—an erotics of the mundane—in which wounding, while never far from the frame, is neither the prerequisite for pleasure, nor the primary indicator for its realness; in which the severity of the grid of hierarchical and penetrative relations, and the subtext of gender that undergirds them, are denaturalized and seen as grid, even while questions of power and legibility remain constructively part of the picture. For the ancient world as well as the contemporary one, and some of the worlds in between, the eventfulness of trauma and *jouissance* might be supplemented by other love stories—the less dramatic but no less distinct or consequential rhythms and impressions that punctuate our lives, but do not puncture them.

DARKENING THE DISCIPLINE

Fantasies of Efficacy and the Art of Redescription

A return of variety to the ancient world's skin tones [on ancient statuary] paints a truer picture. It also asks us to reflect on the current state of those disciplines, fields, and practices connected to historical study.

SARAH BOND, "WHITEWASHING ANCIENT STATUES: WHITENESS, RACISM AND COLOR IN THE ANCIENT WORLD"

Objects have lives of their own: lives, it turns out, that surpass our descriptions. We (I) can tell the stories of objects differently, but they are no passive recipients of our affections. Shape-shifting, burrowing into our imaginations, objects do not stay put. They are not truly pliable, not often or always receptive to our designs, but neither are they fixed. We describe them, bring them to life with our touch, only to realize, sometimes belatedly, that our artistry has been eclipsed by our captivations. The object outdoes us. We try again.

In a tentative conclusion, I'd like to draw our attention back to ancient statuary and the fantasy lives that coalesce around it. This time, however, I focus exclusively on contemporary fantasy lives, and I launch from the heated discourse over the racialized modern history of these ancient artifacts.

White supremacist investments in classical antiquity, including as the origins of "western civilization," have a thick modern history, and one place these investments show up is in the aesthetics of classical sculpture: unlike in antiquity (in which they were painted in vivid hues), these marble depictions of gods, emperors, heroes, and others appear to us now as white. However, the fantasy of white continuity and epic pedigree is not the one I wish to address—in part because it has been criticized (rightfully, obviously) so thoroughly already. Instead, I'd like to scrutinize the counterfantasies and historical redescriptions that emerged *in and around* this critique: a diverse and vibrant, "colorful" antiquity.

The statues themselves are at the center of this discourse even as they are beside the point. What is important about them is the way collectives are imagined in and through them, and the way in which their aesthetic topography becomes a source of political currency. This discourse invites me to ask again, in a slightly different key from chapter 2: what does it mean to do justice to and with history?

Pressing further into the realm of disciplinary attachments, in what follows I open up a line of inquiry into field-based fantasies and objects of study. I wander through the "problem of race," as the euphemism goes, in the study of the ancient world, including and especially biblical and early Christian studies. Indebted to Robyn Wiegman's book *Object Lessons*, a book that gives an account of the desires for justice in identity-based fields of study (women and gender studies, queer studies, whiteness studies, intersectionality, to name a few), I ask: What has happened as race itself has become a privileged, if difficult, object of study in these predominantly white disciplines? What do the political aspirations lodged in certain forms of racialized historiography, specifically in the public realm, tell us about the various fantasies that float in not just these fields, but academic life in this extended political moment? How does this political moment, with the increasing public acceptability of racist violence, inflect or elicit questions of meaning and importance, particularly in the study of the rather remote ancient Mediterranean? And what real (i.e., less romanticized) political possibilities might be carved out or embraced in redescribing these disciplinary fantasies *as fantasies*?

DISCIPLINARY WHITENESS AND ITS SHADOW

In what soon became a flashpoint and exemplar of viral public scholarship, classicist Sarah Bond's article "Why We Need to Start Seeing the Classical World in Color," published in Hyperallergic, a web forum for art, traces the racist history of investments in white marble antiquities. "Most museums and textbooks contain a predominant neon white display of skin tone when it comes to classical statues and sarcophagi. This has an impact on the way we view the antique world. The assemblage of neon whiteness serves to create a false idea of homogeneity—everyone was very white!—across the Mediterranean region."[1] She correctly notes that whiteness was not an ancient concept, and that modern European art historians leveraged white marble statues from antiquity (particularly the Apollo Belvedere now in the Vatican Museum) in order to articulate and diagram racist notions of ideal beauty and humanity. Bond then considers the potential links between the stark and eerie whiteness of these figures and the overwhelming whiteness of classics as a field. "Do we make it easy for people of color who want to study the ancient world? Do they see themselves in the landscape that we present to them?" She ends on something of an exhortation: "It may have taken just one classical statue to influence the construction of race, but it will take many of us to tear it down. We have the power to return color to the ancient world, but it has to start with us."[2]

This seemingly benign article, as much about diversity in an academic discipline as about the aesthetics of race,[3] caught the attention of loud and shadowy conservative internet mouthpieces who, perhaps for the first time, found themselves reading a blog post on a relatively hip art forum. Bond was harassed and threatened, but also hailed by fellow historians for her guts and bravery. In an *Inside Higher Ed* article by Colleen Flaherty entitled "Threats for What She Didn't Say," Bond logged surprise at the fallout: "I knew when I started taking notes on the subject of polychromy many months ago that this column would likely cause a stir within the field, among colleagues and online. . . . I had thought that I was prepared for the internet trolls. After all, I have crossed many proverbial bridges on Twitter—where they usually lurk. However, the hatred and invective I received from this post was more than anything I have ever received to date."[4] The article ends, "Perhaps most distressing about Bond's case, she said, is that 'it seems quite clear that the people who have had the most violent reaction to [her] essay are the ones who have not actually read it,' relying instead on 'distorted and misleading summaries.'"

The article centralizes Bond, but also places her among other academics, including Keeanga-Yamahtta Taylor, Tommy Curry, and Tressie McMillan Cottom, who have seen similar controversy and aggression arise over their public scholarship. Cottom suggests that if institutions want the prestige that comes with public engagement, they must be ready to also defend those scholars who suffer these kinds of repercussions, "[b]ecause public scholarship means pissing people off," and it "doesn't take much to make a controversy."[5]

Bond is not the first or only scholar to raise the issue of polychromy in ancient art, as she herself notes.[6] Nor is she the first to consider it an issue of diversity and representation. Indeed Bond's article and its reception not only pose some important historiographical questions, but provide a snapshot of a number of conundrums within the American academic sphere, specifically the study of antiquity. I'm particularly piqued by the disciplinary "we" whom Bond calls to action, not just their presumed identity but the power she ascribes to them—or shall I say "us"?—especially as it appears in a piece of public scholarship.

I resonate with Bond in her desire for race-critical historiography, and myself have made various kinds of pleas for engaging race and ethnicity as meaningful optics for characterizing the ancient world (this book, for instance). And I share a sense that the ancient world, however remote it may seem, is hardly extraneous to the political present. But given my own affinities with Bond, it feels especially salient to ask: what are the fantasies, the imaginations, at play in Bond's piece and its various receptions? And, a bit more pointedly, to what extent did the conservative backlash and then the defense of Bond by her colleagues, which immediately solidified the sense of "relevance" attending work on antiquity, supply a predominantly white discipline with its own sense of urgency and power? This is not to say there aren't actual dangers associated with having one's work engaged by public audiences—whether by our own volition or by being "outed"—but the risks are most often ones associated with professional peril at the institutional level and tend to follow the usual differentials around race, gender, and queerness. It is rather to ask, what do the risk, and the inflation of controversy through social media, for instance, *also* do? What imaginations about scholars and scholarship do they buttress?

Likewise, we might play out Bond's proposition: does "coloring" the ancient world, marking it as "not-white," make it more friendly, or at least less available to racist recapitulation? On the one hand, Bond situates the production of whiteness in modernity, suggesting that European historians and the "alt-right"/white supremacists would not find themselves truly represented in antiquity. The Romans were not white. On the other, what she longs for is for a wider spectrum of skin hues to be represented in the past, and therefore *available* for identification. The question is, however, identification with whom? Should anybody be especially eager to identify with the Romans, for instance? How about with the nations that Rome conquered, ones who were represented in deeply racialized (and feminized) terms themselves? Where might I place myself (white, of mixed and uncertain eastern European descent) in the landscape of the ancient Mediterranean? Should I step back and realize I'm not there? It would be hard to object to stepping back, but the question that follows then is: Who is one asking, or assuming, to step forward? As whom?

Antiquity was full of pointed representations of "nations" as racialized others, and ethnography was a widespread taxonomic discourse — both official and casual — that sought to make sense of culture collision and changed circumstances through the fabrication of essential if also volatile difference. Even if racial categories in modernity don't align with those of antiquity, antiquity was certainly no less fraught along racial lines. So what, exactly, does finding oneself there do? What are the costs of race-critical scholarship that leans primarily on the epidermalization of race, on race as color, and the values of finding oneself in the past?[7] And how does the emphasis on skin and color in this case perhaps cover for a whiteness that seeks to exit itself?

For so much theoretical literature, fantasy is understood primarily as stabilizing identity over time. In Lacan's mirror, remember, the image of the total body is seen in the mirror and assumed by the one looking to be a psychological reality, a cohesive self. The felt body in fragments becomes one, and does so through retrojection: it was always one, even as the fragments still haunt. So despite or within her emphasis on scenarios that chart tensions and fluctuations of position, in *The Fantasy of Feminist History* Joan Scott's main deployment of fantasy as a historiographical operation is to show how it bridges gaps and creates continuities between subjects or figures across time who would otherwise share little in common.[8] But in Bond's piece, we find that the crux of the fantasy lies in discontinuity, the destabilization of whiteness via time and through recourse to the "more real(istic)" and not-quite-fulfilled hope of darker others seeing themselves reflected back. Identity is either impossible to actualize, or not yet actualized, and the fantasy is one of power: the presumed white subject and architect of the discipline (part of the "we") has the power to disable racist narratives, and perhaps more eerily, the power to provide those darker others with the mirror.

Refusals of white supremacist discourses and white antiracist political sentiment have long been part of the white imaginary, as Robyn Wiegman has shown. She charts a history of whiteness studies, which seeks to critically analyze, contextualize, and ultimately deconstruct whiteness. Wiegman observes how whiteness studies crystallizes the dogged centrality of whiteness in the form of an academic discipline, even as it simultaneously holds out the possibility of an antiracist white subject whose own conscious critical choices can disarticulate them from white supremacist systems and discourses.[9] Whiteness studies has drawn from labor history, in which histories of constructions of whiteness seem to also suggest a kind of mobility of whiteness. If whiteness is associated with class, for instance, and Irish immigrants in the United States opted for social mobility through aligning themselves with whiteness (they in effect "chose" whiteness), then by implication, one can "opt out" of whiteness via certain class—or political—affiliations:

> In this retrieval of the historical as the site of human agency, labor history jump starts, we might say, the critical project of imagining an antiracist white subject in the present, for if whiteness is historically produced and its production requires something more than the physical characteristic of skin color, then whiteness as a form of political identification, if not racial identity, can be undone.[10]

Not far from the argument that "there are no white people in antiquity" (a phrase I myself have uttered in class), the modern story of the production of whiteness in labor history has, in Wiegman's words, "come to define the possibility of the antiracist white subject," with an "emphasis on agency that situates the white humanist subject at the center of social constructionist analysis."[11] But who exactly benefits from the historicizing of whiteness, this "white identificatory mobility"? "The fruit of the social constructionist enterprise is to be found, then, fully on the side of the antiracist white subject," Wiegman observes, "the one that must be rescued from its racial 'self' by marking the difference between identity and political identification . . . a knowing white subject that can write its political commitments against the burden whiteness represents."[12] Wiegman indeed at least twice describes this work as fantasy or romance, a wishful scenario in which one's whiteness is not intractable, in which one can be affiliated (in solidarity?) with racially minoritized people.

Wiegman's book actually chronicles much more than whiteness studies. The "object" in the title *Object Lessons* refers to identity as an object of study, and her book surfaces the ways in which the identity-based disciplines that emerged in concert with liberal political projects continually contended with their vexed relationship to activism and social change. In negotiating this vexed relationship, these fields ended up lending critique an almost exorbitant amount of political power. The movement of inclusivity represented by the move from women to gender to queer to intersectional itself represents a kind of political fantasy of transcending exclusion, according to Wiegman.

However scorching Wiegman's observations of these disciplines or apparatuses of disciplines may be, Wiegman is not interested in rendering futile the project of identity-based critiques. She is compelled by what motivates those critiques and those who perform them—often what affectively motivates them—what their aspirations are, and how those aspirations fail to materialize. Closing her chapter on intersectionality, she writes that

> left theory of any kind does not simply construct an analysis of power as a way of discerning social relations; it lives the complexity of those relations, just as surely as human subjects do. This is why what interests me in *Object Lessons* is not theoretical resolution, as if any of us can master the meaning of the relations we inherit from worldly actions we did not intend. If I am convinced of anything, it is that no matter what we do, mistakes will happen—and that knowing this is no compensation for the fact that living means living unprepared.[13]

So I borrow Wiegman's explorations here not to unveil the uselessness of political aspirations within studies of the ancient world, but to ask what subtends them, and to worry aloud about what happens when we take ourselves and our political gestures too seriously on their own terms, and without recourse to the fantasies they entertain. The fantasies themselves might produce an interesting account of the discipline. Psychoanalytic lines of inquiry impel me, in this case, to wonder at the undertow of disciplinary attachments, and the negotiations of desires for omnipotence and fears of destruction that they entertain. And these are racially inflected desires and fears, for sure.

The field of biblical studies has had its own struggle with politics, and its deep exclusionary practices as a discipline. It has followed the same intellectual trajectory of increasing awareness and inclusivity as identity-based fields. It has done so belatedly following the developments in identity-based fields. Perhaps owing to the moral imperatives emanating from its own primary object of study, biblical studies, at least certain wings of it, has worked out its relationship to politics in a more overt and acute fashion than other adjacent fields. It has generally, though not exclusively, done so by finding politically marginal subjects in ancient texts/history, as well as through attacking that endlessly capacious object of revile, the Roman empire. But as I've hinted above relative to Bond's article, ancient history and the study of the Bible have struggled additionally with something the disciplines that Wiegman charts do not: the question of relevance. In this case, historical and disciplinary questions of race and ethnicity are the ground on which biblical and antiquity studies entertain both political crises and the crises of their own field of study, often mapping them unevenly onto each other.

Less sanguine than Bond, Denise Buell describes her "hesitation" when engaging race and ethnicity as an optic for antiquity.[14] Buell, whose work on "ethnic reasoning" in ancient Christian literature was central to the genealogy of renewed questions of race and ethnicity in the discipline of early Christian studies, notes in fact that race-critical historiography is not just a matter of differentiating ancient discourses and notions from modern ones.[15] It is also about attending to the ways ancient literature has figured in the very making of modern imaginations of race and ethnicity. "In other words," she writes, "I hesitate in part because there *does* seem to be a sense in which ethnicity is 'in' the Bible because this collection of texts is entangled in modern practices of ethnicity and race, as well as nationality, in ways that deserve further exploration. The legacy of New Testament writings as canonical and culturally authoritative even in secular contexts gives me pause, even as it makes their study more urgent and relevant."[16]

In the face of her hesitations, Buell voices her own call to arms, if a significantly less optimistic one than Bond's. She suggests an ethics of haunting, in the vein of Jacques Derrida and Avery Gordon, that "redirects questions about the anachronism or historicity of ethnicity or race."[17] "An orientation to haunting helps articulate the necessity of wrestling with not simply the historical contexts and afterlives of our course materials but also the historical contexts and afterlives of our methods and interpretive frameworks."[18] Buell's sense of urgency and relevance, though solemn, appears in her consistent recourse to injunctive construction: "*We need an approach* that does not simply emphasize the gap between past and the present but also helps account for the transformations and slippages between past and present, and the times between these. *We have to attend* to the spectral possibilities of the texts as well as the various ways that biblical texts have taken material expression over time."[19] Buell closes this piece by addressing the general notion that biblical studies as a discipline is inconsequential—in other words, she is haunted by a sense of *irrelevance*. Countering it, she quotes Benny Liew: "What if biblical materials, in separation from the question of

faith or belief, turn out to have instructive bearing on some of the urgent
issues facing our world today?"[20]

The quote from Liew is taken from his essay in the book *Still at the
Margins: Biblical Scholarship Fifteen Years after 'Voices from the Margin,'* in
which he marks out a broad set of associated quandaries and conserva-
tivisms plaguing biblical studies through the prism of minoritized scholars and scholarship and their reception. Making a comparison to contemporary border politics, Liew observes the ways in which minoritized
scholars and scholarship are seen as interlopers vis-à-vis biblical studies'
"more original" inhabitants, or as imperiling the "rigor" of the discipline,
and notes the ongoing inhospitability of biblical scholarship. The dogma-
tism of and loyalty to historical critical scholarship and the chauvinistic,
singular attraction to the "ancient world" to the exclusion of all others as
relevant to biblical studies continue decades after Vincent Wimbush tren-
chantly critiqued them for their Eurocentrism.[21] Wimbush's own project,
as it was articulated early on, sought to displace the white critic as implicit
subject of biblical studies via an ethnographic focus on African American traditions of interpretation. In his call for "reading darkly," he pro-
vocatively imagines a field-wide abandonment, if not an entirely permanent one, of original languages and ancient history. Wimbush shies away,
however, from the exclusively identitarian implications of his project by
leveraging "darkness" to imply difficult or traumatic experiences at large,
while emphasizing experiences that are collective, and ones undergone by
predominantly dark or diasporic people. Wimbush has held a number of
high-profile and institutionally fraught posts within the academy, including
president of the Society of Biblical Literature. But in a melancholic parable
of the limited potential of politicized critique and perhaps even more the
assimilative power of white disciplines, Wimbush's provocations went generally unheeded.[22]

The margins of biblical studies are both versatile and steep. But as Liew
also notes, biblical scholarship itself is "on the margins" in some sense, with
its cultural currency waning.[23] Liew quickly adds, however, "I bring this up
not to jump on the popular bandwagon that biblical scholarship needs to 'go
public.' I am pretty sure that biblical criticism is always already a part of the
public, and the last thing we need now is yet another binary understanding
that pits 'the academy' and 'the public' in a dualistic framework. . . . Instead
of needing to 'go public,' what we need to talk about is what kind of change
we want to help engineer, what kind of particular public issues we want to

drive and energize our work and/or what particular sectors of the public we are part of and/or hope to engage."[24]

These various calls to ethics of race and ethnicity register a set of felt emergencies and potentialities. For one, they occur at a moment when the various fields touching antiquity studies are "in crisis," as we in the (generally imperiled) humanities like to say. Class enrollments and numbers of majors are dropping, and thus also the job prospects for PhDs in biblical, ancient Christian, and antiquity studies look ever more bleak. Coordinating with identity-based fields of study has, both institutionally and intellectually, a way of keeping biblical studies "alive," as it clamors to make its case for survival in an increasingly perilous educational market. To be "interdisciplinary" is not only to be intellectually cutting-edge or labile but also to be able to fill multiple institutional roles, especially in a small liberal arts college. This is so even as biblical and antiquity studies themselves evince continuing ambivalence about just *how* interdisciplinary, and in which ways, any given scholar should be. "After all," Liew writes, "diversity, pluralism, or minority representation have never been an explicit ethos within the guild of biblical criticism. . . . [E]ven the very thought of a *potential*, let's say, 'all Black' biblical faculty will lead to predictions of doom and rumors of ruin."[25] Returning as if full circle to the issue of polychromy and racialized aesthetics, Liew makes another parallel: "What David Batchelor calls 'chromophobia,' or the fear of corruption through colour, is true not only in the practice and study of Western art, but also the study of the Bible in the Western world."[26] Crucially, however, Liew's definition of chromophobia includes not just an anxiety or fear around people of color crossing into the discipline, but the ways in which people of color might also be corrupting the "pure" reading and historical practices of the field, as well.

ON PUBLIC INTERVENTIONS AND
THE "PUBLIC INTELLECTUAL"

These calls to ethics of race and ethnicity register another set of felt emergencies and potentialities. They specifically register macro or national political concerns, which find themselves continually being worked out through the smaller (infinitely smaller) and enthralling world of a discipline, or the very wide and inviting screen of the ancient world. As Liew implicitly notices, "the public" has regularly been an unwitting and imagined solution to the crisis of relevance, primarily as providing the platform for scholarly or critical intervention. Calling up "the public" does something for us, and we might want to inquire more particularly about how the figures of "the public" and the "public intellectual" function in and as political fantasies of contemporary academic life.

Perhaps no title could be more sought after in contemporary academic life than that of the "public intellectual," a sort of Professor of the People, the real or true educator, who in their historical righteousness is not unlike Joan Scott's characterization of the feminist figure at the podium. The public intellectual stands to inform (or disabuse) a vast array of eager or at least responsive constituencies, who need only to know in clearer terms the nuances of a particular debate, need only to be apprised of some set of data, or to be given long-view history of a certain operating mythology before they can be shaped or changed, or at least become better-informed citizens. These people are best reached, it would seem, through deals with big-tent publishers, appearances on talk shows or history channel programs, contributions to venerable magazines or online venues, or even through a sizeable following on social media. Ideally, all of these venues work in tandem to allow the public intellectual to disseminate their message, which quickly also becomes, we might say, their brand.

The point is not that these kinds of responsive, and persuadable, listeners don't exist, or that these venues don't have impacts or reverberations. It is rather to question the aura of virtue that sometimes surrounds the self-proclaimed title of the "public intellectual" and to ask what *other* than virtue — what circuits and desires — might constitute this set of interlinked fantasies.

The roles and expectations that attend the college professor have changed markedly over the past decades, as most of us know. Academic lives on average mean less job security, more teaching responsibilities, less financial stability, and (often) less authority and autonomy in the classroom than ever before. This has something to do with the changing constituency of academia, which has historically been identified with white men. But it also has to do with the changing economics of postsecondary education, in which increasing bureaucratic and administrative focuses as well as distinct moves toward business models and philosophies have put pressure on faculty members to demonstrate worth and productivity in more quantifiable ways. The now controversial, but still widely applied, rubric of the student evaluation as used in review and promotion processes, for instance, authorizes not just the biases of students, but the students themselves, who thus believe themselves to be (in a sinister recapitulation of Paulo Freire's educational metaphor) recipients of packageable information and skills that will ostensibly put money in their bank.

A certain cultural currency still attaches to having a PhD, however. So it makes sense that we would occasionally leverage our cultural currency to compensate for the otherwise tenuous, if not outright low, status of actually living as an academic. Indeed, big table books at Barnes and Noble make money—at least more money than any more specialized book—and who could blame a guild of writers for wanting compensation for their intellectual labors, especially when they rarely otherwise get it? One question might be, however, whether the fantasy of the "public intellectual"—also a fantasy of upward mobility for some of us—helps us address these material conditions more than it enables them. Another question worth entertaining is how the virtue that surrounds certain iterations of the public intellectual might actually be a *by-product* of predominantly white disciplines such as biblical studies or antiquity studies: we might want to ask about the ways the figure of the (white) public intellectual might provide an alibi for sticky political entanglements.[27]

I would argue that this widely circulating fantasy about public scholarship, at least certain kinds of public scholarship, logs a collective helplessness, reconstituting it as a form of scholarly omnipotence. Deep in the white disciplinary unconscious, there persists the disquieting fantasy of the white savior. So it is worth noting what various forms of racial soul-searching in the discipline, and the aura of nobility that surrounds public interventions, do for those of us entangled in them. That is, to what extent do we imagine ourselves triumphant in destroying the powers that be? To what extent do we imagine our public interventions and racial hand-wringing as saving the field and its purveyors from obscurity and, not incidentally, complicity?

I'm struck by the contrast between Bond's call to darken the ancient world (an emblematic, not singular one) and all that surrounds it and another redescription of the ancient world: Renee Cox's "Yo Mama's Last Supper," an artistic rendition of the biblical scene that showed Cox, a Black woman, standing naked at the center in place of Jesus. In it, all of the disciples appear as Black men—with the exception of Judas, who appears as a white man. Originally displayed at the Brooklyn Museum in 2000–2001, Cox's piece elicited the outrage and defensive posturing of the Catholic League for Religious and Civil Rights, among others, and even provoked the New York City mayor at the time, Rudolph Giuliani, to create a commission to set "decency" standards for publicly funded arts institutions.[28]

Cox, a Catholic, was called "anti-Catholic." Her combatants clarified that their objections were about her nudity, not her Blackness, attempting to cleave her racial identity from her gender and her body ("There would be no problem if you had kept your clothes on").[29] But the subtext was clear as they attempted to discipline and manage the way in which her Blackness could appear in the frame.

Although Cox's piece obviously performs its own race-sensitive redescription of ancient history, it does not do so with any grand historicist conceits. It is self-consciously *not* historicist, in fact, as she personalizes the scene. In another contrast with the polychromy controversy, Cox's response to the public and institutional vitriol she received was wry and playful: the *New York Times* notes that she wanted to send the Catholic League a thank you note for all the free publicity.[30]

Academic disciplines are perhaps not the gatekeepers to history the way those of us trained in those disciplines imagine them to be. As biblical scholars know at least as well as anyone else, the world has no problem doing all kinds of history without us. Then, when things go awry, we show up, experts on the scene, clearing our throats, and beginning with "Well, actually . . ." But how often is "the public" listening to public scholarship beyond outrage or piqued interest? If they were listening, what would change? To what extent do we imagine them hungry for information, wishing contemporary issues to be historicized and parsed for them? Do we imagine that public controversy around scholarship, as in the case of Bond's article, equals political efficacy? And why? Who, exactly, do we imagine when we call up "the public"?

I do not wish to deny significance to what is deemed "public scholarship." After all, nothing fortifies a discipline more than a refusal to look or speak outside the specialized terms of that discipline, and public scholarship can take many forms. I have written and continue to write for publics, and a lot of "public audience" books and articles, op-eds and tweets, have been central to my courses. These kinds of books are often more readable for my students, and usually more constructive, than textbooks explicitly geared toward course adoption. Social media, too, despite its regular function as cathartic echo chamber and hall of mirrors, also means my students can find intellectual communities and virtual mentors and see scholarly responsiveness to their worlds in "real time," so to speak.

However, the fact that I so regularly use these pieces of public scholarship *in the classroom* (and I'm hardly alone) reminds me that most of us in the field don't have to go very far to find "the public." What could be more "public" than an eighteen-year-old economics major taking "Bible, Gender, Sexuality" to meet an interdisciplinary requirement? When would we have a more captive audience? And yet we all know the contingencies and complications of teaching these particular public audience members—sometimes they read, sometimes they don't. They often ask us why in the world they need to know particular things, what difference it makes, and they text during our lectures. They often meet up with the material in ways that alter their orientation to a particular text, issue, cultural force, or relationship—but sometimes we are only incidental to this enterprise. They learn to denaturalize or diffuse the authority that the Bible and other canonical "classics" so acutely emblematize, but maybe only occasionally. They ask really good questions, ones we can't always recognize, let alone answer. Sometimes the figures we implicitly imagine changing with one column, those whom we rhetorically position ourselves toward in the public sphere (those with dogged attachments to preconceived notions) are the very same students we most dread showing up in our classrooms.

Teaching undergraduates in particular demonstrates most thoroughly, I think, how the classroom as scene of political efficacy is not uncomplicated. Indeed, its real democratic potential ironically might exist in teacherly failures of political efficacy, especially if we take political efficacy to mean managing the precise political outcomes of the learning process. That is to say, the classroom is a place where we encounter more distinctly the potentials and pitfalls of educating the public.

If "the public" sometimes provides a stage for fantasies of scholarly relevance, it is also a figure in a romanticized fantasy of *pedagogical* efficacy, in which our readers are always invested and easily persuaded. Outrage and insults like those launched at Bond both interrupt and fortify these fantasies of efficacy, because "the public" is so often the blank slate upon which we write our aspirations for import, and our longings to be architects of change, our fears about whether or not, and how, we are relevant.

LOVING THE DISCIPLINE (A CONCLUSION)

From a while ago E has latched onto the concept that she is someone who feels need to make others smarter—this coming from recognition that she felt responsible for eliciting my intelligent interest. She has asked several people about this and got confirmation except from one colleague whom she clearly feels she has made smarter. Is really shaken by this but still holds on to the concept of herself as making people smarter. (E: "Make them smart" = spank them?)

NOTES FROM EVE SEDGWICK'S PSYCHOTHERAPIST, SHANNON, IN SEDGWICK, A DIALOGUE ON LOVE

Questions of the discipline invariably converge with pedagogical questions. We introduce our students to the discipline, and we sustain or deconstruct the discipline through our students. White disciplines make themselves more "inclusive" via cultivating more diverse students or interested learners generally. Since pedagogical scenes, writ large or small, are the primary scenes in which we stage our relationship to the discipline, I'd like to close this chapter—and this book—with a brief reflection on disciplinary fantasies and attachments, and the ways in which pedagogical scenes, especially ones with implications of professionalization through or into "the field," provide stages for the enactment of these fantasies and attachments.

I want to press the question of the seeming intractability of certain disciplinary attachments ("But what about intellectual *responsibility*?" is the plea of *askesis* that I imagine), and the question of how attachments to the discipline constrain, often quite deeply, not only interactions with others, but political designs within the field. White scholars in antiquity and biblical studies can continue to ask ourselves why these fields are so white, and continue to fret over it. But if diversification tactics of predominantly white (male, cis, straight) fields such as history, antiquity studies, and biblical studies are attempts to exculpate or widen the reach of the discipline, what, exactly, do we make of the fantasy funding the desire to incorporate racialized, queered, and gendered outsiders—in other words, to "discipline" them?[31]

A Dialogue on Love is an account of queer theorist and Proust scholar Eve Sedgwick's self-revelations in psychotherapy, a process she undertook in the aftermath of her diagnosis of breast cancer. It takes the form of both her and her therapist Shannon's descriptions and narrations of their conversations and the subtexts contained therein. While Shannon's descriptions appear only as casual notes (I imagine them first recorded on a yellow legal pad), Sedgwick's tend to be both more elaborated and more edited, and frequently punctuated by her poetry inspired by themes, sensations, or memories that emerge in the therapeutic process.

One of the more riveting slices of their "dialogue on love" involves

Sedgwick's S/M fantasies, in which she is being disciplined or "examined." In contrast to what she describes as a rather orthodox sex life, Sedgwick's fantasizing is composed almost entirely of S/M or disciplinary scenarios. They often have "an institutional pretext—almost a bureaucratic one. They take place in a girls' school, a prison, or a spy agency."[32] The spaces and associations in these fantasies are "quasi-medical," but they converge with associations with childhood and schools—dormitory-like hospital rooms, for instance—and "examination," for example, is a key association for her.[33]

These fantasies tend to be affiliated with a kind of grandiosity or mastery on her part, and Sedgwick's self-perception of "making people smarter." Throughout *A Dialogue on Love*, Shannon is the most frequent object of her (shall we say) pedagogical inclinations, but largely because the proposition of the book foregrounds that relationship. It is nonetheless telling, however, that it is as the patient (subjected, examined, potentially humiliated) that Sedgwick seems most to experience, or at least demonstrate, her own grandiosity.[34] Importantly, that grandiosity doesn't appear as compensation for divestment of power, at least not here. Rather, potential humiliation in the form of vulnerability to scrutiny is itself an opportunity for feeling or demonstrating authority- in this instance, intellectual authority.[35] That is, her potential shame and vulnerability to scrutiny seem, at least on occasion, to increase her sense of command.

As a phenomenology of academic life, this fantasy scenario practically borders on the obvious. *Of course* our own vulnerability to intensified, exacting scrutiny coincides with a sense of our authority. What could or would a dissertation defense, a conference paper, or a tenure review be without that sense of rising to the occasion of our professionalism, or that adrenaline-soaked embodiment of our specialized knowledge so characteristic of these concertedly pedagogical performances? We love the discipline because it enables our authority. We are often at our most teacherly when we fear being schooled.

This is *not* to say that we are the best teachers when we fear being schooled. I'm not out to indict, moralize, or even squirm at the pleasure of potential humiliation or the imaginations of grandiosity—pleasures and imaginations that are deeply threaded into my own attachment to academic life. But we do need to notice that the grandiosity, the exacerbated sense of authority that coincides with, or is a corollary to, the pleasure of exacting scrutiny is not a fantasy that one plays out alone or, for instance, within the deliberately fluid relational space of the psychoanalytic exchange. It often becomes how we determine rigor, what we deem legible, and what counts as a thought worth having and expressing.

The category of "history" is an especially dense site of fantasies of grandiosity tied to exacting scrutiny. "What you are doing is important/beautiful/interesting, but you are not a *historian*," is a refrain I've heard deployed often (and of which I have been the recipient). Christina Sharpe, describing the conundrums Black scholars writing histories of slavery and its afterlives face, for example, observes how "[t]he methods most readily available to us sometimes, oftentimes, force us into positions that run counter to what we know." She goes on:

> That is, our knowledge, of slavery and Black being in slavery, is gained from our studies, yes, but also in excess of those studies; it is gained through the kinds of knowledge from and of the everyday, from what Dionne Brand calls 'sitting in the room with history.' We are expected to discard, discount, disregard, jettison, abandon, and measure those ways of knowing and to act epistemic violence that we know to be violence against others and ourselves. In other words, for Black academics to produce legible work in the academy often means adhering to research methods that are "drafted into the service of a larger destructive force" (Saunders 2008a, 67), thereby doing violence to our own capacities to read, think, and imagine otherwise. Despite knowing otherwise, we are often disciplined into thinking through and along lines that reinscribe our own annihilation.[36]

She is interested in "how we imagine ways of knowing that past, in excess of the fictions of the archive," and, she suggests, "We must become undisciplined."[37]

But I'm curious how often imaginations of "teaching well" correspond with an internalized, hypervigilant enforcement of disciplinary boundaries. In this case, what do the "good students," the ones who succeed, the ones who "get it," do for their teachers? And what, exactly, are they getting, while their teachers enjoy *really giving it* to them? Likewise, as teachers, our sense of efficacy is often confirmed by "the good student." And the "good student" is too often defined not as especially curious, especially thoughtful, or (god forbid) especially creative, but rather as the one who learns the discipline well. The good student in this case allows us to stay in the fantasy of our omnipotence—unless, of course, they learn *too well*, an anxiety for which the tools of the discipline are also especially handy. The corollary figure of the "bad student," the one who gets it wrong, confronts us with the limits of our pedagogical efficacy. She is often also the one the teacher cannot save, and the one through whom the discipline will not properly survive. But as the one who has failed, whom the teacher *must* fail, or who cannot pass the bar, the "bad student" is also sometimes what fortifies the teacher's loyalty to those mechanisms by which the teacher has failed her.[38]

That is to say that attachments to the discipline are sites for fantasies of teacherly efficacy that often actually contravene desires for *political* efficacy. In other words, the question of the "relevance" of a field is periodically construed in the narrowest conceivable way—a way that further calcifies the fantasy of grandiosity and potency. The question for pedagogical scenes, whether "public" or more intimate ones, is not how to make the discipline more relevant or how to convince others of its relevance to them. These questions inevitably center the discipline and its representatives as deliverers of one sort or another. The question (or at least one of them) is: when are the discipline and certain forms of disciplinary rigor and responsibility alibis for the refusal of a certain larger *social and relational* rigor and responsibility? Especially since relational rigor and responsibility are primary to any kind of ethics and political intercession, wouldn't one actually risk losing the pedagogical scene as a site of political change if one overinvests in disciplinary fantasies of teacherly efficacy? Pedagogical scenes are inevitably scenes of success and failure on some level, but their real successes and failures may be different from what we imagine them to be.

I don't mean that scholars don't or can't produce change, or that history and teaching don't do things. I teach and write with a belief, sometimes an inflated one, and sometimes a deflated one, in the dynamic nature of human relations and the efficacy of things well said. We should also distinguish the materials we study from the discipline that frames and arbitrates engagement with them. The point is to ask what happens when, under any circumstances, we lead with the discipline. The point is to observe that whatever political efficacy we might have will need to begin with being present to some overblown, if implicit, hopes to save. It would be wise to stop trying to make the discipline relevant, and to lead instead with the contemporary moment, to lead with our relationships with our students and with each other. Admitting the failure of the discipline as such, and oneself as an agent of it, to be relevant in a given relationship, setting, or moment might actually coincide with an unguarded attentiveness to that relationship, setting, or moment.

Likewise, the notion of professionalized history or interpretation as a form of ethics, a notion raised to the status of dogma in some institutions, like the one I attended, is far from wrong. It is just vastly overestimated, and poorly installed when delivered through the narrow and regulatory mechanisms of the field as such. History as ethics founders when linked more than incidentally or tangentially to the discipline, that is, when it becomes a force field of humiliation and righteousness.

I do not wish to easily or automatically resolve the tensions between disciplinary attachments and certain political desires, even while it seems clear to me that one cannot have both, at least in the way that one might want. I will not deliver an ethics that gets us out of the tension. My goal for now is rather to present the ways that that intractability gets worked out through circulating fantasy figures and scenarios, and to see the real effects of these fantasies on the objects of our pedagogy. I hope that in scrutinizing these fantasies as fantasies, we're more able to see their logics as psychic logics, not necessary ones.

I should also say that we need not dispense with these fantasies themselves, as much as our stultified identifications within them. I've always been charmed by Sedgwick's more specifically pedagogical reflection in *Touching Feeling*, which she begins with a story of her reckoning with the possibility that her cat, who was faithfully bringing her dead mouse after dead mouse, was not presenting her gifts. Rather she was teaching Sedgwick how to hunt. "For persons involved with cats or pedagogy, [this] supposition here may be unsettling in several ways," Sedgwick writes. "First there is the narcissistic wound. Where we had thought to be the powerful or admired, quasi-parental figures to our cats, we are cast instead in the role of clumsy newborns requiring special education. Worse, we have not even learned from this education. With all the cat's careful stage management, we seem especially stupid in having failed to so much as recognize the scene as one of pedagogy. Is it true that we can learn only when we are aware we are being taught?"[39] In this little story, Sedgwick must *redescribe* the pedagogical scene, as she goes from the masterful figure in the exchange to the unwitting student. But in confronting the gap between her aims and those of her cat, she nonetheless learns something about her experience in the classroom. She makes contact with her fantasies of herself as teacher by experiencing the breakdown of those fantasies: her students imagine her, against her own self-understanding, as presenting them with little gifts.

Professionally speaking: if we want our others to be able to live, and I believe that we do, we will need to ask, What do we imagine about those people we teach, those objects of our pedagogical designs? What do we imagine we are teaching them, and why? Better yet, what fantasies of ourselves do we shore up and what allegiances do we pledge in the pedagogical enterprise, that theater of jurisdiction so rich with potential power, so haunted by the risk of failing to deliver?

ACKNOWLEDGMENTS

This book came together over a span of time in which I moved from New York City to a small town in central Ohio steeped in 1950s nostalgia; to an institution, an unexceptional one in this capacity, in which the students who fall outside of the narrow categories of normative acceptability (i.e., brown, black, queer, noncitizen students) suddenly become crippled with various mysterious illnesses, almost upon arrival, and sometimes literally tear their hair out in response to blunt forms of racial and cultural erasure. This is not literary hyperbole: actual vultures still circle over the nature preserve where a Black student of mine hanged himself, half a mile from where a gentle-voiced older man, smiling, wheels my groceries to my car.

This book came together over the years in which my apparently placid thirteen-year marriage fell apart, or perhaps I blew it apart (one can never tell), and in which my stomach regularly and inexplicably winced with a pain that landed me in bed and drew the blood from my face. It came together over a time in which I learned how profoundly I depend on my colleagues (what an inadequate designation) for thinking through my life and work; in which I lost some mentors (or rather lost faith in them), but gained students whose own questions and creative processes taxed, elevated, and gave depth to mine. Over this time, I became more professionalized, more invested in my work, even as I became ever more mad at and disabled by some of the architecture and institutions fundamental to academic life. I plunked down the words of these chapters over the course of the 2016 U.S. election and its fallout, the profound and ongoing disappointments of which revealed to so many of us how beholden we were, unbeknownst to ourselves, to fantasies of progress. #Metoo was trending, a public revelation of collective trauma and objectification (eerily leaving my own field untouched); citizenship was becoming more clearly marked by whiteness, as ICE raids and police violence continued with impunity under the auspices of justice. Children died at the border.

Our writing is skin shed at a particular moment in time. And while I've always been drawn to self-reflexivity in writing, there were moments in writing this book in which self-reflexivity felt painful, even terrible. I had dreams of drowning, of being physically constrained. It was only late in the process that I felt the familiar necessity to speak anecdotally again. I attach no virtue to that necessity. But it occurs to me that if our experiential subtexts are the unseen universe behind our work, as difficult as those subtexts are to measure or see, however much they refuse the light we try to cast on them, we should nonetheless, feeling their vastness and heft, give them their due. Neither do I attach virtue to the politics of this book, which are inevitably complicated. This book is a token of my minor agency, of a desire to paint around some points of collective curiosity and trouble, and the result of an impulse to press harder on the tiny, soft site of academic thought-making.

My thanks go first to Celene Lillie, the mountains to my ocean: for her enduring friendship, hard-won sense of perspective, and loyalty to those people and principles that matter to her—all of which are undervalued in contemporary academic life. No friend has seen me through more embarrassments or heartbreaks, and nobody has been as steady a presence. To Heidi Wendt, who threw me lifelines during our brief overlap in Ohio, and continues to do so: she gave both my ideas and my shape-shifting life a language and gentle recognition when I was most lost in them. Her big historical vision and elegant finessing of the disciplinary terms of legibility have always impressed me; her fierce sense of humor and capacity for nurture sustain me. To Alexis Waller, who regularly slips unseen between teacher, student, and colleague for all those who encounter her: for her conversational generosity and palatial imagination, to which I am perpetually in thrall. She was writing and thinking about fantasy and feelings over this same period. But it is our experiences, overlapping and divergent, with the discipline, academic life, and the dangers of speaking that truly occupy the underground of this book. To Colleen Shantz: if I had to wake up tomorrow as any other person, it would be her. No one mixes depth with levity, analytical precision with relational munificence like she does, and our shared and parallel work on affect made this book's reflection on the materiality of experience what it is. To Jennifer Knust, whose combination of audacity and vulnerability has always culled my admiration: for her confidence in my work, for her tenacity in making our shared field a more livable and compelling place to be, and her unforgettable wisdom on both woman-objects and material things. To

Richard Ascough, for reading pieces of this work throughout its writing, and being a key conversation partner about memorialization, but also for letting me lean hard on him through so many moments of uncertainty, and for letting me witness his own similar moments. To Erin Runions, for many years ago saying as a response to the growing fascist impulses in U.S. politics and culture, "Maybe we should go back to psychoanalysis." That suggestion, like so much of her scholarship, had prescience and real generative force. I take continual inspiration from her theoretical dexterity and overall integrity. To Greg Given, whose literary impulses and delight in scholarly idiosyncrasies always make more space for my own, and who, ever in cahoots with me, understood what I was going for in parts of this book before I did. To Amy Hollywood, for her excitement at this project, and for her book *Acute Melancholia*, which was an object I lustily consumed, only to then find myself posing some resonant questions about trauma, the real, and legibility she asked there, albeit in a different key. To Kyle Wagner, John Modern, and Katie Lofton for their exceptional care with this manuscript, and their faith in the many quirky things in it—I am hugely grateful. Katie deserves special mention not only for being a force for good in this crazy business, but for writing with a level of associative electricity to which I can only aspire. To Judith Perkins, Benny Liew, Brigitte Kahl, Andrew Jacobs, Donovan Shaeffer, Jeremy Schott, Jackie Hidalgo, Lynn Huber, Eric Smith, Sharon Jacob, Ismo Dunderberg, Abby Kulisz, Anna Cwikla, Joe Marchal, and, especially, Tim Beal: for ideas that fed and teased me, but also, variously, their friendship, conversational insight, ways of being in the world, and for encouraging me and/or these ideas in gawky or fledgling phases. To the faculty and students in the Early Christian Studies Workshop at the University of Chicago Divinity School for their tremendously helpful and satisfying engagement with the theoretical grounding of the book. To my students, especially Eva Rosenthal, Cassie Sagness, Rene Guo, and Sarah Curtin. They were my day-to-day conversation partners at Denison as I wrote this, and their curiosities always pushed me forward. To my close and longtime friends Helen Green Allen, Jen McGuire, and Ingrid Michaelson, who are always and ever in it with me. To my dad whose cosmic panorama holds me, and my mom who, in a most Kleinian way, withstood my destruction and survived. To Rocco, for schooling me in whole-heartedness and rebellion.

But I dedicate this book especially to two people. To Carly Daniel-Hughes, with her breathless speech and incomparable laughter: You were the recipient of my weekly half-thoughts, and an abundance of early morning text messages. We traipsed through Chicago, Boston, Santa Rosa, Kingston, San Antonio, San Francisco, and across Greece together and concocted so many plans, so many ideas, of which these chapters are symptoms, consequences, and castoffs. Can anything we write do those moments justice? And finally, I dedicate it to that undisputed master of inscriptions and minor mischief, Phil Harland: You were present at the moment of this book's feverish inception and then, a year later, its furious recalibration. You received each of its pieces with warmth and the full weight of your exactitude. I speak to and about you in more places here than either of us know. You are my most constant interlocutor, an intractable staple of my dream life, my uncommon complement in the unsettled dark — and of course, the source and origin of my impulse toward the real. My love, always.

This book includes material that has been previously published or heavily revised from previous publications. Chapter 2 adapts material from "Babylon's Fall: Figuring Diaspora in and through Ruins," *Bible and Critical Theory* 11.2 (2015): 1–17. Chapter 5 was lightly revised from its earlier publication as "Speaking of Grief and the Grief of Speaking: Martyrs' Speech and the Perils of Translation," *Culture and Religion* 17.4 (2017): 431–49. Finally, chapter 6 was revised from its earlier appearance as "Penetration and Its Discontents: Greco-Roman Sexuality, The Acts of Paul and Thecla, and Theorizing Eros Without the Wound," *Journal of the History of Sexuality*, 27:3 (September 2018): 343–66.

NOTES

INTRODUCTION

1. While this tendency is wide and diffuse rather than particular, and it is sometimes hard to tell when the interest in material culture is "renewed" and when it is simply abiding, some more distinct examples include *Materialising Roman Histories*, ed. Astrid Van Oyen and Martin Pitts (Cambridge: Cambridge University Press, 2017); Jessica Hughes, *Votive Body Parts in Greek and Roman Religion* (Cambridge: Cambridge University Press, 2017); Astrid Van Oyen, *How Things Make History: The Roman Empire and Its Terra Sigillata Pottery* (Amsterdam: Amsterdam University Press, 2016); and Eric Smith, *Jewish Glass and Christian Stone: A Materialist Mapping of the Parting of the Ways* (New York: Routledge, 2018). See also Laura Nasrallah's *Christian Responses to Roman Art and Architecture: The Second-Century Church amid the Spaces of Empire* (New York: Cambridge University Press, 2010); Karen Stern's *Writing on the Wall: Graffiti and the Forgotten Jews of Antiquity* (Princeton: Princeton University Press, 2018); Claudia Moser and Jennifer Knust, *Ritual Matters: Material Remains and Ancient Religion* (Ann Arbor: University of Michigan Press, 2017). Virginia Burrus's *Ancient Christian Ecopoetics: Cosmologies, Saints, Things* (Philadelphia: University of Pennsylvania Press, 2019) has some thematic affinities with this present book. See also the De Gruyter series *Greco-Roman Associations: Texts, Translations, and Commentary*, publishing inscriptions relating to small groups in the ancient world. The materialist turn in religion more generally was signaled by Manuel Vasquez's *More Than Belief: A Materialist Theory of Religion* (New York: Oxford, 2010), and S. Brent Plate, *A History of Religion in 5 ½ Objects: Bringing the Spiritual to Its Senses* (New York: Beacon Press, 2014).

2. Two of the earliest and most influential works in affect theory, which both log disillusionment with the assumptions of the linguistic turn, are philosopher Brian Massumi's *Parables for the Virtual: Movement, Affect, Sensation* (Durham: Duke University Press, 2002) and influential feminist and queer theorist (and Proust scholar) Eve Kosofsky Sedgwick's *Touching Feeling: Affect, Pedagogy, Performativity* (Durham: Duke University Press, 2003). For more on affect theory and its relationship to language, specifically within the fields of religion and biblical studies, see Donovan O. Schaefer, *Religious*

Affects: Animality, Evolution, and Power (Durham: Duke University Press, 2015), especially 1–35; Kotrosits, "How Things Feel: Biblical Studies, Affect Theory, and the (Im)Personal," *Research Perspectives in Biblical Interpretation* 1, no. 1 (2016).

3. In addition to Massumi and Sedgwick, see for instance Kathleen Stewart, *Ordinary Affects* (Durham: Duke University Press, 2007); Ann Cvetkovich, *An Archive of Feelings: Trauma, Sexuality, and Lesbian Public Cultures* (Durham: Duke University Press, 2003) and *Depression: A Public Feeling* (Durham: Duke University Press, 2012); Lauren Berlant, *Cruel Optimism* (Durham: Duke University Press, 2011).

4. See for instance Bruno Latour, *Matter, Materiality, and Material Culture*, ed. P. Graves-Brown (London: Routledge, 2000); Karen Barad, *Meeting the Universe Halfway: Quantum Physics and the Entanglement of Matter and Meaning* (Durham: Duke University Press, 2007); Jane Bennett, *Vibrant Matter: A Political Ecology of Things* (Durham: Duke University Press, 2010); Mel Chen, *Animacies: Biopolitics, Racial Mattering and Queer Affect* (Durham: Duke University Press, 2012); Rosi Braidotti, *The Posthuman* (Cambridge: Polity Press, 2013); Diana Coole and Samantha Frost, eds., *New Materialisms: Ontology, Agency, Politics* (Durham: Duke University Press, 2010).

5. And yet, as Moser and Knust importantly note, "Materials are more stable than other forms of evidence; yet they too decay, change and are moved to new locations, and are put to new purposes. Not every item will be found *in situ*, and only rarely is an object found intact. Things, no less than people, therefore remain subject to circumstances of disrupture and displacement." Indeed. "Ritual Matters: An Introduction," in *Ritual Matters*, 1–10.

6. This is how Eve Sedgwick in fact describes her own attachments to material things and artistic work in "Making Things, Practicing Emptiness," in *The Weather in Proust*, ed. Jonathan Goldberg (Durham: Duke University Press, 2011), 69–122. For a helpful summary and genealogy of new materialism, see Donovan Schaefer, "Heavenbeast: A New Materialist Approach to Ulysses," *Angeliki* 21, no. 2 (June 2016) 119–36. In a different vein, Bruno Latour's essay "The Berlin Key or How to Do Words with Things" takes up the socially constrained limits of objects and their uses and, more specifically, the ways the co-implicated agencies of objects and people work to negotiate social forces and impositions. Latour, *Matter, Materiality, and Material Culture*, 10–21. Latour's essay is an implicit inversion of J. L. Austin's *How to Do Things with Words* (New York: Clarendon, 1962), which was central in poststructuralist theories of speech-acts, performativity, and language (including and especially Eve Sedgwick's work). See Jennifer Knust's "Miscellany Manuscripts and the Christian Canonical Imaginary," in Moser and Knust, *Ritual Matters*, 99–118, which takes up Latour's essay to address the question of how the materiality of manuscripts can interrupt the "canonical imaginary." Knust here performs her own iteration of what I will later describe as "reality testing."

7. See especially Cvetkovich, *Archive of Feelings*; Dian Million, "Felt Theory: An Indigenous Feminist Approach to Affect and History," *Wicazo Sa Review* 24, no. 2 (2009): 53–74; Heather Love, *Feeling Backward: Loss and the Politics of Queer History* (Cambridge: Harvard University Press, 2007).

8. Again, see especially Massumi, *Parables for the Virtual*, and Sedgwick, *Touching Feeling*, as well as my genealogy in "How Things Feel." This integration of humanities and

the hard sciences through affect also appears in the cognitive science wing of the study of religion, as in the work of Colleen Shantz around religious experience—see for instance "Opening the Black Box: New Prospects for Analyzing Religious Experience," in *Experientia*, vol. 2: *Linking Text and Experience*, ed. Shantz and Rodney Werline (Atlanta: Society of Biblical Literature, 2012), 1–16.

9. See Bennett, *Vibrant Matter*.

10. More on this in chapter 1, "Objects Made Real."

11. See Jacques Derrida, "Freud and the Scene of Writing," first published in *Yale French Studies* 48 (1972): 74–114. Psychoanalyst Jacques Lacan, blending Freudian psychoanalysis with linguistic theory, initiated the "linguistic turn" in psychoanalytic theory in the mid-twentieth century (see "On the Instance of the Letter in the Unconscious, or Reason since Freud," in *Écrits*, ed. Bruce Fink [New York: W. W. Norton, 2006]), and was hugely influential in literary studies in the generations that followed.

12. Sigmund Freud, "Civilization and Its Discontents," in *The Standard Edition of the Complete Psychological Works of Sigmund Freud*, trans. James Strachey, vol. 21 (London, 1961), 70.

13. Shane Butler, "Introduction: On the Origin of Deep Classics," in *Deep Classics: Rethinking Classical Reception,* ed. Butler (London: Bloomsbury, 2016), 10.

14. Adam Phillips, *Becoming Freud: The Making of a Psychoanalyst* (New Haven: Yale University Press, 2014), 4–9.

15. Indeed the very notion of the *id* (simply translated: "it") as an aspect of the psyche leaves room for the nonhuman as a fundamental dimension of human experience. Recent expansions of Freudian theory into new materialist and posthumanist theory include an issue of the journal *Studies in Gender and Sexuality* 19, no. 1 (2018), entitled "Nonhuman Encounters: Animals, Objects, Affects, and the Place of Practice," edited by Ann Pellegrini and Katie Gentile, as well as Lana Lin's *Freud's Jaw and Other Lost Objects: Fractured Subjectivity in the Face of Cancer* (New York: Fordham University Press, 2017), which I discuss further on.

16. S. R. F. Price, "The Future of Dreams: From Freud to Artemidorus," *Past and Present* 13, no. 1 (November 1986): 3–37.

17. Ibid., 7.

18. Ibid., 4.

19. This is a generally circulating sentiment, but not a universal one. Psychoanalytic theory has a vibrant, if also marginal, place in biblical and early Christian studies. See for instance Benjamin Dunning, *Specters of Paul: Sexual Difference in Early Christian Thought* (Philadelphia: University of Pennsylvania Press, 2011); Tat-siong Benny Liew and Erin Runions, *Psychoanalytic Meditations between Marx and Postcolonial Readings of the Bible* (Atlanta: Society of Biblical Literature, 2016); and Andrew Jacobs, *Christ Circumcised: A Study in Early Christian History and Difference* (Philadelphia: University of Pennsylvania Press, 2012).

20. This is a different position from that of anthropologist George Devereux, for instance, who argued for a kind of pan-cultural psychology. However, chapter 1 of this book does articulate a relationship between psychoanalytic epistemologies and ethnographic description in ways that are resonant with Devereaux's project. See especially Devereux,

From Anxiety to Method in the Behavioral Sciences (Paris: Mouton, 1967), and *Ethnopsychanalyse complémentariste*, trans. Tina Jolas and Henry Gobard (Paris: Flammarion, 1972).

21. Patricia Cox Miller, *Dreams in Late Antiquity* (Princeton: Princeton University Press, 1994), 22.

22. Ibid., 25. In fact, as Price ("Future of Dreams") notes, Freud takes cues from Greek literature in crafting his own theory of dreams.

23. Miller, *Dreams in Late Antiquity*, 30.

24. Though as Price ("Future of Dreams") notes, Stoic thinkers more often regarded dreams as false and ephemeral productions of the senses, rather than enduring realities.

25. Miller, *Dreams in Late Antiquity*, 28–31; See Artemidorus, *Onir.* 2.39. See also Callistratus, *Ekphraseis* 10, which Miller cites, in which Callistatus notes that the statue of Asklepios is endowed with its own powers.

26. Melanie Klein, *Envy and Gratitude and Other Works* (New York: Vintage, 1997), 251.

27. Joan Wallach Scott, *The Fantasy of Feminist History* (Durham: Duke University Press, 2011), 49.

28. Ibid., 54.

29. Melanie Klein, "A Contribution to the Psychogenesis of Manic-Depressive States," in *Love, Guilt and Reparation and Other Works, 1921–1945* (New York: Simon and Schuster, 1975), 262.

30. Ibid., 268–70.

31. Jessica Benjamin, *Bonds of Love: Psychoanalysis, Feminism, and the Problem of Domination* (New York: Pantheon, 1988), and *Like Subjects, Love Objects: Essays on Recognition and Sexual Difference* (New Haven: Yale University Press, 1995).

32. Anne Anlin Cheng, *The Melancholy of Race: Psychoanalysis, Assimilation, and Hidden Grief* (New York: Oxford University Press, 2000), xi.

33. Ibid., 134.

34. Kyla Wazana Tompkins, *Racial Indigestion: Eating Bodies in the Nineteenth Century* (New York: New York University Press, 2012), 1–2.

35. Chen, *Animacies*; Antonio Viego, *Dead Subjects: Toward a Politics of Loss in Latino Studies* (Durham: Duke University Press, 2007); Russ Castronovo, *Necro Citizenship: Death, Eroticism, and the Public Sphere in the Nineteenth-Century United States* (Durham: Duke University Press, 2001); Christina Sharpe, *In the Wake: On Blackness and Being* (Durham: Duke University Press, 2016); Jasbir Puar, *The Right to Maim: Debility, Capacity, Disability* (Durham: Duke University Press, 2017); Alexander F. Weheliye, *Habeas Viscus: Racializing Assemblages, Biopolitics, and Black Feminist Theories of the Human* (Durham: Duke University Press, 2014).

36. Lin, *Freud's Jaw*, 14.

37. Ibid. Unfortunately, I discovered Lin's book only at the very end of the process of writing this book, so I don't work with it fully here. But the compatibility between the projects is itself interesting.

38. While "diaspora" is clearly a very familiar term for understanding the history of Israel and Judea, the meaning and implications of that term are nearly always taken for granted: a scattered population, exiled from their homeland. I treat diaspora belong-

ing as a set of shared claims, practices, and positions—an improvised and constant renegotiation—rather than a stable or homogenous population, even though that is what diaspora collectives often assert about themselves. Conceptualizing diaspora as (only) separation from homeland naturalizes the borders and content of that homeland, as well as the collective that is said to have originated from it. Homeland is constructed by and out of diasporic circumstances; it is not the referent from which diaspora identity naturally derives. My use of diaspora for ancient literature and social life, then, is meant to gesture to a whole host of reconsidered and colonially structured relationships to one's seemingly more original ethnic collective, no matter where one might have actually lived. My understanding of diaspora is a shared assumption of the last few decades of studies relating to migration, transnational movements, and colonial social conditions.

39. On the "mattering" of certain lives over and against others, made visible to a wider public through the Black Lives Matter movement, see Simone Browne, *Dark Matters: On the Surveillance of Blackness* (Durham: Duke University Press, 2015), and Judith Butler, *Bodies That Matter: On the Discursive Limits of Sex* (New York: Routledge, 1993).

40. In fact, to speak of "the larger social body" is to mix the registers of animate and inanimate: humanity, thingified. Likewise to speak of "the body" in the first place is to objectify it, to disarticulate it from the subjective, experiential, and social forces that compose it.

41. Lacan, "The Mirror Stage as Formative of the *I* Function, as Revealed in Psychoanalytic Experience," in *Écrits*.

42. Two notable exceptions, which have influenced my work here: Cynthia Baker, *Rebuilding the House of Israel: Architectures of Gender in Jewish Antiquity* (Stanford: Stanford University Press, 2002); Erin Runions, *The Babylon Complex: Theopolitical Fantasies of War, Sex, and Sovereignty* (New York: Fordham University Press, 2014).

43. Though as I discuss in the last chapter, the current intensification of nationalism has also upped the ante, so to speak, on politicized descriptions in antiquity.

44. Though attention to ethnicity has certainly grown in studies of the ancient world. For a summary of this scholarship and a perspective on some implications for the study of early Christian literature especially, see Todd Berzon, "Ethnicity and Early Christianity: New Approaches to Religious Kinship and Community" *Currents in Biblical Research* 16, no. 2. (January 2018): 191–227. Ethnicity has been entangled with the notion of race, of course, and so there has been some argument on how to historically differentiate ancient and modern constructions of peoplehood, as well as what each of these terms might be doing for its propagators. See for instance Jeremy McInerney, "Ethnicity: An Introduction," in *A Companion to Ethnicity in the Ancient Mediterranean*, ed. Jeremy McInerney (Chichester, West Sussex: Wiley and Sons, 2014), 1–16.

45. While this debate subtends a lot of scholarly discussions on the ancient world and practices and assumptions related to the gods, two book-length critiques of the category of religion for the study of the ancient world are Brent Nongbri, *Before Religion: A History of a Modern Concept* (New Haven: Yale University Press, 2015), and Carlin A. Barton and Daniel Boyarin, *Imagine No Religion: How Modern Abstractions Hide Ancient Realities* (New York: Fordham University Press, 2016).

46. Clifford Ando, "Sovereignty, Territoriality, and Universalism in the Aftermath of Cara-calla," in *Citizenship and Empire in Europe, 200–1900: The Antonine Constitution after 1800 Years*, ed. Ando (Stuttgart: Franz Steiner, 2016), 17.

47. Anthony Pagden, "Afterword: Roman Citizenship, Empire, and the Challenges of Sov-ereignty," in *Citizenship and Empire in Europe, 200–1900: The Antonine Constitution after 1800 Years*, ed. Clifford Ando (Stuttgart: Franz Steiner, 2016), 248.

48. Ibid.

49. As always, however, "universal" citizenship encompassed only those who counted as full persons and did not include slaves, women, or children.

50. Ando, "Sovereignty, Territoriality, and Universalism," 9.

51. Rey Chow, *Writing Diaspora: Tactics of Intervention in Contemporary Cultural Studies* (Bloomington: Indiana University Press, 1993), 5–6. See Jeremy Schott, *Christianity, Empire, and the Making of Religion in Late Antiquity* (Philadelphia: University of Penn-sylvania Press, 2008), for ancient philosophical contexts for negotiating universalism/particularity, and likewise for a compatible interest in attending to Christian identity production as an unexceptional case of ethnicizing and universalizing discourse.

52. See Steven N. Mason, "*Philosophiai*: Graeco-Roman, Judean and Christian," in *Volun-tary Associations in the Graeco-Roman World*, ed. John S. Kloppenborg and Stephen G. Wilson (New York: Routledge, 1996), 31–58.

53. See Jacobs, *Christ Circumcised*, 6–10. Jacobs also employs psychoanalytic models in his description of Roman power and the imaginations of identity and social life that were constitutive of it, focusing particularly on assimilation and internalization of one's (imaginatively) constructed others.

54. Pagden, "Afterword."

55. For instance, Heidi Wendt argues in fact that the Roman-Jewish war actually *increased* the visibility of and interest in Judean traditions across the empire and gave freelance or institutionally unaffiliated experts in these traditions more traction. See "'Entrusted with the Oracles of God': The Fate of the Judean Writings in Flavian Rome," in *A Most Reliable Witness: Essays in Honor of Ross Shepard Kraemer*, ed. Susan Ashbrook Harvey et al. (Providence, RI: Brown University Press, 2015), 101–9.

56. See Greg Woolf, *Becoming Roman: The Origins of Provincial Civilization in Gaul* (New York: Cambridge University Press, 1998). This case study of Roman Gaul places signal importance on the place of local elites in mediating between Rome and Gaul. Woolf also tracks the way ethnic/cultural difference was eventually parlayed into exaggerated status differentials.

57. For a more extended argument on this, see Maia Kotrosits, *Rethinking Early Christian Identity: Affect, Violence, and Belonging* (Minneapolis: Fortress Press, 2015), chap. 6.

58. Like Schott's *Christianity, Empire, and the Making of Religion in Late Antiquity*, Todd Berzon's *Classifying Christians: Ethnography, Heresiology, and the Limits of Knowledge in Late Antiquity* (Berkeley: University of California Press, 2016) explicitly makes this connection. Berzon sees late ancient Christian writers as harnessing ethnographic dis-course for their own ends, but he does not more thoroughly address this use of ethno-graphic discourse as tied to colonial conditions of the Roman world.

CHAPTER ONE

1. Loraine Daston and Peter Galison, *Objectivity* (New York: Zone Books, 2007), 17. Daston and Galison trace the rise of scientific objectivity in the mid-nineteenth century, a history that includes the creation of "working objects" (as opposed to "natural objects"), which are representative examples, "atlas images, type specimens, or laboratory processes — any manageable, communal representative of the sector of nature under investigation" (19).

2. Anthropologist Michael Jackson has recently observed the "ways in which objects are subject to thought and subjects think about themselves through objects," even suggesting through the work of George Devereux that "the 'new materialism' is a manifestation of Devereux's 'trauma of the unresponsiveness of matter,' a defense against forces over which we have little control (global warming, epidemic diseases, economic collapse)" See Jackson, *Critique of Identity Thinking* (New York: Berghahn Books, 2019), 61. In this book, Jackson evokes the work of Donald W. Winnicott, specifically the notion of transitional objects, a theory on which I elaborate below, to describe the work that lively objects do for human negotiations of reality. Jackson thus still *upholds* a distinction between subjects and material objects. My work differs in that I am interested in what such "lively objects" tell us not about our blunt encounters with inanimate things, or about the ways we form ourselves with and against material objects, or about the way we endow material objects with power, but about what our imaginations about "lively objects" tell us about psychosocial processes of objectification.

3. Ovid, *Met.* 10.243–97.

4. Elsner, *Roman Eyes: Visuality and Subjectivity in Art and Text* (Princeton: Princeton University Press, 2007), 121.

5. Ibid., 125.

6. Ibid., 130.

7. Ibid., 117.

8. Miller, *Dreams in Late Antiquity.*

9. Patricia Cox Miller, *The Corporeal Imagination: Signifying the Holy in Late Ancient Christianity* (Philadelphia: University of Pennsylvania Press, 2009), 109.

10. Ibid., 7.

11. Ibid., 179–80.

12. Mark Goodacre's argument appears in a blogpost: http://ntweblog.blogspot.com/ 2010/10/walking-talking-cross-or-walking.html4 (18 October 2010). I came upon this argument and citation in Paul Foster, "Do Crosses Walk and Talk? A Reconsideration of the Gospel of Peter 10:39–42," *Journal for Theological Studies* 64, no. 1 (April 2013): 89–104. According to Foster, Goodacre later presented a more developed form of the argument at the International Society of Biblical Literature meeting, London, 6 July 2011, "A Walking, Talking Cross or the Walking Talking Crucified One? A Conjectural Emendation in the Gospel of Peter 10.39, 42." In the blogpost he notes that the

major textual "witness" for the Gospel is from the eighth century (P. Cair. 10759), and
he argues that the error was in fact made twice in the text, as the scribe perhaps mis-
recognized the abbreviation (*nomina sacrum*) for "crucified one" (*staurothenta*), and
changed it to "cross" (*stauron*).

13. Foster, "Do Crosses Walk and Talk?," 98.

14. Ibid., 98–99.

15. Foster (ibid., 98) suggests that this is an elaboration of the earthquake at Jesus's death
in the Gospel of Matthew 27:51.

16. Ibid.

17. Ibid., 102–4.

18. Alexis Waller, "The 'Unspeakable Teachings' of the *The Secret Gospel of Mark*: Feelings
and Fantasies in the Making of Christian Histories" in *Religion, Emotion, Sensation:
Affect Theories and Theologies* (New York: Fordham University Press, 2019).

19. Ibid., 3.

20. Ibid., 8.

21. Indeed, Amy Hollywood observes a similar set of negotiations (though her language
distinguishes between the "real" and the "true") in the Christian Middle Ages. Hollywood, *Acute Melancholia and Other Essays: Mysticism, History, and the Study of Religion*
(New York: Columbia University Press, 2016), esp. 3–5.

22. Jesus as body-object, as matter that is both more and less than human, appears across
literature that features him. In the next chapter, I discuss the Gospel of Mark's association of the body of Jesus with the (ruined) temple, and the Letter to the Hebrews
similarly merges Jesus's flesh with the temple veil. The Gospel of John regularly "thing"-
ifies Jesus, as well. See Stephen Moore's *Gospel Jesuses and Other Nonhumans* (Atlanta:
Society of Biblical Literature Press, 2017), which addresses a number of places in the
canonical gospels in which Jesus's body is both more and less than human, in which
divinity and animality, organic and inorganic matter comingle. His project imagines
a Christian theology of the nonhuman Jesus that offers a singular example of what it
means to be human. It seeks to be an ethical response to contemporary colonial and
ecological crises, and yet does so through a surprisingly, if subtly, Christian exception-
alist framework. Jesus is only one figure in a world of objectified others, even in the
literature that features him. See Celene Lillie's discussion of the plot shared by several
extracanonical stories, including the Secret Revelation of John, On the Origin of the
World, and the Reality of the Rulers. In these stories, the creation of the world in Genesis is retold such that Adam and Eve begin as things: lumps of lifeless flesh, lying on the
ground, and at one point Eve escapes rape by the evil rulers by merging her true self
with a tree, leaving "only" her body to be violated. *The Rape of Eve: The Transformation
of Roman Imperial Ideology in Three Early Christian Retellings of Genesis* (Minneapolis:
Fortress Press, 2017).

23. See especially Hayden White, "The Value of Narrativity in the Representation of
Reality," *Critical Inquiry* 7, no. 1 (Autumn 1980): 5–27, and *Metahistory: The Historical
Imagination in Nineteenth-Century Europe* (Baltimore: Johns Hopkins University Press,
1973), and Michel Foucault, *The Archaeology of Knowledge and the Discourse on Lan-*

guage, trans. A. M. Sheridan Smith (New York: Pantheon, 1972). Geertz to be discussed more specifically in what follows.

24. For a critique of the way New Historicism both borrowed from and failed to clearly name its relationship to Foucault, see Suzanne Gearhart, "The Taming of Michel Foucault: New Historicism, Psychoanalysis, and the Subversion of Power," *New Literary History* 28, no. 3 (Summer 1997): 457–80.

25. See for example Stephen Greenblatt, "Toward a Poetics of Culture," in *The New Historicism*, ed. H. Aram Veeser (New York: Routledge, 1989), 1–14.

26. Stephen Greenblatt, "A Touch of the Real," in *The Fate of "Culture": Geertz and Beyond*, ed. Sherry B. Ortner (Berkeley: University of California Press, 1999), 14–15.

27. Clifford Geertz, "Thick Description: Toward an Interpretive Theory of Culture," in *The Interpretation of Cultures* (New York: Basic Books, 1973), 10.

28. Greenblatt, "Touch of the Real," 21.

29. Ibid.

30. Heather Love, "Close Reading and Thin Description," *Public Culture* 25, no. 3 (Fall 2013): 403.

31. Ibid., 403–4. "The field of literary studies is weakened by its refusal to engage with empirical methods," she writes. "[B]y focusing exclusively on meaning, intention, language, and culture, critics have not attended fully to the behavioral components of experience and representation."

32. Ibid., 409.

33. Ibid., 411.

34. Ibid., 402.

35. Ibid., 409, 410. As Geertz writes, "Behavior must be attended to, and with some exactness, because it is through the flow of behavior—or, more precisely, social action—that cultural forms find articulation." *Interpretation of Cultures*, 17.

36. Love, "Close Reading and Thin Description," 414.

37. Ibid., 430.

38. Ibid., 411.

39. Ibid., 412.

40. Of course, Geertz's theory of religion has been central to biblical and early Christian studies. In *The Interpretation of Cultures*, Geertz indeed has recourse to the real/actual and representation in his definition of religion, noting that "sacred symbols function to synthesize a people's ethos—the tone, character, and quality of their life, its moral and aesthetic style and mood—and their world view—the picture they have of the way things in sheer actuality are, their most comprehensive ideas of order. In religious belief and practice, a group's ethos is rendered intellectually reasonable by being shown to represent a way of life ideally adapted to the actual state of affairs the world view describes, while the world view is rendered emotionally convincing by being presented as an image of an actual state of affairs peculiarly well-arranged to accommodate such a way of life." "Religion as a Cultural System," in *The Interpretation of Cultures* (New York: Basic Books, 1973), 95–96.

41. Interestingly, neither has biblical studies really attended to Geertz's later exhortations

in "The Growth of Culture and the Evolution of Mind," for instance, to trace the complex biological factors that contribute to that rational and emotional animal, the human being. In this essay, Geertz waxes on the neurological composition of the human experience and the way it is inextricably tied to cultural symbols, as well as on the ways thinking and feeling (traditionally designated as "rationality" and "emotion") work in complex synergy. Meaning and experience for Geertz are inevitably generated through that synergy of thinking and feeling, as he describes (through a meditation on the work of Hebb and Thompson) the ways in which cultural scenes and scenarios "give specific, explicit, determinate form to the general, diffuse, ongoing flow of bodily sensation . . . imposing upon the continual shifts in sentience to which we are inherently subject a recognizable, meaningful, order, so that we may not only feel but know what we feel and act accordingly." *Interpretation of Cultures*, 80. He writes: "Not only ideas, but emotions too, are cultural artifacts" (81).

42. See Sherry Ortner's introduction to *The Fate of "Culture,"* in which she offers a summary of reception of Geertz up through the late '90s, including the critiques that there was too great a conceit of ethical and political neutrality in Geertz's work, to which some of the essays in that volume respond. See also V. Crapanzano, "Hermes' Dilemma: The Masking of Subversion in Ethnographic Description," in *Writing Culture: The Poetics and Politics of Ethnography*, ed. James Clifford and George Marcus (Berkeley: University of California Press, 1986), 51–76.

43. Ortner, Introduction to *The Fate of "Culture,"* 3.

44. Geertz, "Thick Description: Toward an Interpretive Theory of Culture," *Interpretation of Cultures*, 9.

45. Anand Pandian and Stuart McLean, eds., *Crumpled Paper Boat: Experiments in Ethnographic Writing* (Durham: Duke University Press, 2017),18. The introduction is collectively written by the contributors to the volume.

46. Pandian, "Ethnography and Fiction," in Pandian and McLean, *Crumpled Paper Boat*, 146.

47. Pandian et al., introduction, *Crumpled Paper Boat*, 18.

48. Ibid., 19.

49. Ibid., 21.

50. Ibid., 4.

51. Ibid., 20.

52. Similarly, in an essay called "The Point of Precision," *Representations* 135, no. 1 (Summer 2016): 31–44, Kathleen Stewart (who writes an epilogue to *Crumpled Paper Boat*) speaks of anthropological description in a resonant way. She suggests that "reality itself is incommensurable with any attempt to grasp it," and that "description is an oblique mode of access to its objects; as such, it must become weirdly, robustly realist" (32). This means, for Stewart, catching a glimpse of our objects of description "in motion," or in a state of "flicker" or transition, in which we are uncertain as to what, exactly, they are. That is, she provokes describers to remember the autonomy of their objects of description. Stewart also expresses attraction to the literariness, the interpretive creativity, of the enterprise of description.

53. Pandian et al, *Crumpled Paper Boat*, 23.

54. Ibid., 24.

55. I borrow this pun from Robyn Wiegman (*Object Lessons* [Durham: Duke University Press, 2012]), whose critique of the notion of doing justice with objects of study I discuss more in my final chapter, "Darkening the Discipline."

56. Rey Chow, *The Age of the World Target: Self-Referentiality in War, Theory, and Comparative Work* (Durham: Duke University Press, 2006), 62.

57. Ibid., 60–64.

58. Though Winnicott also notices the mother herself can also act as a transitional object. Donald W. Winnicott, *Playing and Reality* (New York: Routledge, 2005), 6.

59. Ibid., 3.

60. Ibid., 7.

61. Ibid., 13.

62. Ibid.

63. Ibid., 12.

64. Ibid., 18. He follows this statement with, parenthetically, recourse to "arts, religion, etc." — intermediate areas that are in "direct continuity" with children's play. This is to say that religion and arts are described by Winnicott not as "illusion" but rather as *a break from the tension* of inner and outer realities.

65. Ibid., 121.

66. Ibid., 121.

67. See especially Klein, "A Contribution to the Psychogenesis of Manic-Depressive States," in *Love, Guilt, and Reparation and Other Works*.

68. Sedgwick, "Paranoid Reading and Reparative Reading, or, You're So Paranoid, You Probably Think This Essay Is About You," in *Touching Feeling*, 149–51.

69. Benjamin, *Like Subjects, Love Objects*, 35. "Intersubjectivity" or the notion that reality is built relationally has a life and context that precede Benjamin, and the application of intersubjectivity to the enterprise of description of people and the world (or their worlds) has a history. See, for instance, anthropologist Michael Jackson's *Minima Ethnographica: Intersubjectivity and the Anthropological Project* (Chicago: University of Chicago Press, 1998). Jackson, however, is not using the psychoanalytic intonations of intersubjectivity in that work. He does importantly evoke Donald Winnicott's work and the theory of the transitional object here, too, however briefly.

70. Benjamin, *Like Subjects, Love Objects*, 41.

71. Ibid., 184.

72. Ibid., 43.

73. Ibid., 209.

74. See Jacques Lacan, "The Object and the Thing," in which he describes the real as the "excluded interior," both "surplus" and "essential." *The Seminar of Jacques Lacan: The Ethics of Psychoanalysis, Book VII*, ed. Jacques Alain-Miller, trans. Dennis Porter (New York: W. W. Norton, 1997), 101–2. Here Lacan describes the real as having the life of an object, a "thing" (literally: "das Ding"), and particularly a lost thing.

75. See Rey Chow, *Not like a Native Speaker: On Languaging as a Postcolonial Experience* (New York: Columbia University Press, 2014).

76. In some instances, this unyielding presence might look like what Andrea Smith has de-

scribed as "the refusal to be known and the refusal to be infinitely knowable," the tactic of a persistent subject who does not *want* recognition or to be fully seen. Andrea Smith, "Native Studies at the Horizon of Death: Theorizing Ethnographic Entrapment and Settler Self-Reflexivity," in *Theorizing Native Studies*, ed. Audra Simpson and Andrea Smith (Durham: Duke University Press, 2014), 231. The "ethnographic entrapment" in Native studies is, for Smith, a function of the assumption that freedom for Native peoples is contingent on their transparency to colonial culture. This is a problem of the grid, as she notes, in which "the desire to know the Native is itself part of the settler-colonial project to apprehend, contain, and domesticate the potential power of Indigenous peoples to subvert the settler state" (231).

77. The real, or *das Ding*, is "the beyond-of-the-signified." Lacan, "Das Ding," in *Seminar*, 54.

78. See for instance Antonio Viego's race-critical and multiculturally oriented reading of Lacan in *Dead Subjects*.

79. See Derrida's *Monolinguism of the Other; or, The Prosthesis of Origin*, trans. Patrick Mensah (Stanford: Stanford University Press, 1998), which I will discuss more in chapter 5, along with Chow, on the question of translation and violence in martyr stories.

80. See Chow, *Not like a Native Speaker*.

81. Chow, *Age of the World Target*, 71.

82. Ibid., 72–73.

83. Ibid., 76–81.

84. Ibid., 88.

85. This is especially as anthropologists such as Eduardo Kohn have even begun to question what counts as language, and the relationship of human forms of symbolization to other semiotic ecologies. Kohn, *How Forests Think: Toward an Anthropology Beyond the Human* (Berkeley: University of California Press, 2013).

86. Chow, *Age of the World Target*, 86.

CHAPTER TWO

1. For a treatment of the extensive building projects that took place under the rule of Hadrian, for instance, see Mary Boatwright, *Hadrian and the Cities of the Roman Empire* (Princeton: Princeton University Press, 2000).

2. Mary R. Bachvarova, "The Destroyed City in Ancient 'World History' from Agade to Troy," in *The Fall of Cities in the Ancient Mediterranean: Commemoration in Literature, Folk-Song, and Liturgy*, ed. Bachvarova, Dorota Dutsch, and Ann Suter (Cambridge: Cambridge University Press, 2016), 38.

3. Ibid., 37.

4. Ibid. The Exodus and the conquest of Canaan are one prominent biblical example.

5. Ann Laura Stoler, "'The Rot Remains': From Ruins to Ruination," in *Imperial Debris: On Ruins and Ruination*, ed. Stoler (Durham: Duke University Press, 2013), 1–38.

6. Jo-Ann Shelton, "The Fall of Troy in Seneca's *Troades*," in Bachvarova, Dutsch, and Suter, *Fall of Cities in the Ancient Mediterranean*, 203.

7. Alison Keith, "City Lament in Augustan Epic: Antitypes of Rome from Troy to Alba Longa," in Bachvarova, Dutsch, and Suter, *Fall of Cities in the Ancient Mediterranean*, 179–80.

8. Ibid., 180.

9. See ibid. Ovid, *Metamorphoses*, 15.440–45.

10. Shelton, "Fall of Troy in Seneca's *Troades*," 189.

11. Keith, "City Lament in Augustan Epic." Virgil, *Aeneid* 12.887–952.

12. See for instance Hal Taussig, "Melancholy, Colonialism, and Complicity: Complicating Counter-Imperial Readings of Aphrodisias' Sebasteion," in Aliou Cissé Niang and Carolyn Osiek, eds., *Text, Image, and Christians in the Graeco-Roman World: A Festschrift in Honor of David Lee Balch* (Eugene, OR: Pickwick, 2012); Carlin A. Barton, *The Sorrows of the Ancient Romans: The Gladiator and the Monster* (Princeton: Princeton University Press, 1993); Maia Kotrosits, "Seeing Is Feeling: Revelation's Enthroned Lamb and Ancient Visual Affects," *Biblical Interpretation* 22, no. 4 (Fall 2014): 473–502.

13. Shelton, "Fall of Troy in Seneca's *Troades*," 209.

14. See especially John W. Marshall, *Parables of War: Reading John's Jewish Apocalypse* (Waterloo, ON: Wilfred Laurier, 2001), and Jacqueline Hidalgo, *Revelation in Aztlán: Scriptures, Utopias, and the Chicano Movement* (New York: Palgrave, 2016).

15. See Christopher Frilingos, *Spectacles of Empire: Monsters, Martyrs, and the Book of Revelation* (Philadelphia: University of Pennsylvania Press, 2004).

16. For maps of locations of amphitheaters, see S. R. F. Price, *Rituals and Power: The Roman Imperial Cult in Asia Minor* (New York: Cambridge, 1985).

17. Ibid.

18. For the ways images of Rome's conquered nations resonate against Revelation's own gendered and starkly binary imaginations of power, see Lynn Huber, *Thinking and Seeing with Women in Revelation* (New York: T & T Clark, 2013).

19. See for instance Stephen Moore, "'The World Empire Has Become the Empire of Our Lord and His Messiah': Representing Empire in Revelation," *Empire and Apocalypse: Postcolonialism and the New Testament* (Sheffield, UK: Sheffield Phoenix Press, 2006), 97–121; Kotrosits, "Seeing Is Feeling."

20. Runions, *Babylon Complex*, 13. Runions indeed points out that the text negotiates (and leaves somewhat unresolved) the powers of both God and Babylonian technology/progress.

21. Ibid., 15.

22. Cf. Isaiah 47:1, 47:8: "Come down, sit on the ground, virgin daughter of Babylon! Enter the darkness, daughter of the Chaldeans, because you shall no longer be called tender and delicate. . . . Now hear these things, delicate woman, who sits securely, who says in her heart, 'I am, and there is no other.'

23. Jennifer Glancy and Stephen D. Moore, "The Empress and the Brothel Slave," in *Untold Tales From the Book of Revelation: Sex, Gender, Empire and Ecology*, ed. Moore (Atlanta: Society of Biblical Literature, 2014), 103–24.

24. Runions, *Babylon Complex*, 13. She is quoting Jonah Hill.

25. Runions, *Babylon Complex*, 36.

26. Notice that the new Jerusalem has spectacular, highly decorated walls and gates (cf. chap. 21), but the gates "will never be shut by day" and "there will be no night there (21:25), because "nothing unclean will enter it, nor anyone who practices abomination or falsehood" (v. 27).

27. Interpretations of this passage depend heavily on the presumably Christian character of Revelation at large. Elisabeth Schüssler Fiorenza, noting that making allegorical sense of this section is difficult at best, sees the great city and the holy city as symbolic of Jerusalem and the Christian community, respectively. *Revelation: Vision of a Just World* (Minneapolis: Fortress Press, 1991), 78. Adela Yarbro Collins earlier suggested that the two cities are conflated into Jerusalem, and that God's wrath on the city is for the rejection of Jesus, leading her to conclude that Revelation is a Christian text that has a largely strained (albeit formative) relationship to Israel (or "Judaism," for Collins). *Crisis and Catharsis: The Power of the Apocalypse* (Philadelphia: Westminster Press, 1984), 84–86. John Marshall argues against both Collins and Schüssler Fiorenza and suggests that the phrase "where also their Lord was crucified" should be taken not as a literal geographical referent but simply as a reference to the fact that Jesus was crucified by the Romans. *Parables of War*, 170–73.

28. Cf. Kent Brintnall's striking elaboration of this image in the beginning of his essay "Who Weeps for the Sodomite?" which gives a history of pro-LGBT readings of the passage and the stakes of such interpretations: "With the possible exception of Lot and his daughters, it seems virtually no one in the history of the West has obeyed the injunction not to look back on the fiery devastation rained upon the Cities of the Plain. While gendered injustice appears to play a role in the punishment meted out against Lot's wife, when one begins to rack up the shame, terror, anger, and hate experienced by those who have tried to discern—or think that they understand—what happened in Sodom and Gomorrah, and to whom, and why, it may be that no one who has looked back has been left unscathed. . . . The smoldering rubble cautions all who survived the initial blast to be wary lest sodomitic vice—whatever *that* might be—once again catch heaven's attention." Ruin is a kind of contagion that one can't turn away from, and yet in which one fears being implicated. "Who Weeps for the Sodomite?" in *Sexual Disorientations: Queer Temporalities, Affects, Theologies* (New York: Fordham University Press, 2017), 145–60.

29. See Eugene Boring, *Revelation: Interpretation: A Commentary for Teaching and Preaching* (Louisville: Westminster John Knox Press, 1989), 35–60, and Huber, *Thinking and Seeing with Women in Revelation*, 1–9.

30. See especially Seth Schwartz, *Imperialism and Jewish Society: 200 BCE to 640 CE* (Princeton: Princeton University Press, 2001).

31. See Runions, *Babylon Complex*, 10–19. Of course, Babylonia continued to be home to a vibrant Jewish/Judean population long after the exile, eventually generating a strong rabbinic community and the Babylonian Talmud. Cf. Jacob Neusner's five-volume *History of the Jews in Babylonia*, 1965–70. Likewise, Babylonian Jews were hardly sequestered away from Jerusalem: one of Herod's high priest appointees, Hananel, was a

Babylonian, much to the dismay of those with Hasmonean loyalties, for instance. This was probably not exceptional: Herod's larger program of incorporating people associated with Israel but living outside of Judea into the political life of Judea must have included Babylonians. It is interesting to ask what such evocations of Babylon, and Babylon's fall, might have meant in the context of these more geographical and material considerations of first-century diasporic dynamics. On Babylon and Jewish diaspora in late antiquity, see Daniel Boyarin, *A Traveling Homeland: The Babylonian Talmud as Diaspora* (Philadelphia: University of Pennsylvania Press, 2015).

32. See *Antiquities* 1:109–21. Runions, *Babylon Complex*, 46–49. Josephus also recovers the story to stake out some particular positions on governance, as Runions argues.

33. For a summary of some key scholarly positions on Josephus's foggy allegiances, and a nicely observed portrait of Josephus's specific negotiation with cultural memory and Roman systems of benefaction, see Seth Schwartz, *Were the Jews a Mediterranean Society? Reciprocity and Solidarity in Ancient Judaism* (Princeton: Princeton University Press, 2010), 80–109.

34. See Tessa Rajak, *The Jewish Dialogue with Greece and Rome: Studies in Cultural and Social Interaction* (Leiden: Brill, 2002), 81–98.

35. *Antiquities* 11.173; See Shaye J. D. Cohen, *The Beginnings of Jewishness: Boundaries, Varieties, Uncertainties* (Berkeley: University of California Press, 2001). Rajak, *Jewish Dialogue with Greece and Rome*, 138.

36. *Judean Wars*, book 6, chap. 5.

37. The recent critical work on ruins, while paying attention largely to ruins of the past two centuries (the Amazon, the Congo, and post-Holocaust Germany, Detroit or the postindustrial United States at large), illustrates how ruins are fetishized, romanticized, and refigured. See Stoler, *Imperial Debris*; Julia Hell and Andreas Schönle, eds., *Ruins of Modernity* (Durham: Duke University Press, 2010); and Gaston Gordillo, *Rubble: The Afterlife of Destruction* (Durham: Duke Univeristy Press, 2014. One exception to the generally modern interests in these volumes on ruins is an essay by Julia Hell, "Imperial Ruin Gazers, or Why Did Scipio Weep?," in *Ruins of Modernity*, 169–92, in which she compares ancient and modern ruin gazers.

38. See Stoler's introduction, "'The Rot Remains': From Ruins to Ruination," in *Imperial Debris*, 1–35.

39. See Philip A. Harland, "The Declining Polis? Religious Rivalries in Ancient Civic Context," in *Religious Rivalries in the Early Roman Empire and the Rise of Christianity*, ed. Leif E. Vaage. (Waterloo, ON: Wilfrid Laurier University Press, 2006).

40. James Porter, "Ideals and Ruins: Pausanias, Longinus, and the Second Sophistic," in *Pausanias: Travel and Memory in Roman Greece*, ed. Susan E. Alcock, John F. Cherry, and Jaś Elsner (New York: Oxford, 2001), 67.

41. Ibid., 68–69.

42. Ibid., 90.

43. Ibid., 67.

44. Ibid., 67.

45. Ibid., 71–72.

46. Runions, borrowing from the work of Charles Gaines, also discusses the sublime, and

offers a queerly sublime ethics of reading Babylon and Christ. *Babylon Complex*, 213–45.

47. Porter, "Ideals and Ruins," 74. As Porter writes, "at the heart of the account itself is the fundamental shock of contingency . . . that is itself elevated to sublime status" (75).

48. Ibid., 68–69.

49. See Susan E. Alcock's work on Pausanias, among others who imagine Greek pasts, and the relationship between architecture, memory/forgetting, and belonging/identity. *Archaeologies of the Greek Past: Landscape, Monuments, and Memories* (New York: Cambridge University Press, 2002).

50. While ancient laments for fallen cities often appear to be waxing about human mortality in general, the personification of cities (overlapping with the personification of nations) in ancient literature and visual representation points to the ways individuals, collectives, and their associated political geographies implied each other. This was also obviously a gendered enterprise: the depiction of Rome's conquered nations, or at least those nations that loomed large in Rome's imagination, as ethnically stereotyped female figures, often in subjugated poses, is one striking example. See Davina Lopez, *Apostle to the Conquered: Reimagining Paul's Mission* (Minneapolis: Fortress Press, 2008), and Huber, *Thinking and Seeing with Women in Revelation*, 34–55. Although it is also clear that female personifications of a people/place did not always denote subjugation, the gendered dimensions of these representations demonstrate just how deeply individuals, collectives, and geographies were entangled.

51. Originally appearing in the 1948 edition of his book *Solar Throat Slashed*, "Solid" and thirty other poems were deleted from later editions until 1994, and many presume that this was because of the specifically local and political character of these poems. Césaire Aimé, *Solar Throat Slashed: the unexpurgated 1948 edition*, ed. A. James Arnold and Clayton Eshleman (Middletown, CT: Wesleyan University Press, 2011).

52. More recently, Audre Lorde's poem "Coal" merges the exploitation of the natural world with the exploitation of black subjects in the register of coal mining. She writes, "Is the total black, being spoken / From the earth's inside. / There are many kinds of open. / How a diamond comes into a knot of flame / How a sound comes into a work, coloured / By who pays what for speaking." Kathryn Yusoff quotes this poem in a large discussion of the "inhumanities" and a call for rewriting the notion of the Anthropocene (the geological age dominated by humans), centralizing the history of racialized slavery. Yusoff, *A Billion Black Anthropocenes or None* (Minneapolis: University of Minnesota Press, 2018), 84.

53. As Jaś Elsner also points out, "Pausanias' choice of structure—apparently so simple and unreflective—has the virtue of naturalizing, through the relentless 'and next we come to this place' quality of the travel book, his texts' subtle reflection on Greece as other . . . and simultaneously as self in the Greek-speaking pilgrim's confrontation with all that is most essential and most sacred about the Greek tradition." Elsner, "Structuring 'Greece': Pausanias's Periegesis as a Literary Construct," in Alcock, Cherry, and Elsner, *Pausanias: Travel and Memory in Roman Greece*, 5. Elsner connects this naturalization through structure to contemporary readings of Pausanias that simply recon-

struct places in a literal or material way from his texts, rather than understanding his work as specifically literary and ideological.

54. This trajectory is not particular to Daniel, and something like it—in which the protagonist is endangered, escapes death or imprisonment, and then is given recognition or power—occurs in the stories of Joseph and Esther, for example. See John J. Collins, *Daniel, Hermeneia* (Minneapolis: Fortress Press, 1993), 192, as well as George W. E. Nickelsburg, *Resurrection, Immortality, and Eternal Life in Intertestamental Judaism* (Cambridge: Harvard University Press, 1972).

55. W. Lee Humphrey has suggested that Daniel, like the book of Esther, affirms that "at one and the same time the Jew can remain loyal to his heritage and God and yet live a creative, rewarding, and fulfilled life precisely within a foreign setting." "A Lifestyle for Diaspora: A Study of the Tales of Esther and Daniel," *Journal of Biblical Literature* 92 (1973): 223. Humphreys also suggests that the book of Daniel forces the reader to "stretch his [*sic*] credulity to the breaking point" to accept that the figure who remains loyal to God and still ascends through foreign administrations in the first part of the book then condemns those powers as oppressive and against God's plan in the second part of the book (223). Aside from the source questions that attend the book of Daniel, this does point to a larger disjuncture and idealization in the book in which foreign power and loyalty to Israel are completely and fairly easily reconcilable.

56. In fact, it is through the change of heart of these foreign rulers, their sudden loyalty to Israel's god, that the nations are able to come to Yahweh, fulfilling earlier Hebrew scriptural visions (most distinctly in second Isaiah). Cf., e.g., Daniel 4:34, 6:25–27. It is also worth noting that restoration at the end of the book in chapter 12 means not just restoration of a kingdom or a collective, but a kind of personal/subjective restoration through "resurrection," described as becoming like stars.

57. See Kotrosits, "Seeing Is Feeling."

58. As Loren Johns has shown, Revelation's use of *arnion* does not match the Septuagint's preferred term for a burnt offering (*amnos*), and lambs were not the most popular sacrificial animals. Thus, Revelation's use of lamb evokes the more general sense of vulnerability that *amnos* accumulates in Septuagint uses of the term. Loren L. Johns, *The Lamb Christology of the Apocalypse of John* (Tübingen: Mohr Siebeck, 2003). While there is no temple in the new Jerusalem, there is a heavenly temple in Revelation (cf. 11:19, 14:15, 15:5–6). Presumably there is no temple in the new Jerusalem because the new Jerusalem is already thoroughly free from impurity, making a cultic system of purification extraneous, but according to that logic there would be no need for a temple in heaven, either.

59. The history of interpretation is heavy with supersessionist readings of this association that assume that Jesus equals Christianity and the temple equals Judaism. But rather than any kind of supersessionism or replacement theology, or even any kind of grand theological statement at all, it seems the association of Jesus's violent death with the ruined temple simply expresses the ongoing colonial effects of debilitation and decomposition. These effects, by the way, don't get transcended as much as they *catalyze* dreams of sovereignty and projects of belonging—both figured as "restoration."

60. Pressing the question of ruins in Mark further, it seems that the empty tomb scene is strongly reminiscent of the "numinous absence" in Pausanias's ruins, as well.

61. See Maia Kotrosits and Hal Taussig, *Re-reading the Gospel of Mark amidst Pain and Loss* (New York: Palgrave, 2011), and Alexis Waller, "Violent Spectacles and Public Feelings: Trauma and Affect in the Gospel of Mark and the Thunder: Perfect Mind," *Biblical Interpretation* 22, nos. 4–5 (2014): 450–72.

62. Reading the story of the Gerasene demoniac politically is practically commonplace these days, and the cue was largely taken from Ched Myers's work, which uses that pericope as an interpretive key for the rest of the gospel. Myers, *Binding the Strong Man: A Political Reading of Mark's Story of Jesus* (Maryknoll, NY: Orbis Books, 1988).

63. My reading of the Gospel of Mark in this book's various chapters is indebted to the sensitive critique of my earlier work on the Gospel of Mark (*Re-reading the Gospel of Mark*, with Taussig, 2011) by Tat-siong Benny Liew, who rightfully noticed that my/ our treatment of the Gospel of Mark relative to trauma was not attentive enough to the many and deep colonial resonances of the book. Tat-siong Benny Liew, "Haunting Silence: Trauma, Failed Orality, and Mark's Messianic Secret," in Liew and Runions, *Psychoanalytic Mediations between Marxist and Postcolonial Readings of the Bible*, 99– 128. I've also been helped by Liew's diasporic reflections on the gospels, though my approach to diaspora and "early Christian" literature is decidedly more along historicist lines. See for instance Liew, "Tyranny, Boundary and Might: Colonial Mimicry in Mark's Gospel," *Journal for the Study of the New Testament* 77 (1999): 7–31.

64. Though sovereignty is deeply questioned in the Gospel of Mark, healing and some kind of tentative salvation are still possible. In the tradition of Greco-Roman noble death, one is saved in the Gospel of Mark by emulating Jesus — staying faithful even to the point of death, and enduring to the end (e.g., Mark 8:34–35, 13:13).

65. Addressing especially Revelation, Mark, and Daniel as diasporic musings on and through imperial ruin raises larger possibilities for considering "apocalyptic" literature as something other than a distinct category, discrete theology, or comprehensive worldview. What we call "apocalyptic" scenes might have more interpretive purchase as part of a discourse on ruins/ruination, sovereignty, and diaspora.

66. Christ as simultaneously disciplined (non)citizen of Rome and conduit for diasporic belonging in fact parallels Sikh martyrs and Sikh diasporic aspirations for sovereignty as portrayed by Brian Keith Axel. See Kotrosits, *Rethinking Early Christian Identity*, 117–45, where I discuss this parallel at more length.

67. Dale Martin, *The Corinthian Body* (New Haven: Yale University Press, 1999); Margaret Mitchell, *Paul and the Rhetoric of Reconciliation: An Exegetical Investigation of the Language and Composition of 1 Corinthians* (Tübingen: Mohr Siebeck, 1991).

68. 1 Cor. 12:12–17.

69. On women and men and "appropriate" roles/behaviors, see 1 Cor. 5:13, 6:19–10 (sexual immorality); 1 Cor. 7:1–16 (marriage); 1 Cor. 7:25–39 (unmarried); 1 Cor. 7:17–20 (circumcision);1 Cor. 11:1–16 (head coverings).

70. On order at the meal gatherings, see 1 Cor. 5:11 (no meal with sexually immoral people); 1 Cor. 8:4–13 (idol meat not theologically correct); 1 Cor. 10:19 (idol meat is partner

with devil); 1 Cor. 10:27–28 (idol meat is fine when hosted by pagans); 1 Cor. 11:17–34 (on divisions and disagreements).

71. It is not necessarily obvious what "speaking in tongues" means, and Paul's clear stance against it means that his own descriptions should not be taken for granted. It is, at least, a kind of "insider" language: something that *can* be interpreted, but would not be immediately available to outsiders.

72. Maia Kotrosits, "The Rhetoric of Intimate Spaces: Affect and Performance in the Corinthian Correspondence," *Union Seminary Quarterly Review* 62, nos. 3–4 (2011): 134–51.

73. Wendy Brown, *States of Injury: Power and Freedom in Late Modernity* (Princeton: Princeton University Press, 1995).

74. Though his reading departs a bit from my own, I'm again prompted by Benny Liew's colonial and diasporic reading of Paul, the Corinthians, and social bodies in "Melancholia in Diaspora: Reading Paul's Psycho-political Operatives in 1 Corinthians," in his book *What Is Asian American Hermeneutics?: Reading the New Testament* (Honolulu: University of Hawaii Press, 2008). Liew argues that Paul is not out for some kind of nostalgic diasporic purity and that he is rather angling for a "new communal belonging." I don't quite disagree, but Liew's emphasis on the inclusion of the "gentiles" in this new communal belonging feels almost recuperative to me, and I want to stick more closely with the potential implications of what Liew sees as the broken and resurrected body of Jesus as the transfer point for collectivity. And I certainly follow Liew (106–7) in his larger suggestion that Paul is navigating both an acknowledgment and a refusal of diasporic loss.

75. See Martin, *Corinthian Body*, which draws together discourses of disease etiology, gender, and homonoia/concord, among other things, to describe the Corinthian gatherings. The work of the Greco-Roman meals seminar, including Richard Ascough, Hal Taussig, Angela Standhartinger, Matthias Klinghardt, and Carly Daniel-Hughes, among others, demonstrated that Pauline gatherings took place on the symposial model, just like all other associations. The association meals were a comfortable and predictable venue where status, identity, and relationships were negotiated along both hierarchical and more idealized communal lines. Hal Taussig, for instance, describes these meals as working as both heterotopic (in the Foucauldian sense) and utopian spaces at once. That is, they operate as a space that seems to reflect on social order, "perfect" it, and experiment with it, all at the same time. This dynamic at all symposial meals as seen in a lot of the handbooks of Plutarch, for instance, gives us some very clear and precise contexts for the tensions between social stratification and more egalitarian values in the Corinthian correspondence. More recently, Anna Miller has noticed the way democratic discourse informs the Corinthian correspondence and thus connects questions of gender and speaking in the social body to specific delineations of citizenship. Miller, *Corinthian Democracy: Democratic Discourse in First Corinthians* (Princeton: Princeton University Press, 2015).

76. Cavan Concannon has demonstrated how the history of Corinth under the Romans inflects constructions of collectivity—or to use his language, the discourse of ethnicity—for the Corinthians. *When You Were Gentiles: Specters of Ethnicity in Roman Corinth and Paul's Corinthian Correspondence* (New Haven: Yale University Press,

2014). On social stratification in Corinth, see Steven Friesen, Sarah James, and Daniel Showalter, eds., *Corinth in Contrast: Studies in Inequality* (Leiden: Brill, 2003).

77. Bronwen L. Wickkiser, "Asklepios in Greek and Roman Corinth," in *Corinth in Context: Comparative Studies on Religion and Society*, ed. Steve Friesen, Daniel N. Showalter, and James Walters (Leiden: Brill, 2010), 37–66.

78. Ibid., 59.

79. Ibid.

80. Ibid., 59–60. See *Metamorphoses* 15.622–870.

81. Wickkiser, "Asklepios in Greek and Roman Corinth," 60.

82. Brent Hayes Edwards, *The Practice of Diaspora: Literature, Translation, and the Rise of Black Internationalism* (Cambridge: Harvard University Press, 2003), 11.

83. Ibid., 13.

84. Ibid., 13–15.

85. As Antoinette Clark Wire has argued, *The Corinthian Women Prophets: A Reconstruction through Paul's Rhetoric* (Minneapolis: Fortress Press, 1990), 175–76. Paul, too, seems periodically to feel this new vitality and participate with the Corinthians in their experimentation with the boundaries of the body. But of course we also have Paul's worries about being embarrassed or ashamed, and his worries about gender legibility (veiling, speaking, who's "the head").

86. This verse then teeters between the literal and the metaphorical or supraliteral, a tension that characterizes the Corinthian letters and shaped so much of the later history of Christian interpretation, as Margaret M. Mitchell has demonstrated. Indeed, the second-century Christian writer Origen of Alexandria quotes this verse in Second Corinthians to support a spiritualized reading (*On the Principles* 4.1.7). See Mitchell, *Paul, the Corinthians, and the Birth of Christian Hermeneutics* (Cambridge: Cambridge University Press, 2010), especially 50–57. This rhetorical tension—or ambiguity—between literal/material and beyond-the-material might also be understood as a negotiation of "what's real."

87. Liew, "Melancholia in Diaspora," 105.

CHAPTER THREE

1. On differences between the Masoretic text and the old Greek, see Collins, *Daniel* (Minneapolis: Fortress Press, 1993), 236–47.

2. Collins *Daniel*, 246.

3. Greg Woolf, "Monumental Writing and the Expansion of Roman Society in the Early Empire," *Journal of Roman Studies* 86 (1996): 22–39. Woolf indeed provides a bit of a narrative arc for the Roman empire, in that he (after Ramsay Macmullen) notices that epigraphic culture is at its most intense as the Roman empire is also at its height, in the mid-first through mid-second centuries.

4. See Ramsay Macmullen, "The Epigraphic Habit in the Roman Empire," *American Journal of Philology* 103, no. 3 (Autumn 1982): 233–46. Macmullen suggests epigraphy hits its

height in 150 CE. Woolf indeed coins "epigraphic culture" in an adjustment of Ramsey Macmullen's "epigraphic habit."

5. Ramsay Macmullen first diagnosed this phenomenon and, seemingly befuddled by it, suggests simply a "broad psychological shift." Macmullen, "Epigraphic Habit," 246.

6. Woolf, "Monumental Writing," 27. Woolf argues that inscriptions might be thought not as a category in and of itself but as a practice situated within and among other practices such as votive altars (which I discuss more here).

7. Ibid.

8. Ibid., 29.

9. Ibid.

10. Woolf, "Monumental Writing," 37–38.

11. Cassius Dio (76.16.3). See Alexie V. Zadorojnyi, "Shuffling Surfaces: Epigraphy, Power, and Integrity in the Graeco-Roman Narratives," in *Inscriptions and Their Uses in Greek and Latin Literature*, ed. Peter Liddell and Polly Low (New York: Oxford University Press, 2009), 375.

12. See Alexie V. Zadorojnyi, "Transcripts of Dissent? Political Graffiti and Elite Ideology under the Principate," in *Ancient Graffiti in Context*, ed. Jennifer Baird and Claire Taylor (London: Routledge, 2011), 110–33.

13. Peter Homans, *The Ability to Mourn: Disillusionment and the Social Origins of Psychoanalysis* (Chicago: University of Chicago Press, 1989), 270–71. See Sigmund Freud, "Five Lectures on Psychoanalysis," *Standard Edition* 9: 235–41 (London: Hogarth Press, 1957).

14. Angelos Chaniotis, "Affective Epigraphy: Emotions in Public Inscriptions of the Hellenistic Age," *Mediterraneo Antico* 16, no. 2 (2013): 745–60.

15. Ibid., 747.

16. Ibid. As Chaniotis notes, both inscriptions describe a sense of threat and claim resistance to it, but do so once the threat has long passed.

17. Ibid., 756–57.

18. Richard Ascough, Philip A. Harland, and John S. Kloppenborg, eds., *Associations in the Greco-Roman World: A Sourcebook* (Waco, TX: Baylor University Press, 2012), 95.

19. Philip A. Harland, *Greco-Roman Associations: Texts, Translations and Commentary*, vol. 2 (Berlin: De Gruyter, 2014), 58.

20. Ibid., 44.

21. I have chosen these particular inscriptions not just for their poignancy, but for their geographical variety and ordinariness. As such, they demonstrate the experiential subtexts of epigraph culture more broadly.

22. See Susan Alcock, "Tomb Cult and the Post-classical Polis," *American Journal of Archaeology* 95, no. 3 (July 1991): 447–67. She suggests that, for example, the Messenian tomb cult is a "use of the past to unite a previously fragmented population, to define and defend a long-suppressed regional identity."

23. Over the past handful of years, I've found myself following a strand of scholarship on the Gospel of Mark that is pointedly antitriumphalist. Against traditional readings of the gospel that cast Jesus's identity and power as straightforwardly revealed in the story, or that understand Mark as theological myth-making justifying Christian be-

longing, these more recent, antitriumphalist readings summon a haunted, pained Mark that undoes so many later bottled Christian theologies. Mark departs from expected (later) Christian meanings in part because, as I've suggested, it is not at all Christian as a composition. It is rather a negotiation of Israelite/Judean self-understanding, speaking directly to the experience of the Roman Jewish War, including the spectacular destruction of Jerusalem and its temple in 70 CE. Mark depicts a kind of scorched colonial landscape significantly, but only occasionally, punctuated by moments of vitality, wonder, and healing.

24. The inscription is actually a composite of several. See W. Dittenberger, ed., *Orietis Graecae Inscriptiones Selecte* (Hildesheim: Olms, 1960). One translation of the composite text by Craig A. Evans reads: "It seemed good to the Greeks of Asia, in the opinion of the high priest Apollonius of Menophilus Azanitus: 'since Providence, which has ordered all things and is deeply interested in our life, has set in most perfect order by giving us Augustus, whom she filled with virtue that he might benefit humankind, sending him as a savior both for us and for our descendants, that he might end war and arrange all things, and since he, Caesar, by his appearance (excelled even our anticipations), surpassing all previous benefactors, and not even leaving to posterity any hope of surpassing what he has done, and since the birthday of the god Augustus was the beginning of the good tidings for the world that came by reason of him, which Asia resolved in Smyrna . . ." Evans indeed discusses this inscription in the context of the Gospel of Mark's beginning. "Mark's Incipit and the Priene Calendar Inscription: From Jewish Gospel to Greco-Roman Gospel," *Journal of Greco-Roman Judaism and Christianity* 1 (2000): 67–81.

25. Mark archives not only the frustration of literal survival, but the painful cultural divestments that accompany that survival, as we shall see in chapter 5.

26. The Gospel of Mark uses the historical present 151 times, which means the tense strongly inflects the gospel. Just for comparison: the longer gospels of Matthew and Luke use it only twenty times and one time, respectively. Ben Witherington, *The Gospel of Mark: A Socio-rhetorical Commentary* (Grand Rapids, MI: Eerdmans), 2001.

27. As I discuss further in chapter 5, the moment in which Jesus dies has typically been read as a moment of recognition of his divinity or significance. The centurion's words at the moment of Jesus's death are often translated, "Truly, this was God's son!" This hardly suits Mark's larger sense of irony, however, and it doesn't make much sense given that Jesus has just cried out that he's been abandoned by God. The lack of punctuation in Greek allows for a more ironic reading of the centurion's words. See Dennis R. McDonald, *The Homeric Epics and the Gospel of Mark* (New Haven: Yale University Press, 2000), 142–44.

28. Likewise striking for its sense of temporal suspense is one of Mark's major and more characteristic literary devices, intercalation, in which one story begins only to be interrupted by another brief story before the first one can reach its conclusion. The "beginning" of the good news, and the beginning of Mark's story of Jesus, is the middle of Jesus's life. This is obviously troublesome for the other canonical gospels, which try in their own respective ways to get as far back to the beginning of Jesus's story as possible.

Even in its textual afterlife, Mark seems to be perpetually caught in the middle: while the earliest written gospel, it lives its canonical eternity between Matthew and Luke. On intercalations in Mark, see G. Van Oyen, "Intercalation and Irony in the Gospel of Mark," in *The Four Gospels*, ed. F. van Segbroek et al. (Leuven: Peeters, 1992), 2: 949–74.

29. Testifying to this sense of dissatisfaction is a tradition of textual additions that just can't leave that ending alone. Added to the inconclusive ending is the "shorter" ending in which Mary, Mary, and Salome dutifully tell Peter what they have seen, and the "longer" ending in which Jesus appears to Mary Magdalene and some of his disciples, commissions his disciples, and gets "taken up."

30. Mark's relationship to the Greco-Roman noble death tradition is recounted in Burton Mack, *A Myth of Innocence: Mark and Christian Origins* (Philadelphia: Fortress Press, 1988), 247–311, as well as Stephen Patterson, *Beyond the Passion: Rethinking the Death and Life of Jesus* (Minneapolis: Fortress Press, 2004), 39–67. Both Mack and Patterson build on the work of George W. E. Nickelsburg, "Genre and Function of the Markan Passion Narrative," *Harvard Theological Review* 73 (1980): 153–84.

31. It should be noted that most women are not named in Mark, with the exception of Jesus's mother and the women at the empty tomb (Mary, Mary, and Salome).

32. Elisabeth Schussler Fiorenza's *In Memory of Her: A Feminist Theological Reconstruction of Christian Origins* (New York: Crossroads, 1984), 41.

33. Scott, *Fantasy of Feminist Historiography*. Her use of "wo/men" seems to sense this problem but does not quite manage to mitigate it, since it seeks not to account for the difference between ancient and contemporary women but rather to expand the category of figures who would have been erased by patriarchal and androcentric history. She thus actually enlarges and reinforces the field of continuity, rather than disrupting it. On fantasy and feminist historiography and its reverberations at Harvard, see Carly Daniel-Hughes, "Mary Magdalene and the Fantasy Echo: Reflections on the Feminist Historiography of Early Christianity," in *Re-making the World: Christianity and Categories: Essays in Honor of Karen L. King*, ed. Taylor G. Petrey et al. (Tübingen: Mohr Siebeck, 2019), 135–58.

34. Sharpe, *In the Wake*, 1.

35. Ibid., 61.

36. Ibid., 14.

37. Ibid.

38. Ibid., 7.

39. Ibid., 11.

40. Ibid., 76.

41. Ibid., 78.

42. Ibid.

43. Zeb Tortorici, "Visceral Archives of the Body: Consuming the Dead, Digesting the Divine," *GLQ* 20, no. 4 (2014): 407–37.

44. Véronique Dasen, "Healing Images. Gems and Medicine," *Oxford Journal of Archaeology* 33, no. 2 (2014): 183.

45. Ibid., 184.

46. Ibid., 178.

47. Ibid., 178.

48. Ibid.

49. Ibid. Animals, however, are not only associated with the force that needs to be fought off and overcome in healing, but also seen to represent the organ in good working order. The ibis and the phoenix both occur on "digestive gems"—the ibis because it can eat anything, and the phoenix because it could survive without eating. Likewise organs, especially but not only the womb, had a certain representational affiliation with inanimate objects—containers, in particular. Ibid.

50. In *Lose Your Mother,* for instance, Saidiya Hartman gives an account of a political depression in the afterlife of slavery, a depression that is healed not through any kind of diasporic connection to homeland or reclaiming of ancestry in Ghana, but through "excavat[ing] a wound" and getting in touch with the rupture in her story itself. "Hartman seeks a utopia, not of national sovereignty or of cultural nationalism's sense of kinship, but one in which people find ways to move forward by coming together around violence and despair," Cvetkovich writes (*Depression*, 132). Cvetkovich is also interested in the way Jacqui Alexander's work in *This Bridge Called My Back*, as well as "Pedagogies of the Sacred," navigates experiences of colonialism, slavery, and genocide through the language of the sacred. "In her own way, [Alexander] is contributing to new conceptions of neoliberalism and globalization that explore how the operations of biopower target certain populations for destruction or create states of exception and permanent war. She understands liberation to entail a reclaiming of a self whose spirits have been depressed, a process that is a daily practice." The mention of biopower is interesting within Alexander's concertedly spiritual framework, especially through Cvetkovich's observation that "Alexander uses as a foundation for transnational politics and scholarship African-based cosmologies that begin from the premise that all human beings are important and connected" (135–37).

51. Cvetkovich, *Depression*, 139.

52. Ibid., 125.

53. The multiple recensions and the late and complicated manuscript traditions of the letters make both a second-century dating and authenticity a hard case to prove. As J. Gregory Given has argued, Ignatius of Antioch is "entirely the product of modern print culture, and his text emerges for our eyes not from Roman Asia Minor, or even Late Antique manuscripts, but from thorny ecclesiastical, political, and scholarly disputes of the sixteenth to nineteenth centuries." "Ignatius of Antioch and the Historiography of Early Christianity," PhD diss., Harvard University, 2019.

54. In a perhaps similar vein, Ignatius also describes those who "bear the name in wicked deceit" as "raving dogs who bite" (Eph. 7.2).

55. Elisabeth Castelli, *Martyrdom and Memory: Early Christian Culture Making* (New York: Columbia University Press, 2004), 83.

56. While not using the term ecology or biopolitical analytics, the following scholars do analyze the arena for its drama of imperial violence and self-understanding, attending to many actors, participants, and cultural dynamics in the spectacles. Brigitte Kahl,

Galatians Reimagined: Reading with the Eyes of the Vanquished (Minneapolis: Fortress Press, 2014); Allison Futrell, *Blood in the Arena: The Spectacle of Roman Power* (Austin: University of Texas Press, 1997); Frilingos, *Spectacles of Empire*; Barton, *Sorrows of the Ancient Romans.*

57. See Kotrosits, "Seeing Is Feeling."

58. Sacrifice has been naturalized as a (loaded) term around Jesus's death, and while it is clear that Ignatius is borrowing from earlier links between Jesus's death and sacrifice, links that seem especially strong after the practice of sacrifice in Judea was foreclosed by the destruction of the temple, the context for that link itself requires unpacking. First, as Andrew McGowan has argued, there is material context for such a link: associations often met in dining rooms adjoining temples, where sacrifices were performed; this is indeed often where they got their meat for their meals (and what may have been causing problems at the Corinthian gatherings). Association gatherings were also a primary place in which the dead were remembered. So the link between the practice of sacrifice — and its many various meanings — and the remembrance of the dead is not surprising. See McGowan, "Eucharist and Sacrifice: Cultic Tradition and Transformation in Early Christian Meals," in *Mahl und religiöse Identität im frühen Christentum*, ed. Matthias Klinghardt and Hal Taussig (Marburg: Francke Verlag, 2012). See also J. Wright Knust and Z. Varhelyi, eds., *Ancient Mediterranean Sacrifice* (Oxford: Oxford University Press, 2011), for a richer, more complicated picture of practices and meanings associated with the term "sacrifice."

59. Castelli, *Martyrdom and Memory*, 78.

CHAPTER FOUR

1. Benjamin, *Like Subjects, Love Objects*, 149.

2. Clifford Ando, *Imperial Ideology and the Provincial Loyalty in the Roman Empire* (Berkeley: University of California Press, 2000). On the communication and attraction of Roman power, see also Price, *Rituals and Power*, especially 234–48, also discussed more below.

3. Ando, *Imperial Ideology*.

4. Ibid., 336–405. See Carlos Noreña, *Imperial Ideals in the Roman West: Representation, Circulation, Power* (New York: Cambridge University Press, 2011), for another discussion of how Roman propaganda (including visual representation and iconography) created a certain ideological unity across a wide and various empire. Part of Noreña's argument is that representations of Roman power not only had a unifying effect but also managed to further fortify the authority of local elites.

5. See for instance Paul Zanker *The Power of Images in the Age of Augustus*, trans. Alan Shapiro (Ann Arbor: University of Michigan Press, 1990). One of the most striking instances of Roman visual propaganda (and the place of the image of the emperor within it), perhaps, is in the images at the Sebasteion at Aphrodisias.

6. Ibid.

7. See, for instance, Fergus Millar, "The World of the Golden Ass," *Journal of Roman Studies* 71 (1981): esp. 67–71.

8. This might contribute to an understanding of the hesitation about the divinity of emperors in the western empire and Rome itself, for instance, against the more emphatic embrace of the imperial cult in places like Asia Minor.

9. Caroline Vout, *Power and Eroticism in Imperial Rome* (New York: Cambridge University Press, 2007).

10. Ibid., 9.

11. Shadi Bartsch has written specifically on the gaze and its civic and political dynamics within Roman elite male culture. Her description of the penetrative power of the gaze in this culture is resonant with Benjamin's description above. Not only did the gaze have a physical, tactile, and so erotic edge, but it was full of danger and possibility. It was, in short, penetrating. Bartsch, *The Mirror of the Self: Sexuality, Self-Knowledge, and the Gaze in the Early Roman Empire* (Chicago: University of Chicago Press, 2006).

12. Price, *Rituals and Power*.

13. Ibid., 247.

14. It could be in fact that in scholarship, the Roman empire appears less a specific political framework than a figure for violence itself. See Philip A. Harland. "'Do Not Deny Me This Noble Death': Depictions of Violence in the Greek Novels and Apocryphal Acts," *Ancient Narrative* 14 (2017): 129–47.

15. With thanks to Elizabeth Castelli for posing the question this way at the Afterlives of Violence conference at Queen's University, Canada, in September 2016. There was of course the extremity of war and conquest in different places and times across the empire. But one of the most commonly evoked illustrations of the violence of the Romans is the amphitheaters and arena games. These were undoubtedly full of physical cruelty and bloodshed. Yet amphitheaters did not necessarily figure large in the outer provinces. Some estimate that there were only six in all of the Greek East, for instance. No amphitheaters were apparent in Roman Egypt. Hazel Dodge has summarized this archaeological history, though she has also argued that this accounts only for "purpose-built" amphitheaters, and not for other structures that might accommodate similar spectacles of bloodshed. Dodge, "Amphitheaters in the Roman East," in *Roman Amphitheaters and Spectacula, a Twenty-First-Century Perspective*, ed. Tony Wilmott (Oxford: Archaeopress, 2009), 29–46.

16. Ari Bryen's *Violence in Roman Egypt: A Study in Legal Interpretation* (Philadelphia: University of Pennsylvania Press, 2013) parses how violence was understood, described, and mediated in Roman Egypt, as well as playing out the particulars of the way the Roman legal system operated (ad hoc and improvised, not able to meet the demands of the vast number of petitioners consistently). As is consonant with Ben Kelly's study (referenced below), complaints were addressed often on the basis of the status of the person who made them and were not decided on the basis of a code of law as much as they accrued to form legal precedent. In pushing back against contemporary critiques of violence that are overgeneralized and too beholden to contemporary legal/criminal

categories, Bryen seeks a more carefully historical reflection on how acts become violations, and on what basis. He writes, "violence is not a thing or an act (though acts
can indeed be termed violent), but instead an ethical label, one that is located within
matrices of power and of what one considers acceptable and unacceptable. As with all
categories of ethical and moral evaluation it is subject to contest" (52).

17. Translation from Robert D. Sider, *Christian and Pagan in the Roman Empire* (Washington, DC: Catholic University Press of America, 2001), 8–9.

18. Scholars have largely rejected the notion that Tertullian was a cleric, following the work
of Timothy Barnes, *Tertullian: A Historical and Literary Study* (Oxford: Clarendon
Press, 1971), 3–12 and 13–21. They, however, routinely read Tertullian as an architect of
orthodoxy and a figure who contributed to, and even defined, the particular vocabu-
lary of Latin Christianity, for instance, W. H. C. Frend, *The Rise of Christianity* (Minneapolis: Fortress Press, 1984), 282–84; Geoffrey D. Dunn, *Tertullian*, Early Church
Fathers Series (London: Routledge, 2004), 10; Eric Osborn, *Tertullian: First Theologian
of the West* (Cambridge: Cambridge University Press, 1997). The recent encyclopedic
treatment of Christianity in Roman Africa, for example, positions Tertullian as the
first major figure in the development of the African church; see J. Patout Burns Jr. and
Robin Jensen, *Christianity in Roman Africa: The Development of Its Practices and Beliefs*
(Grand Rapids, MI: Eerdmans, 2014). Regarding martyrdom in particular, see Wiebke
Bähnk, *Von der Notwendigkeit: Die Theologie des Martyriums bei Tertullian* (Göttingen:
Vandenhoeck & Ruprecht, 2001). Yet Tertullian's position as an architect of orthodoxy
has also been plagued by questions about his penchant for prophecy and the so-called
"Montanist" movement. In fact, Tertullian's writings have often defied scholars' at-
tempts to plot him in the history of Christianity; see David Wilhite, "Tertullian," in *An-
cient African Christianity: Introduction to a Unique Context and Tradition* (New York:
Routledge, 2017), 108–35.

19. James Rives, *Religion and Authority in Roman Carthage from Augustus to Constantine*
(Oxford: Clarendon Press, 1995), 23.

20. Ibid., 214–15; on the persistence of Libyan and Pheonician languages and cultural practices, see David J. Mattingly, "From One Colonialism to Another: Imperialism and
the Maghreb" and "Identity and Discrepancy," *Imperialism, Power, and Identity: Experiencing the Roman Empire* (Princeton: Princeton University Press, 2011), 236–45. In
the latter essay, Mattingly discusses examples from Roman Tripolitana, to the east of
Africa Proconsularis, and its own province in the fourth century. See also Leslie Dossey, *Peasant and Empire in Christian North Africa* (Berkeley: University of California
Press, 2010), 13; David Wilhite, *Tertullian, the African* (Berlin: Walter DeGruyter Press,
2007), 29; Wilhite, *Ancient African Christianity*, 52–55; and Fergus Millar, "Local Cultures in the Roman Empire: Libyan, Punic, and Latin in Roman Africa," *Journal of
Roman Studies* 58 (1968): 126–34.

21. See Dossey, *Peasant and Empire*. In fact, it takes centuries before Roman-style dwellings
and social customs become the norm for rural populations. The veneration of traditional gods likewise continues into the Roman period, for instance, the cult of Saturn;
see Rives, *Religion and Authority*, 142–51.

22. Rives, *Religion and Authority*, 101–3.

23. Dossey, *Peasant and Empire*, 7; Mattingly, "Landscapes of Imperialism, Africa: A Landscape of Opportunity?," in *Imperialism, Power, and Identity*, 146–66.

24. Rives, *Religion and Authority*, 27.

25. Dossey, *Peasant and Empire*, 15, and David J. Mattingly and R. Bruce Hitchner, "Roman Africa: An Archaeological Review," *Journal of Roman Studies* 85 (1995): especially 180–87.

26. These tasks included tax collection, public and economic order, maintenance of civic structures and cultic festivities, and, not least, running the courts and civic councils. See Rives, *Religion and Authority*, 28–51; Martin Goodman, *The Roman World, 44 BC– AD 180* (London: Routledge, 1997), 111.

27. Mattingly, "From One Colonialism to Another," and "Identity and Discrepancy," in *Imperialism, Power, and Identity*, 63 and 236–45, respectively. Again Mattingly's examples in the second chapter are drawn from Tripolitana, though inscriptional evidence from Roman Africa generally testifies to a similar pattern of local involvement.

28. Take, for instance, the philosopher and novelist Apuleius, who was born in Madauros (west of Carthage) and educated in Athens and Carthage, or the Severan emperors, who hailed from the Punic town of Lepcis Magna, the very town from which Tertullian's own clan, the Septimii, likely came. Wilhite, *Tertullian, the African*, 30.

29. See for instance Greg Woolf, *Tales of the Barbarians: Ethnography and Empire in the Roman West* (Malden, MA: Wiley Blackwell, 2014), especially 32–58.

30. Translation Sider, *Christian and Pagan*, 56–57.

31. Translation Vincent Hunink, *De Pallio* (Amsterdam: J. C. Gieben Press, 2005), found online at http://www.tertullian.org/articles/hunink_de_pallio.htm.

32. Translation Sider, *Christian and Pagan*, 18 (italics added).

33. Ari Bryen, "Martyrdom, Rhetoric, and the Politics of Procedure," *Classical Antiquity* 33, no. 2 (2014): 244. Such fascinations mark Greek novels and philosophical lives, martyrological texts, petitions, various inscriptions, and other Christian sources from the late first and into the third century; see also Bryen, 243 and 276. Maud Gleason has identified a preoccupation with juridical scenes in Apuleius's *Metamorphoses* and the *Apocryphal Acts of the Apostles*. Her analysis distinguishes between "Christian" and non-Christian narratives, as they relate to the body as a guarantor of truth claims. We read this literature as participating in a broader preoccupation with Roman juridical scenes; see Gleason, "Truth Contests and Talking Corpses," in *Constructions of the Classical Body*, ed. James Porter (Ann Arbor: University of Michigan Press, 1999), 287– 313. Brent Shaw has attended to juridical scenes in dreams; while his focus is on Christian literature (a number of his examples are post-Constantinian, so fall outside our discussion), he finds corollaries in Artemidorus and Seneca; see "Judicial Nightmares and Christian Memory," *Journal of Early Christian Studies* 11, no. 4 (2003): 533–63.

34. Bryen examines pre-Decian martyrological texts, based on the view that the Decian legislation changed the political situation of Christians and the methods of interrogation and trial; "Martyrdom, Rhetoric," 254.

35. Ibid., 249.

36. Ibid., 252. Among others, Bryen cites Ando's study.

37. Bryen, "Martyrdom, Rhetoric," 257.

38. Ibid., 259.

39. Inverted in that the accused wields the power of proper judgment, rather than the accused. Brent Shaw, in an analysis that complements Gleason, has considered how such inversions routinely imagined the tortured, suffering body as locus of that truth; see "Body/Power/Identity: Passion of the Martyrs," *Journal of Early Christian Studies* 4, no. 3 (1996): 269–312.

40. Saundra Schwartz, "Chronotypes of Justice in the Greek Novel: Trials in Narrative Spaces," in *Spaces of Justice in the Roman World*, ed. Francesco de Angelis (Leiden: Brill, 2010), 331. See for example the trials of Chaereas and Mithradates in *Chariton* (1.4–6 and 5.4–9, respectively), the trial of Harbrocomes in *Xenophon of Ephesus* (3.12–4.4), and the series of trials in *Heliodorus*.

41. Schwartz, "Chronotypes of Justice," 333. Trial and courtroom scenes are a prominent feature of the Christian imagination. This is true of non-Christian martyrological literature, as well. See for instance Shaw, "Juridical Nightmares and Christian Memory," Herbert A. Musurillo, *The Acts of the Pagan Martyrs: Acta Alexandrinorum* (Oxford: Clarendon Press, 1954).

42. Saundra Schwartz, "The Trial Scene in the Greek Novel and in Acts," in *Contextualizing Acts: Lukan Narrative and Greco-Roman Discourse*, ed. Todd Penner and Caroline Vander Stichele, Symposium 20 (Atlanta: Society of Biblical Literature, 2003), 104.

43. Ibid., 103. Schwartz attempts to infer lived material circumstances and political positionings from the novels' implicit ideologies and referents. But her work also considers the ways these juridical scenes played out the pressures and desires of Greek elite authors and audiences under Rome. While the juridical scenes and authorities in the novels are generally not Roman ones, Schwartz argues that the novels nonetheless represent Greek colonial (and elite) negotiations of Roman rule. The novels' particular interest in trials reflects not only a Greek-centered nostalgia for Greek political autonomy and uphold a sense of cultural superiority but, as Schwartz writes, also reflect a "heightened sensitivity to the tensions and dynamics of living subject to a political order with overlapping legal systems." Schwartz, "Rome in the Greek Novel? Images and Ideas of Empire in Chariton's Persia," *Arethusa* 36 (Fall 2003): 378. See also Schwartz "Chronotypes of Justice," 332.

44. Schwartz, "Trial Scene," 114.

45. Ibid.

46. Ibid., 114–15.

47. Saundra Schwartz, "Dressing Up, Dressing Down: False Enslavement in the Greek Novels," in *Éclats de littérature grecque d'Homère à Pascal Quignard: Mélanges offerts à Suzanne Saïd*, ed. Suzanne Saïd et al. (Paris: Presses Universitaires de Paris Ouest, 2012), 175–89.

48. Angelos Chaniotis, "Under the Watchful Eyes of the Gods: Divine Justice in Hellenistic and Roman Asia Minor," in *The Greco-Roman East: Politics, Culture, Society*, ed. S. Colvin (Cambridge: Cambridge University Press, 2004), 1–43.

49. Ibid., 42. Chaniotis, however, problematically uses the term "secular," a modern notion that artificially separates cultic devotion from civic processes, to refer to Roman authorities and juridical procedures, despite the fact that in these very inscriptions, as

well as in the language and practice around imperial divinity and power that we have recounted above, this separation is nonsensical.

50. Ibid., 2.

51. Benjamin Kelly, *Petitions, Litigation, and Social Control in Roman Egypt* (New York: Oxford University Press, 2011).

52. Ibid., 36.

53. Ibid.

54. Ibid., 37.

55. Ibid., 210–43.

56. In his conclusion, he parallels his work to that of Paul Zanker, whose book *The Power of Images in the Age of Augustus* (Ann Arbor: University of Michigan Press, 1990) sees visual representations as points of transmission of Roman ideology. Kelly, *Petitions, Litigation, and Social Control in Roman Egypt*, 328.

57. Scott, *Fantasy of Feminist History*.

58. It may be that the magistrates were appointed by the town council, rather than elected by the populous, see Rives, *Religion and Authority*, 29.

59. Under Augustus, some governors were appointed by the emperor himself, called *legati Augusti pro praetore*. The practice of the Senate's appointing governors dates to the Republican period and continued into the Imperial; see John Richardson, "Provincial Administration," in *The Oxford Handbook of Roman Law and Society*, ed. Paul J. du Plessis, Clifford Ando, and Kaius Tuori (Oxford: Oxford University Press, 2016), 117.

60. E.g., the *duoviri*. For the pattern in Roman Carthage, see Rives, *Religion and Authority*, 29–39; for the general pattern, see Saskia T. Roselaar, "Local Administration," and Leanne Bablitz, "Roman Courts and Private Arbitration," in du Plessis, Ando, and Tuori, *Oxford Handbook of Roman Law and Society*, 126 and 237.

61. Christopher J. Furman, "Police Functions and Public Order," in du Plessis, Ando, and Tuori, *Oxford Handbook of Roman Law and Society*, 300.

62. Richardson, "Provincial Administration," 120–12, and Roselaar, "Local Administration," 130.

63. Goodman, *Roman World*, 112.

64. On the composition of this legion, see Yann Le Bohec, *The Imperial Roman Army*, rpt. ed. (London: Routledge, 2000), 90 and 174–75. There is also evidence of a garrison in Carthage, and retired veterans populated the region (as they did other Roman colonies); see Mattingly and Hitchner, "Roman Africa," 175.

65. Rome's presence was most apparent in the civic center and less on display in other areas of the Carthaginian territory; see Mattingly and Hitchner, "Roman Africa," 182–83.

66. For instance, the study of "reading communities" by William A. Johnson, *Readers and Reading Culture in the High Roman Empire* (Oxford: Oxford University Press, 2010), and the study of Roman libraries by George W. Houston, *Inside Roman Libraries: Book Collections and Their Management in Antiquity* (Chapel Hill: University of North Carolina Press, 2014). For the circulation of texts amongst Christians, see Harry Y. Gamble, *Books and Readers in the Early Church* (New Haven: Yale University Press, 1995), 82–143, and Karen Haines-Eitzen, *Guardians of Letters: Literacy, Power, and the Transmitters of Early Christian Literature* (Oxford: Oxford University Press, 2000).

67. For example, Tertullian's knowledge of "Marcionism" comes from textual sources that he has amassed, and not from encounters with followers of Marcion in Roman North Africa, because none existed there. David E. Wilhite on Marcionites, "Marcionites in Africa: What Did Tertullian Know and When Did He Invent It?," *Perspectives in Religious Studies* 4 (2016): 437–52. Some of his sources were excerpts of texts; David Rankin, *From Clement to Origen: The Social and Historical Context of the Church Fathers*, 2nd ed. (New York: Routledge, 2016), 57, and Gamble, *Books and Readers*, 113 and 152. It is unclear whether Tertullian's literary sources came from his own private collection, items shared amongst a group of local elites, libraries, or some combination of these venues. Additionally, Tertullian circulated and published his own works and likely uses these same channels to do so; see Gamble, *Books and Readers*, 118–19.

68. This reading most widely advanced in Anglo-American scholarship by Timothy Barnes, who cast doubt on Tertullian's clerical position and advocated for a more sociohistorical reading that attended to his fluency with the second sophistic; see *Tertullian*, especially 211–32. While there remains a tendency amongst scholars of early Christianity to read Tertullian in a trajectory of orthodoxy that culminates in Latin Christianity, historians have also pushed for readings of Tertullian that read him apart from any specifically ecclesiastical or doctrinal context, most recently, Barton and Boyarin, *Imagine No Religion*, 55–118. They write: "Tertullian was not much interested in authorizing an institutional ecclesia. An abstract ecclesia played a part in Tertullian's thought as the imaginary, transcendent, and longed for unity and harmony of Christians" (57).

69. See *De virginibus velandis* and *De carne Christi*. For a discussion of these treatises and how they connect to Tertullian's larger theological interests and polemics, see Carly Daniel-Hughes, *The Salvation of the Flesh in Tertullian of Carthage: Dressing for the Resurrection* (New York: Palgrave Macmillan, 2011), 63–114.

70. Tertullian uses Perpetua's vision of heaven as an exception to the general rule that he posits in which souls and bodies will be reunited in the resurrection. Thomas Heffernan notes that Tertullian provides our first witness to the circulation of the *Martyrdom of Perpetua*, though the vision Tertullian cites is actually attributed to Saturus in the extant manuscripts of this text; see *The Passion of Perpetua and Felicity* (Oxford: Oxford University Press, 2012), 66.

71. The soldier's execution seems to have been in Rome; see Éric Rebillard (citing Le Bohec and Duval), *Christians and Their Many Identities in Late Antiquity: North Africa, 200–450 CE* (Ithaca: Cornell University Press, 2012), 40.

72. Wilhite, *Tertullian, the African*, 164–67.

73. *Apol.* 5.3 and 2.6–7, respectively. Barnes, *Tertullian*, 105.

74. Anthony Birley, "Persecutors and Martyrs in Tertullian's Africa," *Bulletin of the Institute of Archaeology* 29 (1992): 37–86.

75. Cecilia Ames, "Roman Religion in the Vision of Tertullian," in *A Companion to Roman Religion*, ed. Jörg Rüpke (Oxford: Wiley Blackwell, 2011), 457–70.

76. Wilhite, *Tertullian, the Africa*, 21–22 and the detailed study by Robert D. Sider, *Ancient Rhetoric and the Art of Tertullian* (Oxford: Oxford University Press, 1971).

77. *De test. an* 1.5, translation Sider, *Christian and Pagan*, 74.

78. Translation Geoffrey Dunn, *Tertullian*, 115.

79. Translation slightly modified from Dunn, *Tertullian*, 115.

80. *Crudelem deum, qui non intellegit, credit* (Corpus Christianorum Series Latina 2.1082). Translation slightly modified from Dunn, *Tertullian*, 115.

81. Barton and Boyarin, *Imagine No Religion*, 98. We elect not to capitalize *deus* following Carlin Barton, who notes that doing so gives "it both a higher status and very particular Christian flavor," *Imagine No Religion*, 116. As she argues, in Tertullian's writing *deus* is ambiguous, sometimes referring to a particular god, but also referring more generically to a concept that Tertullian treats as shared with Romans and those who did not participate in Christ assemblies.

82. Barton, *Imagine No Religion*, 99.

83. See Millar, "World of the Golden Ass," 66.

84. Judith Perkins has pursued this reading of Tertullian's writings most closely, highlighting his valuation of suffering and pain (a move shared, according to Perkins, by others in the empire). She points to his valorization of the "vulnerable body" in writings like *Adversus Marcionem* or *De carne Christi* as a challenge to Roman cultural values. Contra Perkins, however, it would seem that Tertullian picks up precarity only to locate it elsewhere—precarity is a condition from which Tertullian strives to spare Christ, and it is the condition he regularly assigns to damnable others, or off-loads onto female bodies; see Daniel-Hughes, *Salvation of the Flesh*, especially 60–91.

85. Translation Sider, *Christian and Pagan*, 10.

86. *Sed illud solum exspectator . . . : confessio nominis . . .* (Corpus Christianorum Series Latina 1.87).

87. Dunn, *Tertullian*, 44. Commonly scholars have seen Tertullian's rancor and passion for death to increase over the course of his writing, resulting from the influence of apocalyptic sectarianism (in the form of the "New Prophecy") on his thought. This basic narrative has worked to explain the less palatable parts of Tertullian's writing to his modern readers, and to shield "proto-orthodoxy" from Tertullian's seemingly absolutist rhetoric, his asceticism and moral rigorism.

88. For instance, Judith Perkins, *The Suffering Self: Pain and Narrative Representation in the Early Christian Era* (London: Routledge Press, 1995); Shaw, "Body/Power/Identity; Castelli, *Martyrdom and Memory*; Stephanie Cobb, *Dying to Be Men: Gender and Language in Early Christian Martyr Texts* (New York: Columbia University Press, 2008); Shelly Matthews, *Perfect Martyr: The Stoning of Stephen and the Construction of Christian Identity* (Cambridge: Harvard University Press, 2010).

89. See for example, Daniel-Hughes, "The Perils of Idolatrous Garb: Tertullian and Christian Belonging in Roman Carthage," in *Religious Competition in the Greco-Roman World*, ed. Nathaniel P. DesRosiers and Lily C. Vuong (Atlanta: SBL Press, 2016), 15–26.

90. Rebillard, *Christians and Their Many Identities in Late Antiquity*. See also, Barnes, *Tertullian*, 71, and Burns and Jensen, *Christianity in Roman Africa*, L.

91. See Burns and Jensen, *Christianity in Roman Africa*, 87–88.

92. Associations include synagogues, *ekklesia*, *thiasoi*, and *collegia*. See especially Philip A. Harland, *Dynamics of Identity in the World of the Early Christians: Associations, Judeans, and Cultural Minorities* (New York: T & T Clark, 2009).

93. John S. Kloppenborg and Steve G. Wilson, eds., *Voluntary Associations in the Greco-*

Roman World (New York: Routledge, 2002); Harland, *Dynamics of Identity*, as well as *Associations, Synagogues and Congregations: Claiming a Place in Ancient Mediterranean Society* (Minneapolis: Fortress Press, 2003).

94. In addition to Kotrosits, *Rethinking Christian Identity*, see Brent Shaw's deconstruction of the term Christian as a phenomenon in specific confrontation with Roman power in "The Myth of the Neronian Persecution," *Journal of Roman Studies* 105 (November 2015): 73–100. Also helpful is Birgit van der Lans and Jan Bremmer, "Tacitus and the Persecution of the Christians: An Invention of Tradition?" *Eirene* 53 (2017): 299–331.

95. For the extended argument, see Kotrosits, *Rethinking Early Christian Identity*, 47–84.

96. Kotrosits, *Rethinking Early Christian Identity*, 47–84. HeidiWendt, "*Ea Superstitione*: Christian Martyrdom and the Religion of Freelance Experts," *Journal of Roman Studies* 105 (November 2015): 183–202.

97. Perkins, *Suffering Self*.

98. This of course includes the Acts of the Apostles, which has a history of associations with the martyrological tradition, largely because of its depiction of the stoning of Stephen. It also includes, as I discuss in the next chapter, the Gospel of Mark's "little apocalypse" in Mark 13, which seems to depict a scene of torture and confession (13:11–13), as well as the book of Revelation, which describes the violent death of two "witnesses" (*martys*), both of which have elicited connections to the larger and later body of texts classed as martyrological literature.

99. "There is a battle for us," concludes Tertullian in his *Apologeticum*, "because we are called to trial in court so that we may fight there for the truth. . . . Carry on, good magistrates; you will become much better in the eyes of the people if you sacrifice the Christians for them. Crucify us—torture us—condemn us—destroy us! Your injustice is proof of our innocence" (*Apol.* 50.2 and 12).

CHAPTER FIVE

1. See especially Judith Butler's *Bodies That Matter*, published in 1993, which restaged dimensions of her earlier argument about the discursive construction of sex in *Gender Trouble*, and did so with a pointed attention to the ways the very materialization of bodies is part of social-discursive and regulatory machinery, especially after pushback on the linguistic/discursive (and thus apparently nonmaterial) framing of her argument. In her first chapter, Butler waxes on the pun of "matter" in her title: "*Materia* in Latin denotes the stuff out of which things are made, not only the timber for houses and ships but whatever serves as nourishment for infants: nutrients that act as extensions of the mother's body. Insofar as matter appears in these cases to be invested with a certain capacity to originate and to compose that for which it also supplies the principle of legibility, then matter is clearly defined by a certain power of creation and rationality that is for the most part divested from the more modern empirical deployments of the term. To speak within these classical contexts of *bodies that matter* is not an idle pun, for to be material means to materialize, where the principle of that materialization is

precisely what 'matters' about that body, its very intelligibility. In this sense, to know the significance of something is to know how and why it matters, where 'to matter' means at once 'to materialize' and 'to mean'" (32).

2. On the concepts of deconstruction and *différance*, see especially the essays in *Writing and Difference*, trans. Alan Bass, rpt. ed. (Chicago: University of Chicago Press, 1993).

3. Derrida, *Monolinguism of the Other*.

4. Ibid., 1.

5. Ibid., 45.

6. "Quite far from dissolving the always relative specificity, however cruel, of situatons of linguistic oppression or colonial expropriation, this prudent and differentiated univer-salization must account, and I would even say that it is the only way one can account, for the *determinable* possibility of a subservience and a hegemony. And even account for a terror inside languages (inside languages there is a terror, soft, discreet, or glaring; that is our subject). For contrary to what one is often tempted to believe, the master is nothing. And he does not have exclusive possession of anything. Because the master does not possess exclusively, and *naturally*, what he calls his language, because, what-ever he wants or does, he cannot maintain any relations of property or identity that are natural, national, congenital, or ontological, with it, because he can give substance to and articulate [*dire*] this appropriation only in the course of an unnatural process of politico-phantasmatic constructions, because language is not his natural possession, he can, thanks to that very fact, pretend historically, through the rape of a cultural usur-pation, which means always essentially colonial, to appropriate it in order to impose it as 'his own.'" Ibid., 23.

7. As Derrida recounts, Jews of Algeria received French citizenship in 1870, only to have it revoked, and then regained, over the course of the next eighty years.

8. Derrida, *Monolinguism of the Other*, 39 (emphasis mine).

9. Chow, *Not Like a Native Speaker*, 30.

10. Derrida, *Monolinguism of the Other*, 50.

11. The word also has distinctly Christian intonations, as his use of terms like "universal hostage," "sacrifice," and "messenicity," suggest.

12. Indeed despite the tensions between universals and cultural and political specificities that characterize this text, Derrida's legacy has fallen strongly on the side of the abstract and universalizing. This is not surprising, of course, since so many of Derrida's other texts theorize precisely in that vein.

13. Given the critique of "martyrdom literature" as a category presented in the previous chapter, I am more interested in the more expansive category of noble death traditions of which these later stories are partaking, and from which the term "martyr" derives.

14. The evidence for bilingualism in antiquity is plentiful and widespread, and gives a stronger sense of context for these reflections. J. N. Adams, Mark Janse, and Simon Swain, eds., *Bilingualism in Ancient Society: Language Contact and the Written Word* (New York: Oxford University Press, 2003). Though one need not speak multiple lan-guages to be caught in the problem of dominant languages (as Derrida shows).

15. See Daniel Boyarin, *Dying for God: Martyrdom and the Making of Christianity and*

Judaism (Stanford: Stanford University Press, 1999); Virginia Burrus, *Saving Shame: Martyrs, Saints, and Other Abject Subjects* (Philadelphia: University of Pennsylvania Press, 2007); Castelli, *Martyrdom and Memory*; Cobb, *Dying to Be Men*; Perkins, *Suffering Self* and *Roman Imperial Identities in the Early Christian Era* (New York: Routledge, 2009).

16. In Mark 1:23–34, Jesus has his first encounter with an unclean spirit, who says, "What do you want with us, Jesus the Nazarene? Have you come to destroy us? I know you, who you are: the holy one of God!" (1:24). Interestingly, Jesus is identified here geographically (from Nazareth) as well as being called the "holy one of God." But in this scene people have already begun talking, and "reports about him went out in all the countryside surrounding Galilee" (1:28). In the episode immediately following, the "whole city" is at the door of the house where he is healing (1:33), and the text says he "doesn't permit the demons to speak because they knew him" (1:35). That obviously doesn't work for long, since the Gerasene demoniac speaks to and names him later (5:7–8).

17. See also Mark 1:44 and 3:12, for instance.

18. In 3:14 he forms the group of twelve disciples to be sent out to "proclaim" (*kerussein*) and drive out demons.

19. This trial ("and you will stand before governors and kings for the sake of me as a testimony [*marturion*] to them . . .") has often been interpreted as an instance of persecution against early followers of Jesus. However, Mark 13 seems to be mishmash of references to various forms of strife plaguing the Judean community from both without and within, including the chaos and cataclysm of the Roman-Judean war. Not incidentally, the chapter mentions "false prophets and false Christs" who perform signs and wonders "so as to deceive" (13:21), suggesting that perhaps one of the struggles for Judeans following Jesus was how to determine authenticity and expertise. Heidi Wendt's work has illustrated how this language was common rhetoric for the independent or "freelance" experts on (ethnically coded) religious traditions who pervaded the social world of the ancient Mediterranean. She has also suggested that such figures were seen as suspicious by imperial authorities, in part because they had no official links to cultural/social/religious institutions, and they were regularly subject to legislation trying to target and describe them. Indeed, she suggests that one way to understand "martyrdom" is that so-called Christian martyrs were such freelance experts, since the punishments and accusations were so similar. See Wendt, *At the Temple Gates: The Religion of Freelance Experts in the Roman Empire* (New York: Oxford University Press, 2016), and "*Ea Superstitione.*"

20. See Adela Yarbro Collins, *Mark: A Commentary*, Hermeneia (Minneapolis: Fortress Press, 2007), 730–32.

21. See Ludger Schenke, *Der gekreuzigte Christus: Versuch einer literarkristischen und traditionsgeschichtlen Bestimmung der vormarkinischen Passionsgeschichte* (Stuttgart: Katholisches Bibelwerk, 1974).

22. See Collins, *Mark*, 734, 755.

23. This is the way Stanley Stowers has treated Paul's claims to authority and specialized

knowledge with the Corinthians, for example. See Stowers, "Kinds of Myths, Meals, and Power: Paul and the Corinthians," in *Redescribing Paul and the Corinthians*, ed. Ron Cameron and Merrill P. Miller (Atlanta: Society of Biblical Literature, 2011).

24. One might add that these voices become one to painfully ironic effect: "*Alethos utos o anthropos uios theou*" spoken by the torturer seems to mock, rather than proclaim in earnest.

25. More on the exemplary and symbolic status of Hebrew heroes at large below. On the exemplary status of the heroes of noble death narratives, see Patterson, *Beyond the Passion*, 39–52. Patterson is building on the earlier work of Nickelsburg, *Resurrection, Immortality, and Eternal Life in Intertestamental Judaism*.

26. Chow writes, "In addition to inducing in the colonized an unfulfillable yearning for linguistic purity and thus a general sense of incompetence and disability, this mono-linguism of the other legitimates itself by getting rid of likely competitors, by making sure that native languages such as Arabic and Berber become increasingly marginal and useless. . . . The monolinguism of the colonizer means that the development and re-finement of the mind that come with the literary, philosophical and humanistic learn-ing . . . were in Algeria's case allowed to take place only in French." *Not like a Native Speaker*, 24.

27. As Chow's other work has shown. See Chow, *Writing Diaspora*.

28. See also Stuart Hall, "Cultural Identity and Diaspora," in *Theorizing Diaspora*, ed. Jana Evans Braziel and Anita Mannur (Malden, MA: Blackwell, 2003).

29. The French philosopher Louis Althusser theorizes the production of identity through state institutions, and to illustrate this dynamic (which he terms "interpellation") he used the example of the police officer calling out to someone on the street, and the "someone" turning in response. The juridical framing is an important one, and has been taken up in the history of philosophy and contemporary theory by many thinkers, Michel Foucault and Judith Butler being two of the most prominent. Althusser, *Lenin and Philosophy and Other Essays* (New York: Monthly Review Press, 1971). See for in-stance Butler's longest elaboration of interpellation as a concept in *The Psychic Life of Power: Theories in Subjection* (Stanford: Stanford University Press, 1993).

30. Chow, *Not like a Native Speaker*, 7.

31. Chow also notes, quite significantly, that Fanon's work prefigures ("foreshadows") Althusser's scene of interpellation. Ibid., 4.

32. Ibid., 3.

33. Ibid., 5.

34. See Mark 5:41, 7:34, 14:36, 15:34.

35. "When far away from home, it is often the taste of something familiar that reminds us not only of what we have eaten before, but also of who we are. To be sure, there is noth-ing extraordinary about such a revelation, but what is unusual is that it is consumption, normally considered a passive, unproductive act, that serves as the agent of generating cultural difference, at a time when such difference is thought to be lost or in the pro-cess of disappearing." Chow, *Not like a Native Speaker*, 85–86.

36. Page DuBois, *Torture and Truth* (New York: Routledge, 1991), 35–36.

37. Pseudo-Linus, Martyrdom of the Blessed Apostle Paul. The earlier version notes that

it was only after Paul stopped speaking, and was silent, that the executioner cut off his head.

38. "In total disregard for the Law, Jason changed the nation's whole mode of life and its polity; not only did he lay out a gymnasium on the citadel of our native land but he also rescinded the service of the Temple" (4 Macc. 4:19–21).

39. Steven N. Mason, "*Philosophiai*: Graeco-Roman, Judean and Christian," in *Voluntary Associations in the Graeco-Roman World*, ed. John S. Kloppenborg and Stephen G. Wilson (New York: Routledge, 1996), 42–43.

40. Ibid., 35–36.

41. See Wendt, "*Ea Superstitione*."

42. See Rajak for instance on the overassimilation of "Jewish martyrdom" to "Christian martyrdom," and what she describes as the full entanglement of Greek elements with Jewish ones in the story. *Jewish Dialogue with Greece and Rome*, 99–124. Rajak also highlights the ethnic/national investments in 4 Maccabees, but the implicit suggestion is of course that there is something "more Greek" about 4 Maccabees, and thus more culturally mixed. Boyarin for instance posits 4 Maccabees as arising contemporaneously with and/or geographically close to Ignatius, Polycarp, and the martyrs of Lyons. These texts share a "cultural world." *Dying for God*, 115–17. Boyarin in this book posits that the distinction between Jew and Christian makes little sense, though he is hardly consistent on this point. He understands Christian as a referential identity, for instance, throughout the book. But I do agree with Boyarin about shared cultural worlds, literary interaction across our presumed identity categories, and general indistinctions between these categories.

43. See especially Jana Evans Braziel and Anita Mannur, eds., *Theorizing Diaspora* (Malden, MA: Wiley-Blackwell, 2003); Brian Keith Axel, *The Nation's Tortured Body: Violence, Representation, and the Formation of a Sikh 'Diaspora'* (Durham: Duke University Press, 2001); Chow, *Writing Diaspora*.

44. Kotrosits, *Rethinking Early Christian Identity* and "Diaspora Theory and the End of Early Christianity and Early Christian Identity," presented at the Annual Meeting for the Society of Biblical Literature, San Diego, 22–25 November 2014.

45. Tessa Rajak has observed not just the "nationalist" and masculinist aspirations of 4 Maccabees, but the thoroughly "de-personalized" character of the story. Not only are the mother and the sons never named, but Eleazar itself is a "generic name, given in both the Letter of Aristeas and in 3 Maccabees to the venerable priest in the story." Rajak continues that this tendency, one she ascribes to "Jewish martyrology," "discourages any possible focus on personalities and, ultimately, to curb the cult of individuals. The martyrs must represent Israel as a whole." Jesus's death in the Gospel of Mark, as I've read it above, fits this description, substantiating Rajak's observation—though she contrasts this tendency to the later Christian martyr cult and, of course, would not place Mark as "Jewish martyrology." But Rajak's point additionally corroborates a reading of these kinds of stories as not really about the singularity of heroes at all, and as perhaps holding more unexceptional experiences of violence and grief. Rajak, *Jewish Dialogue with Greece and Rome*, 118.

46. See especially Cobb, *Dying to Be Men*, chap. 4.

47. Likewise, the transformation of Eleazar's old and feeble body into an athletic and virile physicality under torture is a fantasy that *registers* vulnerability as much as it offers an imagination of overcoming it.

48. As Steve Mason has shown, part of that identification is clearly about cooperation with foreign rulers. Daniel seemingly offers Josephus the possibility that "a Jew may participate fully in the apparatus of foreign government *without* becoming tainted by the association." "Josephus, Daniel and the Flavian House," in *Josephus and the History of the Greco-Roman Period: Essays in Memory of Morton Smith*, ed. Fausto Parente and Joseph Sievers (Leiden: Brill, 1994), 164. Though it's obvious that both Daniel and Josephus both express the complications of that cooperation.

49. Translation from David L. Eastman, *The Ancient Martyrdom Accounts of Peter and Paul* (Atlanta: Society of Biblical Literature Press, 2015).

50. This is also echoed in the extracanonical Gospel of Truth, for instance, in which the Father's inaccessibility, abandonment, and implication in violence regarding those for whom he ostensibly cares are continually affectively revalenced as and with pleasurable experience. In that text, Jesus's death on a "tree" becomes fruit that one can enjoy guiltlessly. See Kotrosits, *Rethinking Early Christian Identity*, chap. 6.

51. See chapter 2. "I desire the bread of God, which is the flesh of Jesus Christ, from the seed of David; and for drink I desire his blood, which is imperishable love" (Rom. 7.3).

52. Again, the recent debates surrounding the dating and authenticity of Ignatius's letters mean that his use of the term Christian and his references to *christianismos* are far from firm ground on which to build any notion of a second-century social phenomenon.

53. As Ignatius writes, "For me, ask only that I have power both inside and out, that I not only speak but also have the desire, that I not only be called a Christian but also be found one. For if I am found a Christian, I can also be called one, and then be faithful, when I am no longer visible in the world" (Romans 3:2). He writes to the Magnesians that "it is fitting not only to be called Christians, but also to be Christians" (4:1). The notion that for Ignatius, his Christian-ness is in question until he dies, that he anticipates the revelation of his being Christian in the arena, would seem to confirm that 'Christian' carries the valence of imperial targeting, if not torture-induced truth production, rather than being an identity with obvious or given content. The 'truth' of being a Christian, for Ignatius, is revealed primarily in the crosshairs of state discipline. Indeed the only real content to "being Christian" for Ignatius is imitating Christ in death (as someone else who died under the auspices of the state): he hopes to become worthy of "the name" by dying honorably and voluntarily. In anticipation of his death, he figures himself as Christ, or as about to "attain" Christ, thus becoming a "sacrifice" for those in the *ekklesiai*. Consonant with the noble death traditions that shaped understandings and representations of Jesus's death, for Ignatius, "Christian" is what gives *meaning* to his death or, put differently, what *rescues his death from meaninglessness*, rather than what causes it.

54. On the power to name in the ancient world, and the ambivalences around that power, see Perkins, *Roman Imperial Identities*, chap. 6.

CHAPTER SIX

1. Brooke Holmes discusses this scene in the context of medical diagnosis and bodily symptoms, noting Ovid's description of the pulse of the woman-statue (who is only later named Galatea), which "leaps to meet the thumb that takes it," as well as her blush at Pygmalion's kisses. "The blush," Holmes writes, "provoked by an encounter between two people, subject to praise and blame, realized at the intersection of the voluntary and the involuntary—deftly captures the complexity of Galatea's change from object to subject." *The Symptom and the Subject* (Princeton: Princeton University Press, 2010), 193.

2. This is of course not necessarily how asceticism should be read, as I'll discuss below.

3. On the history of this consensus, as well as an important critique of its epistemology and historiographical motors, see James Davidson, "Dover, Foucault and Greek Homosexuality: Penetration and the Truth of Sex," *Past and Present*, no. 170 (2001): 3–51. Davidson specifically states, however, that his aim is "not to provide a comprehensive alternative theory of Greek sexuality, so much as to examine the will to truth which insists on taking as its object of knowledge the undisclosed details of the sexual acts of a distant culture" (7).

4. It's worth noting here Foucault's critique of "the repressive hypothesis" in *The History of Sexuality*, which deconstructs the opposition between surface and depth, as well as Eve Sedgwick's observation that the repressive hypothesis gets displaced in the Foucauldian project of unveiling hidden violence and carries its own structural (surface/depth) binaries. Sedgwick indeed suggests affect, texture, and touching as conceptualities that might divert readers and critics away from the repeated impulse to reveal/uncover hidden truths. My own compatible considerations, clearly indebted to Sedgwick, to follow. Sedgwick, *Touching Feeling*, especially 1–25, 123–51.

5. Trauma would be (and has been) the more obvious association with dark matter, and for good reasons, since it is sometimes hard to account for, or make an account of, and there is little evidence in the traditional sense. But it seems important to note that traumatic experiences are not the *only* kinds of experiences that get written out, written away, or don't quite materialize at all.

6. K. J. Dover, *Greek Homosexuality* (Cambridge: Harvard University Press, 1978). Michel Foucault, *The History of Sexuality*, vol. 1: *An Introduction*, trans. Robert Hurley (1978; New York: Vintage, 1990).

7. Foucault articulates sexuality as a technology of power and does so specifically in response to the "repressive hypothesis," which he so famously discredits. "Let there be no misunderstanding:" he writes, "I do not claim that sex has not been prohibited barred or masked or misapprehended since the classical age; nor do I even assert that it has suffered these things any less from that period on than before. I do not maintain that the prohibition of sex is a ruse; but it is a ruse to make prohibition into the basic and constitutive element from which one would be able to write the history of

what has been said concerning sex starting from the modern epoch. All these negative elements—defenses, censorships, denials—which the repressive hypothesis groups
together in one great central mechanism destined to say no, are doubtless only component parts that have a local and tactical role to play in a transformation into discourse,
a *technology of power*, and a will to knowledge that are far from being reducible to the
former." *History of Sexuality*, 1: 12 (emphasis mine). The "classical age" here refers not
to antiquity, of course, but rather to the century or so following the Renaissance.

8. David M. Halperin, *One Hundred Years of Homosexuality and Other Essays on Greek
Love* (New York: Routledge, 1989), 30.

9. The penetration grid and the active/passive binary it implies have been central to some
of the most vaunted, and often cited, texts of Early Christian Studies on gender and
sexuality. See, for example, Dale Martin's *Sex and the Single Savior: Gender and Sexuality in Biblical Interpretation* (Louisville, KY: Westminster John Knox Press, 2006);
Jennifer Knust, *Abandoned to Lust: Sexual Slander and Ancient Christianity* (New York:
Columbia University Press, 2006); and a number of the essays in Stephen D. Moore
and Janice Capel Anderson, eds., *New Testament Masculinities* (Atlanta: Society of Bib-
lical Literature, 2003), especially Diana M. Swancutt, "'The Disease of Effemination':
The Charge of Effeminacy and the Verdict of God (Romans 1:18–2:16)," 193–233, and
Stephen D. Moore, "'O Man, Who Art Thou?': Masculinity Studies and New Testament
Studies," 1–22. Kyle Harper's *From Shame to Sin: Christian Transformation of Sexual
Morality in Late Antiquity* (Cambridge: Harvard University Press, 2013), specifically
makes use of the penetration grid and the active/passive binary to describe social relations in antiquity generally. Likewise, Davina Lopez's *Apostle to the Conquered* specifically attends to the gendered and sexualized representation of Roman conquest,
suggesting that the penetration grid structures relationships between Rome and its
conquered peoples. There has been, however, some recent discontent with the association between being penetrated and passivity, as in Joseph Marchal's "Bottoming Out:
Rethinking the Reception of Receptivity," in *Bodies on the Verge: Queering Pauline
Epistles and Interpretations*, ed. Joseph Marchal (Atlanta: Society of Biblical Literature
Press, 2019), 209–38.

10. Davidson, "Dover, Foucault and Greek Homosexuality."

11. See for instance, James Davidson, *The Greeks and Greek Love: A Radical Reappraisal of
Homosexuality in Ancient Greece* (London: Weidenfeld and Nicolson, 2007). See also T.
K. Hubbard, "Popular Perceptions of Elite Homosexuality in Classical Athens," *Arion*,
3rd ser., 6, no. 1 (1998): 48–78, more about which will be said below. For an important
framing and characterization of this debate, see Amy Richlin, "Sexuality and History,"
in *The SAGE Handbook of Historical Theory*, ed. Nancy Partner and Sarah Foot (London: Sage, 2013), 294–310.

12. Hubbard, "Popular Perceptions," 71.

13. On the other end of the spectrum, Amy Richlin has criticized the predominantly male
focus of this intellectual genealogy and doubled down on the violence inherent in
ancient sexuality. See Richlin, *Garden of Priapus: Sexuality and Aggression in Roman
Humor* (New York: Oxford University Press, 1992).

14. Bernadette J. Brooten, *Love between Women: Early Christian Responses to Female Homoeroticism* (Chicago: University of Chicago Press, 1996).

15. Ibid., 8–9.

16. For a similar argument regarding non-Christian Roman texts, see Judith P. Hallett, "Female Homoeroticism and the Denial of Reality in Latin Literature," in *Roman Sexualities*, ed. Hallett and Marilyn B. Skinner (Princeton: Princeton University Press, 1997), 255–73.

17. See also Deborah Kamen and Sarah Levin-Richardson, "Revisiting Roman Sexuality: Agency and the Conceptualization of Penetrated Males," in *Sex in Antiquity: Exploring Gender and Sexuality in the Ancient World*, ed. Mark Masterson, Nancy Sorkin Rabinowitz, and James Robson (New York: Routledge, 2014), 449–60. Kamen and Levin-Richardson accept the penetration paradigm but seek to decouple penetration from the active-passive binary.

18. Page duBois, *Sappho Is Burning* (Chicago: University of Chicago Press, 1997), 145.

19. Ibid., 14.

20. Brooke Holmes, *Gender: Antiquity and Its Legacy* (New York: Oxford University Press, 2012), 81.

21. Ibid., 98–100.

22. Halperin, *One Hundred Years*, 32–39.

23. Ibid., 86.

24. Ibid.

25. Ibid., 130.

26. Ibid., 132. Likewise in the *Symposium* there is both an acknowledgment of and a resistance to a certain passivity or "enslavement" in desire, especially if one's desire is focused toward the forms or the "ocean of the beautiful" (210D) rather than on the singular beautiful body itself. As Diotima describes in the *Symposium*, "He who would proceed rightly in this business must not merely begin from his youth to encounter beautiful bodies. In the first place, indeed, if his conductor guides him aright, he must be in love with one particular body, and engender beautiful converse therein; but next he must remark how the beauty attached to this or that body is cognate to that which is attached to any other, and that if he means to ensue beauty in form, it is gross folly not to regard as one and the same the beauty belonging to all; and so, having grasped this truth, he must make himself a lover of all beautiful bodies, and slacken the stress of his feeling for one by contemning it and counting it a trifle. But his next advance will be to set a higher value on the beauty of souls than on that of the body, so that however little the grace that may bloom in any likely soul it shall suffice for loving and caring, and for bringing forth and soliciting such converse as will tend to the betterment of the young; and that finally he may be constrained to contemplate the beautiful as appearing in our observances and our laws, and to behold it all bound together in kinship and so estimate the body's beauty as a slight affair. From observances he should be led on to the branches of knowledge, that there also he may behold a province of beauty, and by looking thus on beauty in the mass may escape from the mean, meticulous slavery of a single instance, where he must centre all his care, like a lackey, upon the beauty of a

particular child or man or single observance" (210A–D). And then later: "So when a
man by the right method of boy-loving ascends from these particulars and begins to
descry that beauty, he is almost able to lay hold of the final secret. Such is the right approach or induction to the love-matters" (211B–C), trans. W. R. M Lamb, *Loeb Classical
Library* (Cambridge: Harvard University Press, 1925).

27. Halperin, *One Hundred Years of Homosexuality*, 147–49.

28. See for instance, Luce Irigaray, *Speculum of the Other Woman*, trans. Gillian G. Gill
(New York: Cornell University Press, 1985), and Julia Kristeva, *Powers of Horror*, trans.
Leon Roudiez (New York: Columbia University Press, 1982), esp. 56–112, 157–73.

29. Halperin, *One Hundred Years of Homosexuality*, 145.

30. Luce Irigaray, *The Sex Which Is Not One*, trans. Catherine Porter (New York: Cornell
University Press, 1985), 23.

31. Ibid.

32. Ibid., 24.

33. Ibid., 25.

34. See Judith Butler's critique of Irigaray along these lines in *Bodies That Matter*, 11–22.
Rosi Braidotti and Diana Fuss, however, have mitigated this charge, treating Irigaray's
essentialisms as "strategic," or necessary rhetorical tools, rather than as an ontological
position. Braidotti, "The Politics of Ontological Difference," in *Between Feminism and
Psychoanalysis*, ed. Teresa Brennan (New York: Routledge, 1989), 89–105. See also Margaret Whitford's essay "Rereading Irigaray," pp. 106–26 in this same volume. See also
Diana Fuss, *Essentially Speaking: Feminism, Nature, and Difference* (New York: Routledge, 1989), 55–72. See also Amy Hollywood's rendition of Butler's critique and her
engaging reading of Irigaray on penetration, woundedness, and (women's) sexuality,
"'That Glorious Slit': Irigaray and the Medieval Devotion to Christ's Side Wound," in
Acute Melancholia, 171–88. As Hollywood notices, Irigaray explicitly moves away from
associations of the female sex with woundedness, associations that were part of Irigaray's earlier work in *Speculum of the Other Woman*, and that—not insignificantly—
were inspired by medieval mystical devotions of women to Christ's wound.

35. Leo Bersani, *Is the Rectum a Grave? and Other Essays* (Chicago: University of Chicago
Press, 2009).

36. Cvetkovich, *Archive of Feelings*, 63.

37. Bersani, "Is the Rectum a Grave?," 3.

38. Cvetkovich, *Archive of Feelings*, 63.

39. Ibid.

40. Ibid.

41. See especially her chapter "Trauma and Touch: Butch-Femme Sexualities," in *Archive
of Feelings*, 49–82.

42. Likewise, although Cvetkovich is particularly interested in lesbian experiences and
cultures, she is not necessarily tied to any kind of identitarian framing as much as she
is interested in those experiences as they are resonant and perhaps even transferable
ones, and especially as they intervene in dominant national narratives. See *Archive of
Feelings*, introduction.

43. See for instance Sara Ahmed's description of wounding and pain in *The Cultural Poli-*

tics of Emotion (New York: Routledge, 2004), 20–41, as well as Cvetkovich's rendition of Freud's account of traumatized subject as protective organism in *Archive of Feelings*, 52–55.

44. Some questions around the *kinaidos* include to what extent this is simply a blanket term for sexual deviance, or whether it describes a certain sexual preference or identity. In his attempt to broaden discussions of appetite and eros in the classical period, James N. Davidson has suggested that the uses and implications of the term *kinaidos* challenge the active/passive model, and that it is more about exhibiting a kind of "womanish desire" than about sexual humiliation. Davidson, *Courtesans and Fishcakes: The Consuming Passions of Classical Athens* (Chicago: University of Chicago Press, 1997). Ruth Mazo Karras notes, however, that the passivity of the *kinaidos* (at least in Halperin's description) is "anatomical" rather than "affective." Karras, "Active/Passive, Acts/Passions: Greek and Roman Sexualities," *American Historical Review* 105, no. 4 (October 2000): 1259. Again, Deborah Kamen and Sarah Levin-Richardson, in "Revisiting Roman Sexuality," stage a disentanglement of the active/passive binary from penetration. See also Holmes's thorough summary of scholarship on the *kinaidos* in *Gender*, 93–93, 102–4.

45. For a breakdown of this terminology see Brooten, *Love between Women*, 4–9.

46. Irigaray, *The Sex Which Is Not One*, 90.

47. Ibid., 106–18.

48. Interestingly, while there has been debate about the extent to which sexuality in the Greek classical period was overdetermined by active/passive models, there is less debate for the Roman period. See Davidson, *Courtesans and Fishcakes*; Richlin, *Garden of Priapus*; Hallett and Skinner, *Roman Sexualities*. See discussion in Karras, "Active/Passive," 1260. Yet I wonder whether this idea that Roman culture was more bluntly hierarchical and binary might implicitly align with narratives of Roman culture as a bastardization or as representing a decline of classical Greek culture. I don't differentiate Greek and Roman periods strongly here, either from each other or from that hazy and expansive moment we call "the present," largely because of the critiques of historians and theorists such as Carla Freccero and Joan Scott who have noticed the ways in which periodization and hard historical differentiation often work inadvertently to stabilize identities in a given context (ancient or, more often, modern). See Freccero, "Queer Times," *South Atlantic Quarterly* 106, no. 3 (2006): 485–94 and *Queer/Early/Modern* (Durham: Duke University Press, 2005).

49. As both Joan Scott and Carolyn Dinshaw have (differently) argued. Scott, *Fantasy of Feminist History*; Carolyn Dinshaw, *Getting Medieval: Sexualities and Communities, Pre- and Postmodern* (Durham: Duke University Press, 1999).

50. On Thecla and her popularity in late antiquity, see Stephen J. Davis, *The Cult of St. Thecla: A Tradition of Women's Piety in Late Antiquity* (New York: Oxford University Press, 2008). Critical edition in James Barrier, *The Acts of Paul and Thecla: A Critical Introduction and Commentary* (Tübingen: Mohr Siebeck, 2009). The translation here is borrowed from Celene Lillie's translation in *A New New Testament: A Bible for the Twenty-First Century Combining Traditional and Newly Discovered Texts*, ed. Hal Taussig (New York: Mariner Press, 2015), 337–46.

51. See, for instance, Matt A. Jackson-McCabe, "Women and Eros in Greek Magic and The Acts of Paul and Thecla," in *Women and Gender in Ancient Religions: Interdisciplinary Approaches*, ed. Stephen P. Ahearne-Kroll, Paul A. Holloway, and James Kelhoffer (Tübingen: Mohr Siebeck, 2010), 267–78; and Eung Chun Park, "Agneia as a Sublime Form of Eros in the Acts of Paul and Thecla," in *Distant Voices Drawing Near: Essays in Honor of Antoinette Clark Wire*, ed. Holly Hearon (Collegeville, MN: Liturgical Press, 2004), 215–26. Park in fact draws a strict contrast between the figures of Thecla and Diotima. Rosie Ratcliffe's treatment of the text sees the figure of Thecla as an androcentric construction and the text itself as "pornographic," which is to say that Ratcliffe notices how the text exudes or archives a kind of eroticism, if one overdetermined (in her understanding) by male desires. Ratcliffe, "Violating the Inviolate Body: Thecla Uncut," in *The Body in Biblical, Christian, and Jewish Texts*, ed. Joan E. Taylor (New York: Bloomsbury, 2014), 184–209. One pivotal and indeed game-changing exception to the reading of asceticism as renunciation of desire is Virginia Burrus's work, to be discussed below.

52. In the vein of scholarship that reads the Acts of Paul and Thecla as anxious about (and attempting to avoid or blot out) eros, Jennifer Eyl suggests that because Thecla does not see Paul at first, the narrative manages to skirt the usual conventions of the Greek novel (the genre to which the Acts of Paul and Thecla belongs), in which "love at first sight" catalyzes the narrative. In Eyl's analysis, in other words, the avoidance of the "love at first sight" trope is a symptom of the text's allergy to eros. Eyl, "Why Thekla Does Not See Paul: Visual Perception and the Displacement of Eros in the Acts of Paul and Thekla," in *The Ancient Novel and Early Christian and Jewish Narrative: Fictional Intersections*, ed. Judith Perkins and Mariliá Futre Pinheiro (Groningen: Barkhuis, 2013), 3–19.

53. In several manuscript versions, the text ends with a continuation of this pattern of threat and resilience. Many "violent young men" are sent to "ruin" her, but she evades them, not incidentally through recourse to a kind of hardened state that manages to preserve her vitality: she enters a rock, and it descends into the earth. This section, however, does not appear in the earliest manuscript traditions, and it might tend to place her more strongly (and retrojectively) in the martyrdom tradition. See Jeremy W. Barrier, *The Acts of Paul and Thecla: A Critical Edition and Commentary* (Tübingen: Mohr Siebeck, 2009), 188.

54. On violence in Greek novels, see Harland, "'Do Not Deny Me This Noble Death.'" On marriage as a happy ending in Greek novels and the ways that early Christian literature riffs on that trope, see Perkins, *Suffering Self*, 41–76. On the Acts of Paul and Thecla specifically as a counter to the marital plot, see Melissa Aubin, "Reversing Romance? The Acts of Paul and Thecla and the Ancient Novel," in *Ancient Fiction and Early Christian Narrative*, ed. Ronald F. Hock, J. Bradley Chance, and Judith Perkins (Atlanta: Scholars Press, 1998), 257–72.

55. Perkins, *Suffering Self*, 41–76.

56. Ibid., 15–40.

57. See also Cobb, *Dying to Be Men*, and Boyarin, *Dying for God*, chap. 3, which chart (to different degrees) the ways in which sexuality, gender, the active/passive binary infuse

ancient literary texts about Christian martyrs. Boyarin, borrowing from Burrus, treats Thecla specifically.

58. Virginia Burrus, "Word and Flesh: The Bodies and Sexuality of Ascetic Women," *Journal of Feminist Studies in Religion* 10, no.1 (Spring 1994): 31. See also Burrus's "The Heretical Woman as Symbol in Alexander, Athanasius, Epiphanius, and Jerome," *Harvard Theological Review* 84, no. 3 (July 1991): 229–48.

59. Burrus, "Word and Flesh," 50.

60. Burrus writes that while she has "pushed beyond the 'word' of the dominant construction of ascetic women's sexuality," she has not made contact with "actual 'flesh' but rather more words—words which are, however, more revealing of the elusive flesh, representing the utterance of that flesh." "Word and Flesh," 50. It seems to me, though, that the notion of affective archives mitigates this poststructuralist tension between "word and flesh" a bit, since texts can act as "repositories of felt experiences" (to quote Ann Cvetkovich) or conduits for sensation.

61. Burrus, *The Sex Lives of Saints: An Erotics of Ancient Hagiography* (Philadelphia: University of Pennsylvania Press, 2007).

62. Ibid., 15.

63. Ibid., 14.

64. I am even cautious about calling these pleasures "sublimation," as if they are secondary to sex, or as if sex is the more direct or foundational pleasure.

65. On the realness of joy, especially against the hallowed place accorded pain and trauma with respect to the real, see Hollywood, "The Unspeakability of Trauma, the Unspeakability of Joy," in *Acute Melancholia*.

1. Sarah E. Bond, "Why We Need to Start Seeing the Classical World in Color," Hyperallergic, 7 June 2017. https://hyperallergic.com/383776/why-we-need-to-start-seeing-the-classical-world-in-color/.

2. Ibid. The whiteness of Classics was a subject of specific heated debate at the Future of Classics panel at the 2019 AIASCS annual meeting in San Diego. Bond, Dan-el Padilla Peralta, and Mary Boatwright (the SCS president at the time) all have responded to a racist tirade of one attendee of the panel, and the responses to that tirade. See https://classicalstudies.org/scs-news/scs-president-and-executive-director, https://sarahemilybond.com/2019/03/04/my-statement-on-the-future-of-classics-panel-and-the-aftermath/, and https://medium.com/@danelpadillaperalta/some-thoughts-on-aia-scs-2019-d6a480a1812a. In the wake of this panel, numerous classics departments in various institutions have issued diversity statements.

3. See also her article from Forbes, excerpted in the epigraph above. Following that statement excerpted above, Bond writes, "My field is dominated by white folks. We have known for a long time that we have a diversity problem, and one way to address this might be to emphasize what an integral part people of color played within Mediterranean history." It is a curious statement, given that "people of color" is a term that arises only as the anti-thesis to whiteness and is no less modern a construction than whiteness. And would ancient "people of color" be "integral" to/integrated into that history? It seems rather that they would be the very actors of that history itself.

4. Colleen Flaherty, "Threats for What She Didn't Say," *Inside Higher Ed*, June 19, 2017.

5. Ibid.

6. "How Coloring Books Can Teach Us about Diversity in Ancient Times," Hyperallergic, 11 August 2107. See also the later piece by Margaret Talbot, "The Myth of Whiteness in Classical Sculpture," *New Yorker*, 29 October 2018.

7. See Kyla Wazana Tompkins's *Racial Indigestion*, in which she borrows from critical eating studies to read "orificially," which provokes a "move beyond the concern with skin and boundary that has dominated body studies, and thus away from an investment in surfaces that I want to argue is the intellectually limited inheritance of the epidermal ontology of race," 3. Compatibly, Rey Chow's *Not like a Native Speaker* addresses the racial "intonations" of language, thus moving racial optics beyond questions of skin, or even body.

8. Scott, *Fantasy of Feminist History*, especially 45–67.

9. Wiegman, *Object Lessons*, 137–96.

10. Ibid., 173.

11. Ibid., 174.

12. Ibid.

13. Ibid., 343.

14. Denise Buell, "Challenges and Strategies for Speaking about Ethnicity in New Testament Studies," *Svensk Exegetisk Arsbok* 49 (2014): 33–51.

15. See Denise Buell, *Why This New Race? Ethnic Reasoning in Early Christianity* (New York: Columbia University Press, 2005).

16. Buell, "Challenges and Strategies," 37.

17. Ibid., 45.

18. Ibid., 46.

19. Ibid., 37. Emphasis mine.

20. Ibid., 50.

21. Vincent L. Wimbush, "Reading Darkness, Reading Scriptures," in *African-Americans and the Bible: Sacred Texts and Social Textures*, ed. Wimbush (New York: Continuum, 2000).

22. As Hal Taussig has repeatedly observed.

23. Tat-siong Benny Liew, "When Margins Become Common Ground: Questions of and for Biblical Studies," in *Still at the Margins: Biblical Scholarship Fifteen Years after 'Voices from the Margins,'* ed. R. S. Sugirtharajah (London: T & T Clark, 2008), 50.

24. Ibid., 51. In an eerie fulfillment of Liew's observation, and as I wrote this chapter, Liew's work was the center of a conservative-propaganda-machine-engineered "controversy" about his scholarship queering the figure of Jesus. We are perhaps all "public intellectuals" in that our work could unexpectedly enter public discourse.

25. Ibid., 44.

26. Ibid.

27. That the white public intellectual provides an alibi for a closed field might be part of the reason why when people of color engage in public forms of scholarship, that scholarship is sometimes seen as being at odds with other academic work, or even slandered as "unrigorous" or excessively political.

28. https://www.nytimes.com/2001/02/21/nyregion/yo-mama-artist-takes-on-catholic-critic.html.

29. Ibid.

30. Ibid.

31. Sara Ahmed, *On Being Included: Racism and Diversity in Institutional Life* (Durham: Duke University Press, 2012), in particular has charted the ironies and failures of institutionalized diversity work.

32. Eve Kosofsky Sedgwick, *A Dialogue on Love* (New York: Beacon Press, 2000), 47.

33. Ibid.

34. She begins the book, "Apparently, it's as patient that I wish to emerge," in part because she began psychotherapy in the wake of her breast cancer diagnosis.

35. She does experience a change in her concept of power over the course of therapy. See especially Sedgwick, *Dialogue on Love*, 203.

36. Sharpe, *In the Wake*, 12–13, quoting Patricia Saunders, "Defending the Dead, Confronting the Archive: A Conversation with NourbeSe Philip," *small axe* 26 (June 2008): 63–79.

37. Sharpe, *In the Wake*, 13.

38. Loving the discipline can also take the form of rebellion against the discipline, of course, and it seems to me that forms of rebellion against the discipline are too often carefully titrated or stipulated ones. Notice that what Sharpe recommends, however, is not revising the discipline, or deconstructing the discipline, but becoming "undisciplined."

39. Sedgwick, *Touching Feeling*, 153.

BIBLIOGRAPHY

Ahearne-Kroll, Stephen P., Paul A. Holloway, and James Kelhoffer, eds. *Women and Gender in Ancient Religions: Interdisciplinary Approaches.* Tübingen: Mohr Siebeck, 2010.

Ahmed, Sara. *The Cultural Politics of Emotion.* New York: Routledge, 2004.

_____. *On Being Included: Racism and Diversity in Institutional Life.* Durham: Duke University Press, 2012.

Alcock, Susan E. *Archaeologies of the Greek Past: Landscape, Monuments, and Memories.* New York: Cambridge University Press, 2002.

_____. "Tomb Cult and the Postclassical Polis." *American Journal of Archaeology* 95, no. 3 (July 1991): 447–67.

Althusser, Louis. *Lenin and Philosophy and Other Essays.* New York: Monthly Review Press, 1971.

Ames, Cecilia. "Roman Religion in the Vision of Tertullian." In *A Companion to Roman Religion*, ed. Jörg Rüpke, 457–70. Oxford: Wiley Blackwell, 2011.

Ando, Clifford. *Imperial Ideology and Provincial Loyalty in the Roman Empire.* Berkeley: University of California Press, 2000.

_____. *The Matter of the Gods: Religion and the Roman Empire.* Berkeley: University of California Press, 2008.

Ascough, Richard, Philip A. Harland, and John S. Kloppenborg, eds. *Associations in the Greco-Roman World: A Sourcebook.* Waco, TX: Baylor University Press, 2012.

Axel, Brian Keith. "The Diasporic Imaginary." *Public Culture* 14, no. 2 (2002): 411–28.

_____. *The Nation's Tortured Body: Violence, Representation, and the Formation of a Sikh 'Diaspora.'* Durham: Duke University Press, 2001.

Bablitz, Leanne. "Roman Courts and Private Arbitration." In *The Oxford Handbook of Roman Law and Society*, ed. Paul J. du Plessis, Clifford Ando, and Kaius Tuori, 234–44. Oxford: Oxford University Press, 2016.

Bachvarova, Mary R. "The Destroyed City in Ancient 'World History' from Agade to Troy." In *The Fall of Cities in the Mediterranean: Commemoration in Literature, Folk-Song, and Liturgy*, ed. Mary R. Bachvarova, Dorota Dutsch, and Ann Suter, 36–68. Cambridge: Cambridge University Press, 2016.

Bähnk, Wiebke. *Von der Notwendigkeit: Die Theologie des Martyriums bei Tertullian.* Göttingen: Vandenhoeck & Ruprecht, 2001.

Baird, Jennifer, and Claire Taylor. *Ancient Graffiti in Context.* New York: Routledge, 2011.

Baker, Cynthia. *Rebuilding the House of Israel: Architectures of Gender in Jewish Antiquity.* Stanford: Stanford University Press, 2002.

Barnes, Timothy. *Tertullian: A Historical and Literary Study.* Oxford: Clarendon Press, 1971.

Barton, Carlin A. *The Sorrows of the Ancient Romans: The Gladiator and the Monster.* Princeton: Princeton University Press, 1993.

Barton, Carlin A., and Daniel Boyarin. *Imagine No Religion: How Modern Abstractions Hide Ancient Realities.* New York: Fordham University Press, 2016.

Bartsch, Shadi. *The Mirror of the Self: Sexuality, Self-Knowledge, and the Gaze in the Early Roman Empire.* Chicago: University of Chicago Press, 2006.

Benjamin, Jessica. *Bonds of Love: Psychoanalysis, Feminism, and the Problem of Domination.* New York: Pantheon, 1988.

_____. *Like Subjects, Love Objects: Essays on Recognition and Sexual Difference.* New Haven: Yale University Press, 1995.

Bennett, Jane. *The Enchantment of Modern Life: Attachments, Crossings, Ethics.* Princeton: Princeton University Press, 2001.

_____. *Vibrant Matter: A Political Ecology of Things.* Durham: Duke University Press, 2010.

Berlant, Lauren. *Cruel Optimism.* Durham: Duke University Press, 2011.

Bersani, Leo. *Is the Rectum a Grave? and Other Essays.* Chicago: University of Chicago Press, 2009.

Berzon, Todd. *Classifying Christians: Ethnography, Heresiology, and the Limits of Knowledge in Late Antiquity.* Berkeley: University of California Press, 2016.

_____. "Ethnicity and Early Christianity: New Approaches to Religious Kinship and Community." *Currents in Biblical Research* 16, no. 2 (January 2018): 191–227.

Boring, M. Eugene. *Revelation: Interpretation.* Louisville: Westminster John Knox Press, 1989.

Boyarin, Daniel. *Dying for God: Martyrdom and the Making of Christianity and Judaism.* Stanford: Stanford University Press, 1999.

_____. *A Traveling Homeland: The Babylonian Talmud as Diaspora.* Philadelphia: University of Pennsylvania Press, 2015.

Braidotti, Rosi. *The Posthuman.* Cambridge, UK: Polity Press, 2013.

Braziel, Jana Evans, and Anita Mannur, eds. *Theorizing Diaspora.* Malden, MA: Blackwell, 2003.

Brennan, Teresa, ed. *Between Feminism and Psychoanalysis.* New York: Routledge, 1989.

Brent, Allen. *Cyprian and Roman Carthage.* Cambridge: Cambridge University Press, 2010.

Brintnall, Kent L. "Who Weeps for the Sodomite?" In *Sexual Disorientations: Queer Temporalities, Affects, Theologies,* ed. Kent Brintnall, Joseph Marchal, and Stephen Moore, 145–60. New York: Fordham University Press, 2017.

Brooten, Bernadette. *Love between Women: Early Christian Responses to Female Homoeroticism.* Chicago: University of Chicago Press, 1996.

Brown, Wendy. *States of Injury: Power and Freedom in Late Modernity.* Princeton: Princeton University Press, 1995.

Browne, Simone. *Dark Matters: On the Surveillance of Blackness.* Durham: Duke University Press, 2015.

Bryen, Ari Z. "Martyrdom, Rhetoric, and the Politics of Procedure." *Classical Antiquity* 33, no. 2 (2014): 243–80.

_____. *Violence in Roman Egypt: A Study in Legal Interpretation*. Philadelphia: University of Pennsylvania Press, 2013.

Buell, Denise. "Challenges and Strategies for Speaking about Ethnicity in New Testament Studies." *Svensk Exegetisk Arsbok* 49 (2014): 33–51.

_____. *Why This New Race? Ethnic Reasoning in Early Christianity*. New York: Columbia University Press, 2005.

Burns, J. Patout, Jr., and Robin Jensen. *Christianity in Roman Africa: The Development of Its Practices and Beliefs*. Grand Rapids, MI: Eerdmans Press, 2014.

Burrus, Virginia. *Ancient Christian Ecopoetics: Cosmologies, Saints, Things*. Philadelphia: University of Pennsylvania Press, 2019.

_____. "The Heretical Woman as Symbol in Alexander, Athanasius, Epiphanius, and Jerome." *Harvard Theological Review* 84, no. 3. (July 1991): 229–48.

_____. *The Sex Lives of Saints: An Erotics of Ancient Hagiography*. Philadelphia: University of Pennsylvania Press, 2007.

_____. "Word and Flesh: The Bodies and Sexuality of Ascetic Women." *Journal of Feminist Studies in Religion* 10, no. 1 (Spring 1994): 27–51.

Butler, Judith. *Bodies That Matter: On the Discursive Limits of Sex*. New York: Routledge, 1993.

Butler, Shane, ed. *Deep Classics: Rethinking Classical Reception*. London: Bloomsbury, 2016.

Cagnat, René. 'Un temple de la gens Augusta à Carthage.' *Comptes Rendus des Séances, Académie des Inscriptions et Belles-Lettres* 57 (1913): 680–86.

Castelli, Elisabeth. *Martyrdom and Memory: Early Christian Culture Making*. New York: Columbia University Press, 2004.

Castronovo, Russ. *Necro Citizenship: Death, Eroticism, and the Public Sphere in the Nineteenth-Century United States*. Durham: Duke University Press, 2001.

Césaire, Aimé. *Solar Throat Slashed: the unexpurgated 1948 edition*. Ed. A. James Arnold and Clayton Eshleman. Middletown, CT: Wesleyan University Press, 2011.

Chaniotis, Angelos. "Affective Epigraphy: Emotions in Public Inscriptions of the Hellenistic Age." *Mediterraneo Antico* 16, no. 2 (2013): 745–60.

_____. "Under the Watchful Eyes of the Gods: Divine Justice in Hellenistic and Roman Asia Minor." In *The Greco-Roman East: Politics, Culture, Society*, ed. S. Colvin. Cambridge: Cambridge University Press, 2004.

Chen, Mel Y. *Animacies: Biopolitics, Racial Mattering, and Queer Affect*. Durham: Duke University Press, 2012.

Cheng, Anne Anlin. *The Melancholy of Race: Psychoanalysis, Assimilation, and Hidden Grief*. New York: Oxford University Press, 2000.

Chow, Rey. *The Age of the World Target: Self-Referentiality in War, Theory, and Comparative Work*. Durham: Duke University Press, 2006.

_____. *Not like a Native Speaker: On Languaging as a Postcolonial Experience*. New York: Columbia University Press, 2014.

Clifford, James, and George Marcus, eds. *Writing Culture: The Poetics and Politics of Ethnography*. Berkeley: University of California Press, 1986.

Cobb, Stephanie. *Dying to Be Men: Gender and Language in Early Christian Martyr Texts.* New York: Columbia University Press, 2008.

Cohen, Shaye J. D. *The Beginnings of Jewishness: Boundaries, Varieties, Uncertainties.* Berkeley: University of California Press, 2001.

Collins, Adela Yarbro. *Crisis and Catharsis: The Power of the Apocalypse.* Philadelphia: Westminster Press, 1984.

_____. *Mark: A Commentary. Hermeneia.* Minneapolis: Fortress Press, 2007.

Collins, John J. *Daniel. Hermeneia.* Minneapolis: Fortress Press, 1993.

Concannon, Cavan. *When You Were Gentiles: Specters of Ethnicity in Roman Corinth and Paul's Corinthian Correspondence.* New Haven: Yale University Press, 2014.

Coole, Diana, and Samantha Frost, eds. *New Materialisms: Ontology, Agency, Politics.* Durham: Duke University Press, 2010.

Cvetkovich, Ann. *An Archive of Feelings: Trauma, Sexuality, and Lesbian Public Cultures.* Durham: Duke University Press, 2003.

_____. *Depression: A Public Feeling.* Durham: Duke University Press, 2012.

Daniel-Hughes, Carly. "Mary Magdalene and the Fantasy Echo: Reflections on the Feminist Historiography of Early Christianity." In *Re-making the World: Christianity and Categories. Essays in Honor of Karen L. King*, ed. Taylor G. Petrey et al. Tübingen: Mohr Siebeck, 2019.

_____. "The Perils of Idolatrous Garb: Tertullian and Christian Belonging in Roman Carthage." In *Religious Competition in the Greco-Roman World*, ed. Nathaniel P. DesRosiers and Lily C. Vuong, 15–26. Atlanta: SBL Press, 2016.

_____. *The Salvation of the Flesh in Tertullian of Carthage: Dressing for the Resurrection.* New York: Palgrave Macmillan, 2011.

Dasen, Véronique. "Healing Images. Gems and Medicine." *Oxford Journal of Archaeology* 33, no. 2 (2014): 177–91.

Daston, Lorraine, and Peter Galison. *Objectivity.* New York: Zone Books, 2007.

Davidson, James. "Dover, Foucault and Greek Homosexuality: Penetration and the Truth of Sex." *Past and Present*, no. 170 (February 2001): 3–51.

_____. *The Greeks and Greek Love: A Radical Reappraisal of Homosexuality in Ancient Greece.* London: Weidenfeld and Nicolson, 2007.

Davis, Stephen J. *The Cult of St. Thecla: A Tradition of Women's Piety in Late Antiquity.* New York: Oxford University Press, 2008.

Derrida, Jacques. "Freud and the Scene of Writing." *Yale French Studies* 48 (1972): 74–114.

_____. *Monolinguism of the Other: or, the Prosthesis of Origin.* Trans. Patrick Mensah. Stanford: Stanford University Press, 1998.

_____. *Writing and Difference.* Trans. Alan Bass. Rpt. ed. Chicago: University of Chicago Press, 1993.

Devereux, George. *Ethnopsychanalyse complémentariste.* Trans. Tina Jolas and Henry Gobard. Paris: Flammarion, 1972.

_____. *From Anxiety to Method in the Behavioral Sciences.* Paris: Mouton, 1967.

Dinshaw, Carolyn. *Getting Medieval: Sexualities and Communities, Pre- and Postmodern.* Durham: Duke University Press, 1999.

_____. *How Soon Is Now? Medieval Texts, Amateur Readers, and the Queerness of Time*. Durham: Duke University Press, 2012.

Dossey, Leslie. *Peasant and Empire in Christian North Africa*. Berkeley: University of California Press, 2010.

Dover, K. J. *Greek Homosexuality*. Cambridge: Harvard University Press, 1978.

DuBois, Page. *Sappho Is Burning*. Chicago: University of Chicago Press, 1997.

_____. *Torture and Truth*. New York: Routledge, 1991.

Dunn, Geoffrey D. *Tertullian*. Early Church Fathers Series. London: Routledge, 2004.

Dunning, Benjamin. *Specters of Paul: Sexual Difference in Early Christian Thought*. Philadelphia: University of Pennsylvania Press, 2011.

Eastman, David L. *The Ancient Martyrdom Accounts of Peter and Paul*. Atlanta: Society of Biblical Literature Press, 2015.

Edwards, Brent Hayes. *The Practice of Diaspora: Literature, Translation, and the Rise of Black Internationalism*. Cambridge: Harvard University Press, 2003.

Elsner, Jaś. *Roman Eyes: Visuality and Subjectivity in Art and Text*. Princeton: Princeton University Press, 2007.

_____. "Structuring 'Greece': Pausanias's Periegesis as a Literary Construct." In *Pausanias: Travel and Memory in Roman Greece*, ed. Susan E. Alcock, John F. Cherry, and Jaś Elsner, 3–20. New York: Oxford, 2001.

Fiorenza, Elisabeth Schüssler. *Revelation: Vision of a Just World*. Minneapolis: Fortress Press, 1991.

Foster, Paul. "Do Crosses Walk and Talk? A Reconsideration of the Gospel of Peter 10:39–42." *Journal for Theological Studies* 64, no. 1 (April 2013): 89–104.

Foucault, Michel. *The Archaeology of Knowledge and the Discourse on Language*. Trans. A. M. Sheridan Smith. New York: Pantheon, 1972.

_____. *The History of Sexuality*, vol. 1: *An Introduction*. Trans. Robert Hurley. 1978; New York: Vintage, 1990.

Freccero, Carla. *Queer/Early/Modern*. Durham: Duke University Press, 2005.

Frend, W. H. C. *The Rise of Christianity*. Minneapolis: Fortress Press, 1984.

Freud, Sigmund. *The Standard Edition of the Complete Psychological Works of Sigmund Freud*. Trans. James Strachey. London, 1961.

Frilingos, Christopher. *Spectacles of Empire: Monsters, Martyrs, and the Book of Revelation*. Philadelphia: University of Pennsylvania Press, 2004.

Fuhrmann, Christopher J. "Police Functions and Public Order." In *The Oxford Handbook of Roman Law and Society*, ed. Paul J. du Plessis, Clifford Ando, and Kaius Tuori, 297–309. Oxford: Oxford University Press, 2016.

Futrell, Allison. *Blood in the Arena: The Spectacle of Roman Power*. Austin: University of Texas Press, 1997.

Gamble, Harry Y. *Books and Readers in the Early Church*. New Haven: Yale University Press, 1995.

Gearhart, Suzanne. "The Taming of Michel Foucault: New Historicism, Psychoanalysis, and the Subversion of Power." *New Literary History* 28, no. 3 (Summer 1997): 457–80.

Geertz, Clifford. *The Interpretation of Cultures*. New York: Basic Books, 1973.

Given, J. Gregory. "Ignatius of Antioch and the Historiography of Early Christianity." PhD diss., Harvard University, 2019.

Glancy, Jennifer, and Stephen D. Moore. "The Empress and the Brothel Slave." In *Untold Tales from the Book of Revelation: Sex, Gender, Empire and Ecology*, ed. Moore, 103–24. Atlanta: Society of Biblical Literature, 2014.

Goodman, Martin. *The Roman World, 44 BC–AD 180*. London: Routledge, 1997.

Gordillo, Gaston. *Rubble: The Afterlife of Destruction*. Durham: Duke University Press, 2014.

Haines-Eitzen, Karen. *Guardians of Letters: Literacy, Power, and the Transmitters of Early Christian Literature*. Oxford: Oxford University Press, 2000.

Hallett, Judith P., and Marilyn Skinner, eds. *Roman Sexualities*. Princeton: Princeton University Press, 1997.

Halperin, David M. *One Hundred Years of Homosexuality and Other Essays on Greek Love*. New York: Routledge, 1989.

Harland, Philip A. *Associations, Synagogues, and Congregations: Claiming a Place in Ancient Mediterranean Society*. Minneapolis: Fortress Press, 2003.

———. "The Declining Polis? Religious Rivalries in Ancient Civic Context." In *Religious Rivalries in the Early Roman Empire and the Rise of Christianity*, ed. Leif E. Vaage. Waterloo, ON: Wilfrid Laurier University Press, 2006.

———. "'Do Not Deny Me This Noble Death': Depictions of Violence in the Greek Novels and Apocryphal Acts." *Ancient Narrative* 14 (2017): 129–47.

———. *Dynamics of Identity in the World of the Early Christians: Associations, Judeans, and Cultural Minorities*. New York: T & T Clark, 2009.

Harvey, Susan Ashbrook, Nathaniel P. DesRosiers, Shira Lander, Jacqueline Z. Pastis, and Daniel Ulluci, eds. *A Most Reliable Witness: Essays in Honor of Ross Shepard Kraemer*. Providence: Brown University Press, 2015.

Hearon, Holly, ed. *Distant Voices Drawing Near: Essays in Honor of Antoinette Clark Wire*. Collegeville, MN: Liturgical Press, 2004.

Heffernan, Thomas. *The Passion of Perpetua and Felicity*. Oxford: Oxford University Press, 2012.

Hell, Julia, and Andreas Schönle. *Ruins of Modernity*. Durham: Duke University Press, 2010.

Hidalgo, Jacqueline. *Revelation in Aztlán: Scriptures, Utopias, and the Chicano Movement*. New York: Palgrave, 2016.

Hock, Ronald, J. Bradley Chance, and Judith Perkins, eds. *Ancient Fiction and Early Christian Narrative*. Atlanta: Scholars Press, 1998.

Hollywood, Amy. *Acute Melancholia and Other Essays: Mysticism, History, and the Study of Religion*. New York: Columbia University Press, 2016.

Holmes, Brooke. *Gender: Antiquity and Its Legacy*. New York: Oxford University Press, 2012.

———. *The Symptom and the Subject: The Emergence of the Physical Body in Ancient Greece*. Princeton: Princeton University Press, 2010.

Houston, George W. *Inside Roman Libraries: Book Collections and Their Management in Antiquity*. Chapel Hill: University of North Carolina Press, 2014.

Hubbard, T. K. "Popular Perceptions of Elite Homosexuality in Classical Athens." *Arion*, 3rd ser., 6, no.1 (1998): 48–78.

Huber, Lynn. *Thinking and Seeing with Women in Revelation*. New York: T & T Clark, 2013.

Hughes, Jessica. *Votive Body Parts in Greek and Roman Religion*. Cambridge: Cambridge University Press, 2017.

Humphrey, W. Lee. "A Lifestyle for Diaspora: A Study of the Tales of Esther and Daniel." *Journal of Biblical Literature* 92 (1973): 211–23.

Irigaray, Luce. *The Sex Which Is Not One*. Trans. Catherine Porter. Ithaca: Cornell University Press, 1985.

_____. *Speculum of the Other Woman*. Trans. Gillian G. Gill. Ithaca: Cornell University Press, 1985.

Jackson, Michael. *Critique of Identity Thinking*. New York: Berghahn Books, 2019.

_____. *Minima Ethnographica: Intersubjectivity and the Anthropological Project*. Chicago: University of Chicago Press, 1998.

Jacobs, Andrew. *Christ Circumcised: A Study in Early Christian History and Difference*. Philadelphia: University of Pennsylvania Press, 2012.

Johns, Loren L. *The Lamb Christology of the Apocalypse of John*. Tübingen: Mohr Siebeck, 2003.

Johnson, William A. *Readers and Reading Culture in the High Roman Empire*. Oxford: Oxford University Press, 2010.

Kahl, Brigitte. *Galatians Reimagined: Reading with the Eyes of the Vanquished*. Minneapolis: Fortress Press, 2014.

Karras, Ruth Mazo. "Active/Passive, Acts/Passions: Greek and Roman Sexualities." *American Historical Review* 105, no. 4 (October 2000): 1250–65.

Keith, Alison. "City Lament in Augustan Epic: Antitypes of Rome from Troy to Alba Longa." In *The Fall of Cities in the Mediterranean: Commemoration in Literature, Folk-Song, and Liturgy*, ed. Mary R. Bachvarova, Dorota Dutsch, and Ann Suter, 156–82. Cambridge: Cambridge University Press, 2016.

Kelly, Benjamin. *Petitions, Litigation, and Social Control in Roman Egypt*. New York: Oxford University Press, 2011.

Klein, Melanie. *Envy and Gratitude and Other Works*. New York: Vintage, 1997.

_____. *Love, Guilt, and Reparation, and Other Works, 1921–1945*. New York: Simon and Schuster, 1975.

Kloppenborg, John S., and Steve G. Wilson, eds. *Voluntary Associations in the Greco-Roman World*. New York: Routledge, 2002.

Knust, Jennifer. *Abandoned to Lust: Sexual Slander and Ancient Christianity*. New York: Columbia University Press, 2006.

Kotrosits, Maia. *How Things Feel: Biblical Studies, Affect Theory, and the (Im)Personal*. Leiden: Brill, 2016.

_____. *Rethinking Early Christian Identity: Affect, Violence, and Belonging*. Minneapolis: Fortress Press, 2015.

_____. "The Rhetoric of Intimate Spaces: Affect and Performance in the Corinthian Correspondence." *Union Seminary Quarterly Review* 62, nos. 3–4 (2011): 134–51.

_____. "Seeing Is Feeling: Revelation's Enthroned Lamb and Ancient Visual Affects." *Biblical Interpretation* 22, no. 4 (Fall 2014): 473–502.

Kotrosits, Maia, and Hal Taussig. *Re-reading the Gospel of Mark amidst Pain and Loss.* New York: Palgrave, 2011.

Kristeva, Julia. *Desire in Language: A Semiotic Approach to Literature and Art.* Trans. Leon Roudiez. New York: Columbia University Press, 1980.

_____. *Powers of Horror: An Essay on Abjection.* Trans. Leon Roudiez. New York: Columbia University Press, 1982.

_____. *Revolution of Poetic Language.* New York: Columbia University Press, 1984.

Lacan, Jacques. *Écrits.* Ed. Bruce Fink. New York: W. W. Norton, 2006.

_____. *The Seminar of Jacques Lacan: The Ethics of Psychoanalysis, Book VII.* Ed. Jacques Alain-Miller. Trans. Dennis Porter. New York: W. W. Norton, 1997.

Le Bohec, Yann. *The Imperial Roman Army.* Rpt. ed. London: Routledge, 2000.

Liddell, Peter, and Polly Low, eds. *Inscriptions and Their Uses in Greek and Latin Literature.* New York: Oxford University Press, 2009.

Liew, Tat-siong Benny. "Haunting Silence: Trauma, Failed Orality, and Mark's Messianic Secret." In *Psychoanalytic Mediations between Marxist and Postcolonial Readings of the Bible*, ed. Tat-siong Liew and Erin Runions, 99–128. Atlanta: Society of Biblical Literature, 2016.

_____. "Tyranny, Boundary and Might: Colonial Mimicry in Mark's Gospel." *Journal for the Study of the New Testament* 77 (1999): 7–31.

_____. *What Is Asian American Hermeneutics?: Reading the New Testament.* Honolulu: University of Hawaii Press, 2008.

Lillie, Celene. *The Rape of Eve: The Transformation of Roman Imperial Ideology in Three Early Christian Retellings of Genesis.* Minneapolis: Fortress Press, 2017.

Lin, Lana. *Freud's Jaw and Other Lost Objects: Fractured Subjectivity in the Face of Cancer.* New York: Fordham University Press, 2017.

Lopez, Davina C. *Apostle to the Conquered: Reimagining Paul's Mission.* Minneapolis: Fortress Press, 2008.

Love, Heather. "Close but Not Deep: Literary Ethics and the Descriptive Turn." *New Literary History* 21, no. 2 (2010): 371–91.

_____. "Close Reading and Thin Description." *Public Culture* 25, no. 3 (Fall 2013): 401–34.

_____. *Feeling Backward: Loss and the Politics of Queer History.* Cambridge: Harvard University Press, 2007.

Macmullen, Ramsay. "The Epigraphic Habit in the Roman Empire." *American Journal of Philology* 103, no. 3 (Autumn 1982): 233–46.

Marchal, Joseph. "Bottoming Out: Rethinking the Reception of Receptivity." In *Bodies on the Verge: Queering Pauline Epistles and Interpretations*, ed. Joseph Marchal, 209–38. Atlanta: Society of Biblical Literature Press, 2019.

Marshall, John W. *Parables of War: Reading John's Jewish Apocalypse.* Waterloo, ON: Wilfred Laurier, 2001.

Martin, Dale. *The Corinthian Body.* New Haven: Yale University Press, 1999.

_____. *Sex and the Single Savior: Gender and Sexuality in Biblical Interpretation.* Louisville, KY: Westminster John Knox Press, 2006.

Massumi, Brian. *Parables for the Virtual: Movement, Affect, Sensation.* Durham: Duke University Press, 2002.

Masterson, Mark, Nancy Sorkin Rabinowitz, and James Robson, eds. *Sex in Antiquity: Exploring Gender and Sexuality in the Ancient World.* New York: Routledge, 2014.

Matthews, Shelly. *Perfect Martyr: The Stoning of Stephen and the Construction of Christian Identity.* Cambridge: Harvard University Press, 2010.

Mattingly, David J. *Imperialism, Power, and Identity: Experiencing the Roman Empire.* Princeton: Princeton University Press, 2011.

Mattingly, David J., and R. Bruce Hitchner. "Roman Africa: An Archaeological Review." *Journal of Roman Studies* 85 (1995): 165–213.

McCallum, E. L., and Mikko Tuhkanen, eds. *Queer Times, Queer Becomings.* New York: SUNY Press, 2011.

McDonald, Dennis R. *The Homeric Epics and the Gospel of Mark.* New Haven: Yale University Press, 2000.

McInerney, Jeremy, ed. *A Companion to Ethnicity in the Ancient Mediterranean.* Chichester, West Sussex, UK: Wiley and Sons, 2014.

Millar, Fergus. "Local Cultures in the Roman Empire: Libyan, Punic, and Latin in Roman Africa." *Journal of Roman Studies* 58 (1968): 126–34.

Miller, Anna. *Corinthian Democracy: Democratic Discourse in First Corinthians.* Princeton: Princeton University Press, 2015.

Miller, Patricia Cox. *The Corporeal Imagination: Signifying the Holy in Late Ancient Christianity.* Philadelphia: University of Pennsylvania Press, 2009.

_____. *Dreams in Late Antiquity.* Princeton: Princeton University Press, 1994.

Million, Dian. "Felt Theory: An Indigenous Feminist Approach to Affect and History." *Wicazo Sa Review* 24, no. 2 (2009): 53–74.

Mitchell, Margaret. *Paul and the Rhetoric of Reconciliation: An Exegetical Investigation of the Language and Composition of 1 Corinthians.* Tübingen: Mohr Siebeck, 1991.

_____. *Paul, the Corinthians and the Birth of Christian Hermeneutics.* Cambridge: Cambridge University Press, 2010.

Moore, Stephen D. "'The World Empire Has Become the Empire of Our Lord and His Messiah': Representing Empire in Revelation." In *Empire and Apocalypse: Postcolonialism and the New Testament.* Sheffield, UK: Sheffield Phoenix Press, 2006.

Moore, Stephen D., and Janice Capel Anderson. *New Testament Masculinities.* Atlanta: Society of Biblical Literature, 2003.

Moser, Claudia, and Jennifer Knust, eds. *Ritual Matters: Material Remains and Ancient Religion.* Ann Arbor: University of Michigan Press, 2017.

Myers, Ched. *Binding the Strong Man: A Political Reading of Mark's Story of Jesus.* Maryknoll, NY: Orbis Books, 1988.

Nasrallah, Laura. *Christian Responses to Roman Art and Architecture: The Second Century Church amid the Spaces of Empire.* New York: Cambridge University Press, 2010.

Nickelsburg, George W. E. *Resurrection, Immortality, and Eternal Life in Intertestamental Judaism.* Cambridge: Harvard University Press, 1972.

Nongbri, Bren. *Before Religion: A History of a Modern Concept.* New Haven: Yale University Press, 2015.

Noreña, Carlos. *Imperial Ideals in the Roman West: Representation, Circulation, Power*. New York: Cambridge University Press, 2011.

Ortner, Sherry B., ed. *The Fate of "Culture": Geertz and Beyond*. Berkeley: University of California Press, 1999.

Osborn, Eric. *Tertullian: First Theologian of the West*. Cambridge: Cambridge University Press, 1997.

Pandian, Anand, and Stuart McLean, eds. *Crumpled Paper Boat: Experiments in Ethnographic Writing*. Durham: Duke University Press, 2017.

Patterson, Stephen. *Beyond the Passion: Rethinking the Death and Life of Jesus*. Minneapolis: Fortress Press, 2004.

Pellegrini, Ann, and Katie Gentile, eds. "Nonhuman Encounters: Animals, Objects, Affects and the Place of Practice." *Studies in Gender and Sexuality* 19, no. 1 (2018).

Perkins, Judith. *Roman Imperial Identities in the Early Christian Era*. New York: Routledge, 2009.

_____. *The Suffering Self: Pain and Narrative Representation in the Early Christian Era*. London: Routledge, 1995.

Perkins, Judith, and Mariliá Futre Pinheiro, eds. *The Ancient Novel and Early Christian and Jewish Narrative: Fictional Intersections*. Groningen: Barkhuis, 2013.

Phillips, Adam. *Becoming Freud: The Making of a Psychoanalyst*. New Haven: Yale University Press, 2014.

Porter, James. "Ideals and Ruins: Pausanias, Longinus, and the Second Sophistic." In *Pausanias: Travel and Memory in Roman Greece*, ed. Susan E. Alcock, John F. Cherry, and Jaś Elsner, 63–92. New York: Oxford, 2001.

Price, S. R. F. "The Future of Dreams: From Freud to Artemidorus." *Past and Present* 13, no. 1 (November 1986): 3–37.

_____. *Rituals and Power: The Roman Imperial Cult in Asia Minor*. New York: Cambridge University Press, 1985.

Puar, Jasbir K. *The Right to Maim: Debility, Capacity, Disability*. Durham: Duke University Press, 2017.

_____. *Terrorist Assemblages: Homonationalism in Queer Times*. Durham: Duke University Press, 2007.

Rajak, Tessa. *The Jewish Dialogue with Greece and Rome: Studies in Cultural and Social Interaction*. Leiden: Brill, 2002.

Rankin, David. *From Clement to Origen: The Social and Historical Context of the Church Fathers*. 2nd ed. New York: Routledge, 2016.

Rebillard, Éric. *Christians and Their Many Identities in Late Antiquity: North Africa, 200–450 CE*. Ithaca: Cornell University Press, 2012.

Richardson, John. "Provincial Administration." In *The Oxford Handbook of Roman Law and Society*, ed. Paul J. du Plessis, Clifford Ando, and Kaius Tuori, 111–23. Oxford: Oxford University Press, 2016.

Richlin, Amy. *Garden of Priapus: Sexuality and Aggression in Roman Humor*. New York: Oxford University Press, 1992.

_____. "Sexuality and History." In *The SAGE Handbook of Historical Theory*, ed. Nancy Partner and Sarah Foot, 294–310. London: Sage, 2012.

Rives, James. *Religion and Authority in Roman Carthage from Augustus to Constantine.* Oxford: Clarendon Press, 1995.

Roselaar, Saskia T. "Local Administration." In The Oxford Handbook of Roman Law and Society, eds. Paul du Plessis, Clifford Ando, and Kaius Tuori, 124–36. Oxford: Oxford University Press, 2016.

Runions, Erin. *The Babylon Complex: Theopolitical Fantasies of War, Sex and Sovereignty.* New York: Fordham University Press, 2014.

Schaefer, Donovan. "Heavenbeast: A New Materialist Approach to Ulysses." *Angeliki* 21, no. 2 (June 2016): 119–36.

_____. *Religious Affects: Animality, Evolution, and Power.* Durham: Duke University Press, 2015.

Schott, Jeremy. *Christianity, Empire, and the Making of Religion in Late Antiquity.* Philadelphia: University of Pennsylvania Press, 2008.

Schüssler Fiorenza, Elisabeth. *In Memory of Her: A Feminist Theological Reconstruction of Christian Origins.* New York: Crossroads, 1984.

Schwartz, Saundra. "Chronotypes of Justice in the Greek Novel: Trials in Narrative Spaces." In *Spaces of Justice in the Roman World*, ed. Francesco de Angelis. Leiden: Brill, 2010.

_____. "Dressing Up, Dressing Down: False Enslavement in the Greek Novels." In *Éclats de littérature grecque d'Homère à Pascal Quignard: Mélanges offerts à Suzanne Saïd*, ed. Suzanne Saïd et al., 175–89. Paris: Presses Universitaires de Paris Ouest, 2012.

_____. "Rome in the Greek Novel? Images and Ideas of Empire in Chariton's Persia." *Arethusa* 36, no. 3 (Fall 2003): 375–94.

_____. "The Trial Scene in the Greek Novel and in Acts." In *Contextualizing Acts: Lukan Narrative and Greco-Roman Discourse*, ed. Todd Penner and Caroline Vander Stichele. Symposium 20. Atlanta: Society of Biblical Literature, 2003.

Schwartz, Seth. *Imperialism and Jewish Society: 200 BCE to 640 CE.* Princeton: Princeton University Press, 2001.

_____. *Were the Jews a Mediterranean Society? Reciprocity and Solidarity in Ancient Judaism.* Princeton: Princeton University Press, 2010.

Scott, Joan W. *The Fantasy of Feminist History.* Durham: Duke University Press, 2011.

Sedgwick, Eve Kosofsky. *A Dialogue on Love.* New York: Beacon Press, 2000.

_____. *Touching Feeling: Affect, Pedagogy, Performativity.* Durham: Duke University Press, 2003.

_____. *The Weather in Proust.* Durham: Duke University Press, 2011.

Shantz, Colleen, and Rodney Werline, eds. *Experientia*, vol. 2: *Linking Text and Experience.* Atlanta: Society of Biblical Literature, 2012.

Sharpe, Christina. *In the Wake: On Blackness and Being.* Durham: Duke University Press, 2016.

Shaw, Brent. "Body/Power/Identity: Passions of the Martyrs." *Journal of Early Christian Studies* 4, no. 3 (1996): 269–312.

_____. "The Myth of the Neronian Persecution." *Journal of Roman Studies* 105 (November 2015): 73–100.

Shelton, Jo-Ann. "The Fall of Troy in Seneca's *Troades.*" In *The Fall of Cities in the Mediter-*

ranean: Commemoration in Literature, Folk-Song, and Liturgy, ed. Mary R. Bachvarova, Dorota Dutsch, and Ann Suter, 183–211. Cambridge: Cambridge University Press, 2016.

Sider, Robert D. *Ancient Rhetoric and the Art of Tertullian*. Oxford: Oxford University Press, 1971.

———. *Christian and Pagan in the Roman Empire*. Washington, DC: Catholic University Press of America, 2001.

Smith, Andrea. "Native Studies at the Horizon of Death: Theorizing Ethnographic Entrapment and Settler Self-Reflexivity." In *Theorizing Native Studies*, ed. Audra Simpson and Andrea Smith, 208–34. Durham: Duke University Press, 2014.

Stern, Karen. *Writing on the Wall: Graffiti and the Forgotten Jews of Antiquity*. Princeton: Princeton University Press, 2018.

Stewart, Kathleen. *Ordinary Affects*. Durham: Duke University Press, 2007.

———. "The Point of Precision." *Representations* 135, no. 1 (Summer 2016): 31–44.

Stoler, Ann Laura. *Imperial Debris: On Ruins and Ruination*. Durham: Duke University Press 2013.

———. "'The Rot Remains': From Ruins to Ruination." In *Imperial Debris: On Ruins and Ruination*, ed. Ann Stoler, 1–38. Durham: Duke University Press, 2013.

Sugirtharajah, R. S., ed. *Still at the Margins: Biblical Scholarship Fifteen Years after "Voices from the Margins."* London: T & T Clark, 2008.

Taussig, Hal. "Melancholy, Colonialism, and Complicity: Complicating Counter-Imperial Readings of Aphrodisias' *Sebasteion*." In *Text, Image, and Christians in the Graeco-Roman World: A Festschrift in Honor of David Lee Balch*, ed. Aliou Cissé Niang and Carolyn Osiek. Eugene, OR: Pickwick, 2012.

Taylor, Joan E., ed. *The Body in Biblical, Christian and Jewish Texts*. New York: Bloomsbury, 2014.

Tertullian. *De Pallio (On the mantle)*. Trans. Vincent Hunink. Amsterdam: J. C. Gieben Press, 2005. Accessed February 10, 2018. http://www.tertullian.org/articles/hunink_de_pallio.htm.

Tompkins, Kyla Wazana. *Racial Indigestion: Eating Bodies in the Nineteenth Century*. New York: New York University Press, 2012.

Tortorici, Zeb. "Visceral Archives of the Body: Consuming the Dead, Digesting the Divine." *GLQ* 20, no. 4 (2014): 407–37.

Van der Lans, Birgit, and Jan Bremmer. "Tacitus and the Persecution of the Christians: An Invention of Tradition." *Eirene* 53 (2017): 299–331.

Van Oyen, Astrid. *How Things Make History: The Roman Empire and Its Terra Sigillata Pottery*. Amsterdam: Amsterdam University Press, 2016.

Van Oyen, Astrid, and Martin Pitts, eds. *Materialising Roman Histories*. New York: Cambridge University Press, 2017.

Veeser, H. Aram. *The New Historicism*. New York: Routledge, 1989.

Viego, Antonio. *Dead Subjects: Toward a Politics of Loss in Latino Studies*. Durham: Duke University Press, 2007.

Vout, Caroline. *Power and Eroticism in Imperial Rome*. New York: Cambridge University Press, 2007.

Waller, Alexis. "Touching Philip: Intertextuality, Texture, and Affect in the Gospel of Philip and Scholarly Handlings of It." MDiv thesis, Union Theological Seminary, New York, 2013.

_____. "The 'Unspeakable Teachings' of *The Secret Gospel of Mark*: Feelings and Fantasies in the Making of Christian Histories." In *Religion, Emotion, Sensation: Affect Theories and Theologies*, ed. Karen Bray and Stephen D. Moore. New York: Fordham University Press, 2019.

_____. "Violent Spectacles and Public Feelings: Trauma and Affect in the Gospel of Mark and the Thunder: Perfect Mind." *Biblical Interpretation* 22, nos. 4–5 (2014): 450–72.

Weheliye, Alexander G. *Habeas Viscus: Racializing Assemblages, Biopolitics, and Black Feminist Theories of the Human*. Durham: Duke University Press, 2014.

Wendt, Heidi. *At the Temple Gates: The Religion of Freelance Experts in the Roman Empire*. New York: Oxford University Press, 2016.

_____. "*Ea Superstitione*: Christian Martyrdom and the Religion of Freelance Experts." *Journal of Roman Studies* 105 (November 2015): 183–202.

White, Hayden. *Metahistory: The Historical Imagination in Nineteenth-Century Europe*. Baltimore: Johns Hopkins University Press, 1973.

Wickkiser, Bronwen L. "Asklepios in Greek and Roman Corinth." In *Corinth in Context: Comparative Studies on Religion and Society*, ed. Steve Friesen, Daniel N. Showalter, and James Walters, 37–66. Leiden: Brill, 2010.

Wiegman, Robyn. *Object Lessons*. Durham: Duke University Press, 2012.

Wilhite, David E. "Marcionites in Africa: What Did Tertullian Know and When Did He Invent It?" *Perspectives in Religious Studies* 4 (2016): 437–52.

_____. "Tertullian." In *Ancient African Christianity: Introduction to a Unique Context and Tradition*. New York: Routledge, 2017.

_____. *Tertullian, the African*. Berlin: Walter DeGruyter Press, 2007.

Wimbush, Vincent, ed. *African Americans and the Bible: Sacred Texts and Social Textures*. New York: Continuum, 2001.

Winnicott, Donald W. *Playing and Reality*. New York: Routledge, 2005.

Wire, Antoinette Clark. *The Corinthian Women Prophets: A Reconstruction through Paul's Rhetoric*. Minneapolis: Fortress Press, 1990.

Witherington, Ben. *The Gospel of Mark: A Socio-historical Commentary*. Grand Rapids, MI: Eerdmans, 2001.

Woolf, Greg. *Becoming Roman: The Origins of Provincial Civilization in Gaul*. New York: Cambridge University Press, 1998.

_____. "Monumental Writing and the Expansion of Roman Society in the Early Empire." *Journal of Roman Studies* 86 (1996): 22–39.

Yusoff, Kathryn. *A Billion Black Anthropocenes or None*. Minneapolis: University of Minnesota Press, 2018.

Zanker, Paul. *The Power of Images in the Age of Augustus*. Trans. Alan Shapiro. Ann Arbor: University of Michigan Press, 1990.

INDEX

Printed in Great Britain
by Amazon

40361210R00139